Mrs Wordsmith®

STORYTELLER'S ILLUSTRATED DICTIONARY™

mrswordsmith.com

INSPIRING WORDS THAT WILL BLOW YOUR MIND!

You're a writer now, with a pen in one hand and the *Storyteller's Illustrated Dictionary* in the other.

You've got stories inside, bursting to come out.

What are you waiting for?
Astonish yourself!

conquer
p. 18

ACTION

WRITE A STORY WITH ...

ACTION NOUNS

unicycle
p. 36

disguise
p. 37

spray paint
p. 41

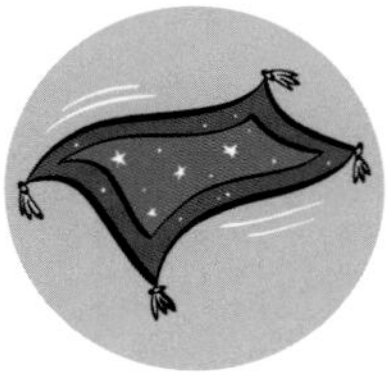

flying carpet
p. 44

CHARACTER

WRITE A STORY WITH ...

gargantuan
p. 54

CHARACTER NOUNS

troll
p. 72

cyborg
p. 73

pincer
p. 77

mohawk
p. 79

EMOTION

WRITE A STORY WITH ...

wistful

p. 94

SETTING

WRITE A STORY WITH ...

secluded

p. 119

SETTING NOUNS

fortress
p. 127

penthouse
p. 134

tree house
p. 135

canyon
p. 137

igloo
p. 138

submarine
p. 140

delta
p. 141

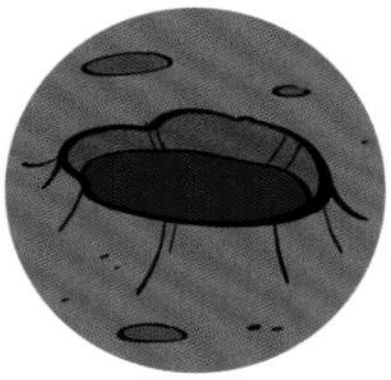

crater
p. 144

TASTE & SMELL

WRITE A STORY WITH ...

savor
p. 155

TASTE & SMELL NOUNS

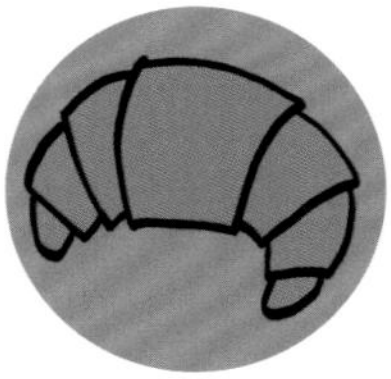

croissant
p. 168

cauliflower
p. 172

lobster
p. 174

dumplings
p. 176

WEATHER

WRITE A STORY WITH ...

WEATHER NOUNS

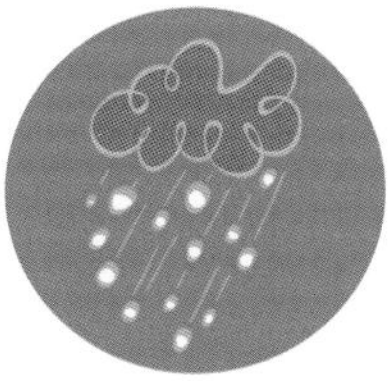

hail
p. 200

tsunami
p. 201

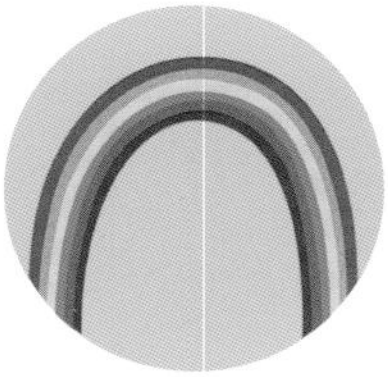

rainbow
p. 202

gale
p. 203

GET TO KNOW YOUR ILLUSTRATED DICTIONARY

This dictionary is filled with hundreds of words to take your storytelling to the next level. Each word is accompanied by a definition and three word pairs (words that frequently appear with it in stories). Some word pairs go before the storytelling word, and some go after. If you aren't sure how to use the word pairs, just check the examples on the right-hand side of the page.

Storytelling word and definition

Here, you'll find incredible words to use in your stories!

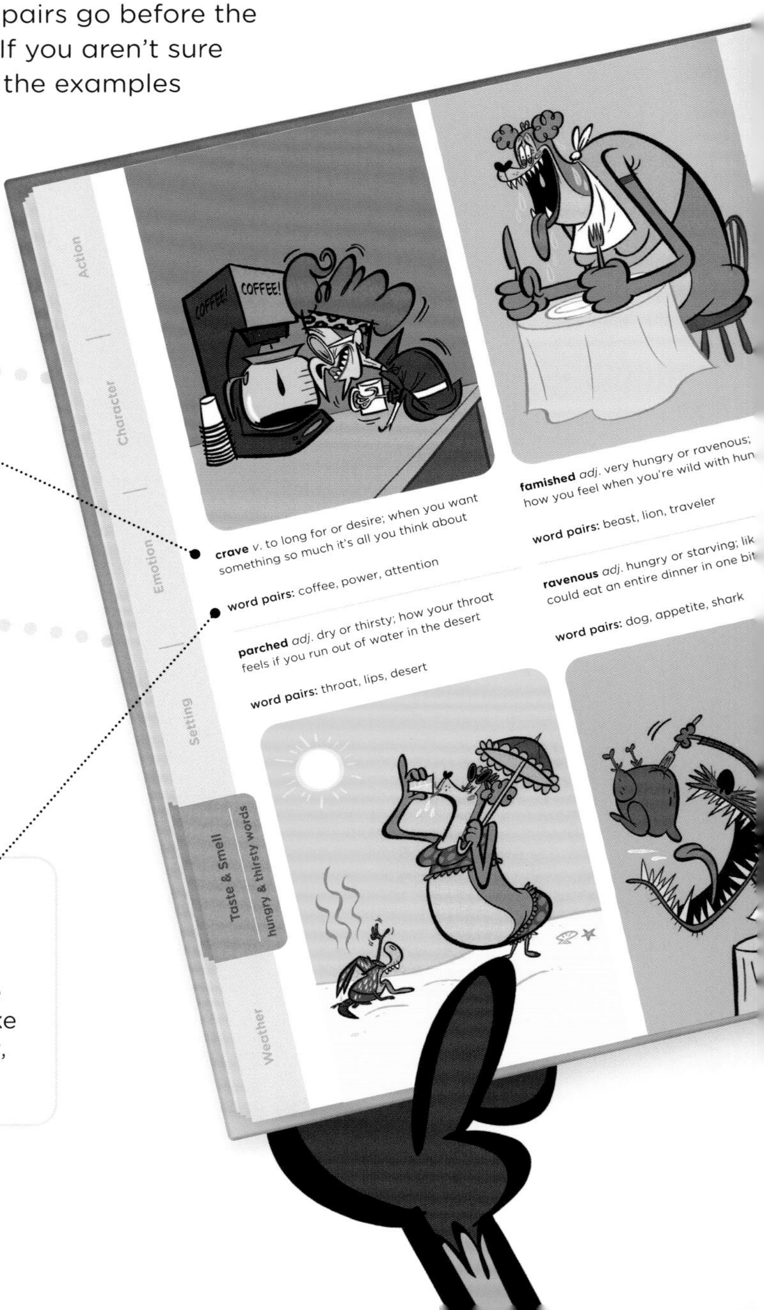
Action
Character
Emotion
Setting
Taste & Smell
hungry & thirsty words
Weather
COFFEE!
COFFEE!
crave v. to long for or desire; when you want something so much it's all you think about
word pairs: coffee, power, attention
parched adj. dry or thirsty; how your throat feels if you run out of water in the desert
word pairs: throat, lips, desert
famished adj. very hungry or ravenous; how you feel when you're wild with hun
word pairs: beast, lion, traveler
ravenous adj. hungry or starving; lik could eat an entire dinner in one bit
word pairs: dog, appetite, shark

Word pairs

These are words that are frequently used alongside the main word in stories, like **crave coffee**, **crave power**, and **crave attention**.

Action
Character
Emotion
Setting
Taste & Smell
hungry & thirsty words
Weather
hungry & thirsty words
insatiable adj. greedy or impossible to satisfy; so hungry you never fill up
word pairs: appetite, greed, curiosity
voracious adj. greedy or very hungry; like having a never-ending hunger for hamburgers
word pairs: appetite, predator, reader
word pair after:
crave coffee
famished beast
insatiable appetite
parched throat
ravenous dog
voracious appetite
159

Category tab

These color-coded tabs will help you navigate your way through this book.

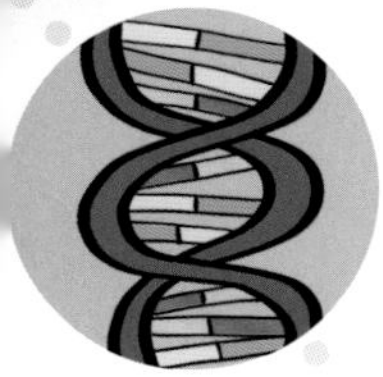

ADD DETAIL TO YOUR STORIES

The noun sections in this book have all the nouns and word pairs you need to kick your creativity into overdrive. Whether you're writing an action adventure involving a **leaky canoe** and a **ridiculous disguise** or a romance based around an **elaborate sandcastle** and a **devastating heartbreak**, these pages are sure to help.

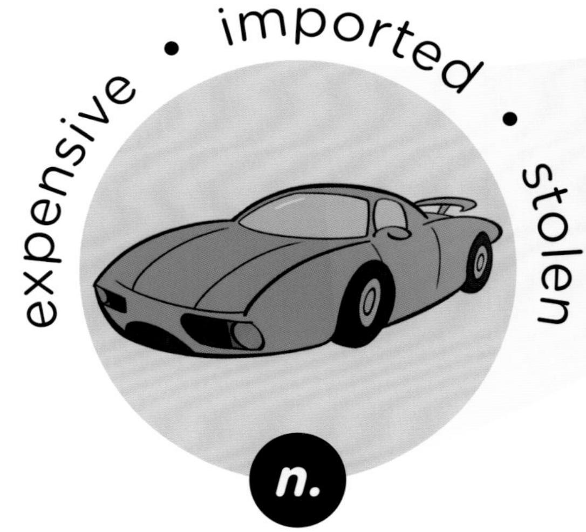

sports car

Oz spent all of her savings on an **expensive sports car**.

Oz's **imported sports car** was absolutely terrible for the environment.

Oz raced away from the police in the **stolen sports car**.

Word pairs

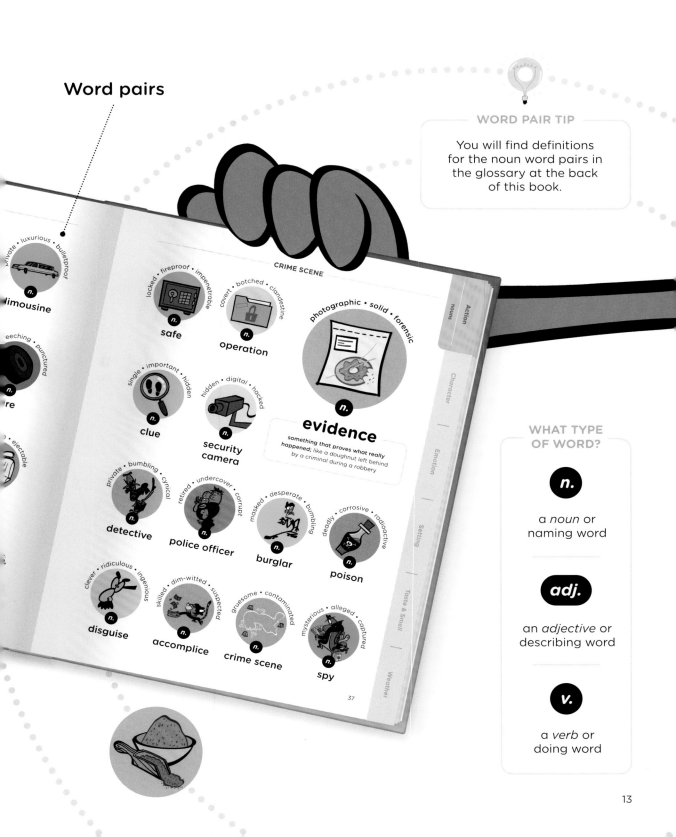

WORD PAIR TIP

You will find definitions for the noun word pairs in the glossary at the back of this book.

WHAT TYPE OF WORD?

n.

a *noun* or naming word

adj.

an *adjective* or describing word

v.

a *verb* or doing word

conquer

ACTION

commotion *n*. chaos or uproar; like animals set loose in a kitchen causing a crazy mess

word pairs: wild, loud, sudden

devastating *adj*. terrible or destructive; like flinging a bowling ball along the dinner table

word pairs: effect, loss, earthquake

---

rebellious *adj*. naughty or disobedient; like a giraffe who draws on the walls

word pairs: artist, attitude, teenager

turbulent *adj*. violent and unstable; like a plane that gets knocked around by heavy clouds

word pairs: flight, water, history

chaotic words

word pair before:

wild **commotion**
cause **havoc**

word pair after:

devastating effect
rebellious artist
turbulent flight
unruly hair

havoc *n*. damage or chaos; like the mess caused by a giant bear smashing through a city

word pairs: cause, wreak, unleash

---

unruly *adj*. wild, rowdy, and rebellious; like long, frizzy hair at the beach

word pairs: hair, class, crowd

ambush *n.* a surprise attack by somebody who has been hiding and waiting

word pairs: sudden, surprise, violent

conquer *v.* to defeat or get control over; like an army taking over new land

word pairs: a country, the world, your fears

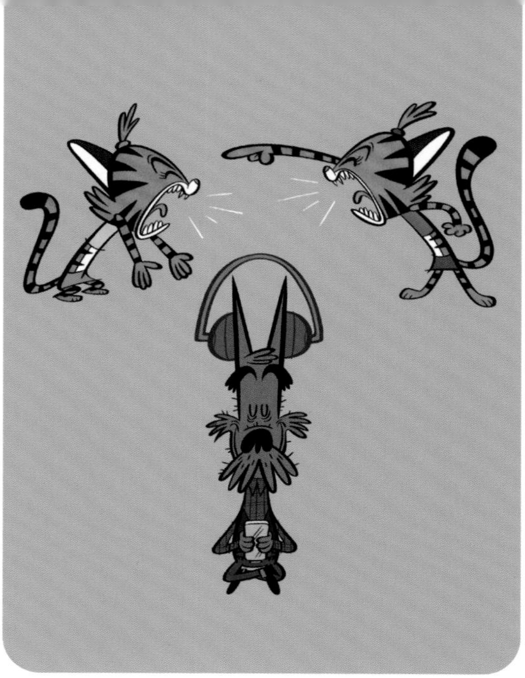

bicker *v.* to argue over silly things; like sisters arguing about nothing

word pairs: constantly, playfully, childishly

feud *n.* a conflict that is never settled; like people fighting about the same thing for years

word pairs: bitter, long-running, vicious

bombard *v.* to attack or overwhelm; like showering someone with gifts on their birthday

word pairs: with gifts, with questions, with arrows

siege *n.* a blockade or assault; when soldiers surround the enemy until they surrender

word pairs: brutal, long, bloody

fighting words

word pair before:

sudden **ambush**
bitter **feud**
brutal **siege**

word pair after:

bicker constantly
bombard with gifts
conquer a country

backbreaking *adj*. exhausting or crushing; like lifting something so heavy it hurts your spine

word pairs: work, effort, burden

exhausted *adj*. worn out or very tired; when you are so tired you sleep deeply for hours

word pairs: employee, voice, athlete

laborious *adj*. difficult or exhausting; like the job of pushing big, heavy boulders uphill

word pairs: chore, process, undertaking

overwhelming *adj*. overpowering or immense; like carrying a busload of stuff on your shoulders

word pairs: pressure, majority, urge

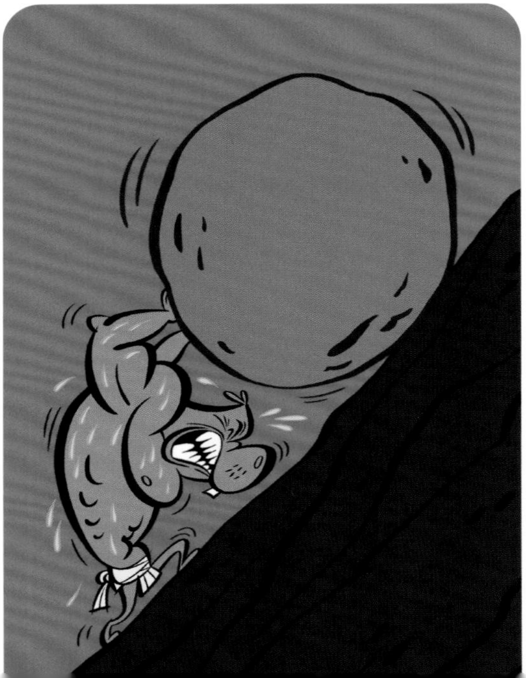

grueling *adj.* difficult or draining; like the effort of carrying a huge bear

word pairs: work, climb, schedule

tedious *adj.* boring or dull; like having to work through an endless pile of homework

word pairs: paperwork, task, process

hard-working words

word pair after:

backbreaking work
exhausted employee
grueling work
laborious chore
overwhelming pressure
tedious paperwork

gawk *v.* to gape or stare openly; like a tourist wandering around with eyes wide open

word pairs: stupidly, openly, rudely

gaze *v.* to stare or look deep in thought; like looking longingly at an ice cream

word pairs: lovingly, longingly, blankly

---

peer *v.* to peek or stare; like looking over your shoulder to see what's going on

word pairs: down, inside, curiously

scrutinize *v.* to inspect or study; like when you look at something up close and in detail

word pairs: details, faces, evidence

glimpse *v.* to see briefly or get a quick look; like spotting a mouse out of the corner of your eye

word pairs: a mouse, the sea, the truth

---

squint *v.* to look through half-closed eyes; like when you shield your eyes from the sun

word pairs: slightly, curiously, suspiciously

looking words

word pair after:

gawk stupidly
gaze lovingly
glimpse a mouse
peer down
scrutinize details
squint slightly

drowsy *adj*. sleepy or dopey; how you feel when your alarm clock goes off

word pairs: driver, voice, afternoon

sluggish *adj*. slow, lazy, or lifeless; how you feel when you get up too early in the morning

word pairs: start, river, pace

lounge *v*. to lie around or laze; like someone lying in the sun sipping a cool drink

word pairs: comfortably, luxuriously, lazily

soothing *adj*. calming or comforting; like a sweet song that makes you feel peaceful

word pairs: lullaby, voice, bath

pampered *adj*. spoiled or coddled; like having an indulgent mud bath at a fancy hotel

word pairs: body, guest, lifestyle

unwind *v*. to rest or relax; like when you stretch out on the couch after a long day at work

word pairs: completely, finally, mentally

relaxing words

word pair after:

drowsy driver
lounge comfortably
pampered body
sluggish start
soothing lullaby
unwind completely

charge *v.* to run or lunge toward; rushing toward a target as fast as you can

word pairs: suddenly, furiously, headlong

dart *v.* to sprint or bolt; running somewhere suddenly and rapidly

word pairs: forward, ahead, away

hurtle *v.* to rush or move very quickly; like a big asteroid plunging toward Earth

word pairs: asteroids, trains, spaceships

scamper *v.* to scurry or dash; how you would run if you were very excited

word pairs: away, inside, hurriedly

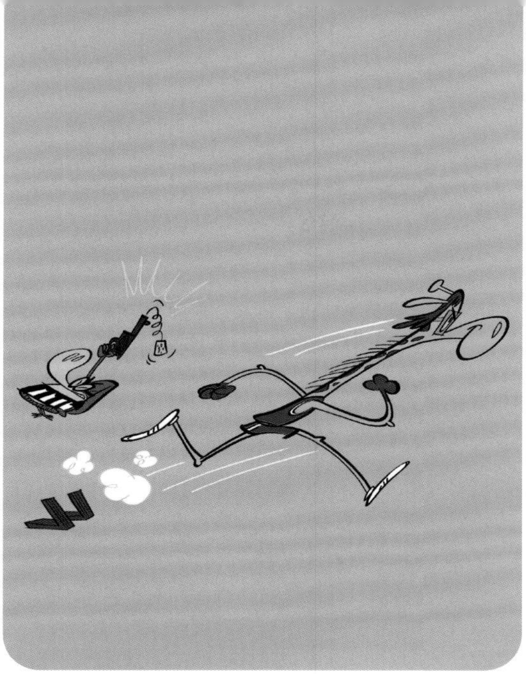

dash *v.* to run or rush; like a sprinter running at full speed toward the finish line

word pairs: frantically, suddenly, toward

---

scurry *v.* to scamper or scuttle; like a scared armadillo trying to outrun a huge wave

word pairs: quickly, away, frantically

running words

word pair before:

asteroids **hurtle**

word pair after:

charge suddenly
dart forward
dash frantically
scamper away
scurry quickly

blurt *v.* to cry out or say suddenly; like shouting out when it's someone else's turn

word pairs: suddenly, accidentally, awkwardly

drone *v.* to hum or make a continuous dull sound; like someone reading out a boring list

word pairs: endlessly, away, monotonously

sneer *v.* to smirk or smile nastily; like a mean smile when others make mistakes

word pairs: arrogantly, nastily, sarcastically

squeal *v.* to wail or yelp; the high-pitched sound someone makes when they're surprised

word pairs: loudly, excitedly, shrilly

protest *v.* to disagree or challenge; like refusing to work until someone listens to you

word pairs: strongly, peacefully, vehemently

---

whimper *v.* to whine or sniffle; like the soft crying sound when someone is sad or in pain

word pairs: softly, sadly, feebly

speaking words

word pair before:

strongly **protest**

word pair after:

blurt suddenly
drone endlessly
sneer arrogantly
squeal loudly
whimper softly

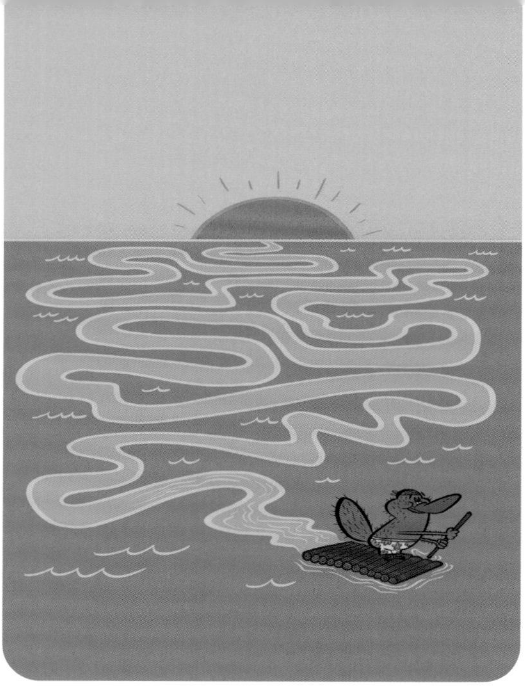

meander *v.* to wander or follow a bendy path; like a sailor roaming across the sea

word pairs: slowly, sluggishly, aimlessly

---

swagger *v.* to strut or stride; how you walk when you are feeling on top of the world

word pairs: confidently, arrogantly, boisterously

skulk *v.* to creep or prowl; when you lie low or move carefully to avoid being seen

word pairs: around, behind, sneakily

---

traverse *v.* to cross or travel through; like a hiker making their way across steep hills

word pairs: mountains, deserts, the globe

stagger *v.* to stumble or walk unsteadily; how you walk after a coconut falls on your head

word pairs: about, downstairs, dizzily

trudge *v.* to plod or walk slowly with heavy steps; like a tired dog walking out of the sea

word pairs: slowly, wearily, reluctantly

walking words

word pair after:

meander slowly
skulk around
stagger about
swagger confidently
traverse mountains
trudge slowly

douse *v.* to drench or put out with water; like pouring a bucket of water over a bonfire

word pairs: flames, a blaze, embers

drenched *adj.* very wet or soaked; like when you've had a bucket of water thrown over you

word pairs: hair, clothes, earth

plunge *v.* to dive or plummet; like when you jump off the highest rock into deep water

word pairs: down, headlong, recklessly

squirt *v.* to spray or splatter; like firing a water blaster in all directions

word pairs: water, ketchup, venom

immerse *v.* to dunk or plunge; like pushing someone right to the bottom of a tank of water

word pairs: fully, partly, quickly

---

submerged *adj.* completely underwater; like a diver at the bottom of the sea

word pairs: diver, feet, shipwreck

wet words

word pair before:

fully **immerse**

word pair after:

douse flames
drenched hair
plunge down
squirt water
submerged diver

210

astonishing action nouns

Add drama and suspense to your stories with these nouns and word pairs. Build a **multistory blanket fort** with an **alleged spy** or destroy some **forensic evidence** with an **agile gymnast**. This section is action packed.

parked • rickety • abandoned

n.
bicycle

classic • electric • driverless

n.
car

amazing • enchanted • driverless
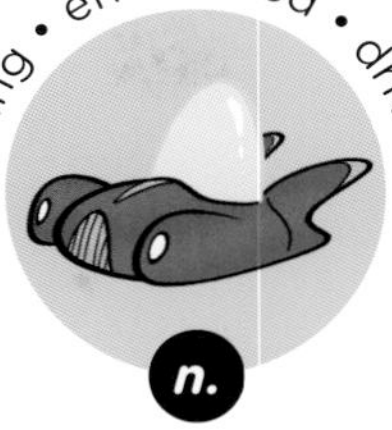
n.
flying car

protective • dented • scuffed

n.
bumper

powerful • purring • turbocharged
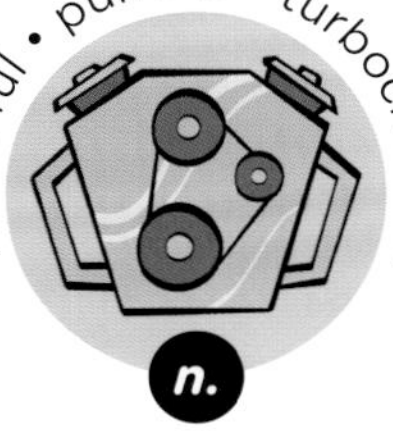
n.
engine

dim • blinding • distant

n.
headlights

digital • futuristic • intuitive
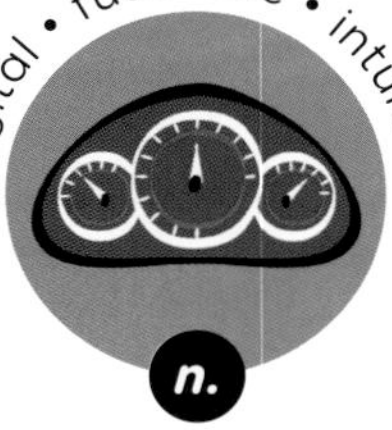
n.
dashboard

packed • double-decker • jolting

n.
bus

large • burnt-out • clanking

n.
caravan

leaky • drifting • capsized
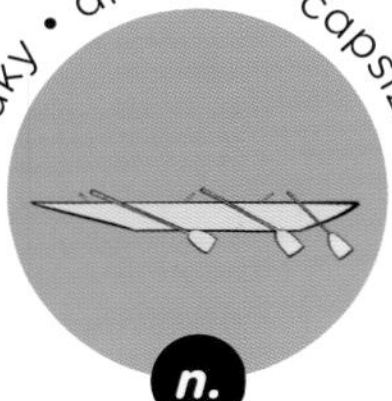
n.
canoe

overnight • sunken • overloaded

n.
ferry

lightweight • crude • motorized
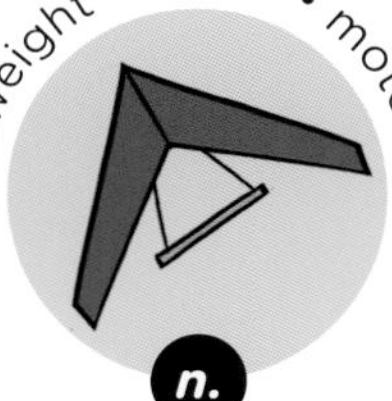
n.
hang glider

private • paper • crashed

n.
airplane

giant • airborne • deflated

n.
blimp

magical • runaway • splintered

n.
broomstick

circling • low-flying • whirling

n.
helicopter

HIGH-SPEED CHASE

huge • rising • breathtaking

n.

hot air balloon

torn • built-in • billowing

n.

parachute

crowded • superfast • derailed

n.

train

private • luxurious • bulletproof

n.

limousine

expensive • imported • stolen

n.

sports car

fast • noisy • turbocharged

n.

motorcycle

private • cruising • palatial

n.

yacht

spare • screeching • punctured

n.

tire

heated • crooked • leather-clad

n.

steering wheel

electric • folding • compact

n.

scooter

giant • wobbly • lopsided

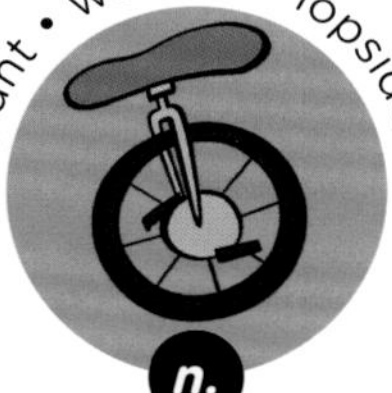

n.

unicycle

bouncy • plush • ejectable

n.

seats

dirty • smashed • bulletproof

n.

windshield

rented • two-person • powerful

n.

jet ski

powerful • elegant • military

n.

speedboat

pirate • sinking • derelict

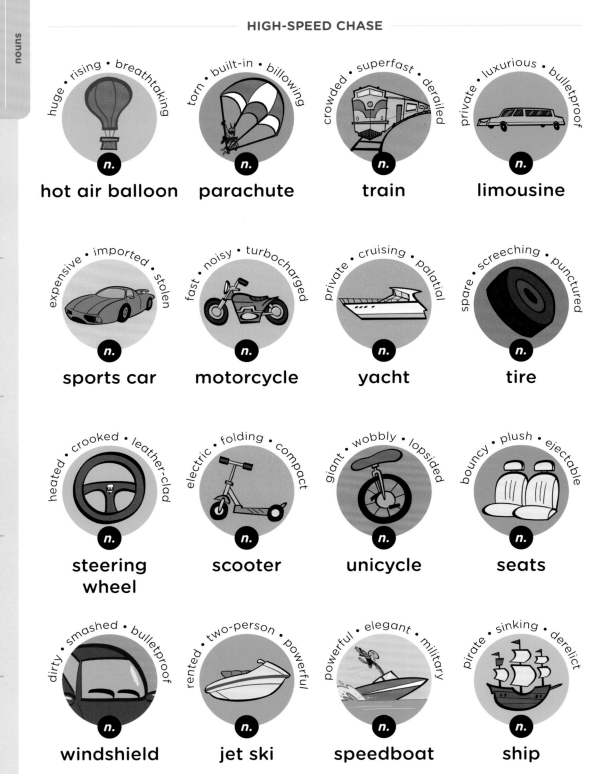

n.

ship

locked • fireproof • impenetrable

n.

safe

covert • botched • clandestine

n.

operation

photographic • solid • forensic

n.

evidence

something that proves what really happened; like a doughnut left behind by a criminal during a robbery

single • important • hidden

n.

clue

hidden • digital • hacked

n.

security camera

private • bumbling • cynical

n.

detective

retired • undercover • corrupt

n.

police officer

masked • desperate • bumbling

n.

burglar

deadly • corrosive • radioactive

n.

poison

clever • ridiculous • ingenious

n.

disguise

skilled • dim-witted • suspected

n.

accomplice

gruesome • contaminated

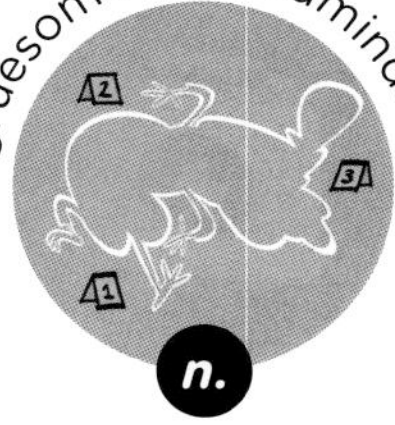

n.

crime scene

mysterious • alleged • captured

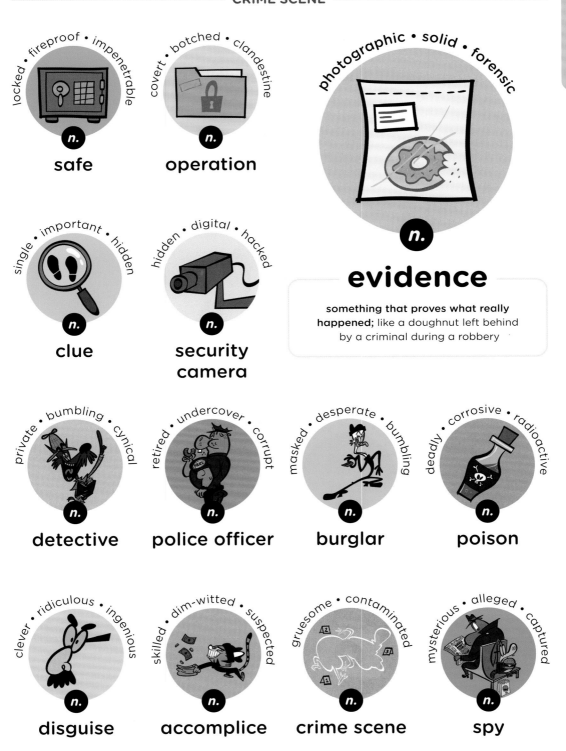

n.

spy

CRIME SCENE

accurate • fake • unbeatable

n.

lie detector

a machine that shows if you're lying; something connected to you that flashes and beeps when you don't tell the truth

key • credible • hostile

n.

witness

powerful • dim • rechargeable

n.

flashlight

armed • fleeing • unidentified

n.

suspect

deadly • cunning • elaborate

n.

trap

CRISIS

cramped • capsized • unsinkable

n.

lifeboat

electric • back-up • solar

n.

generator

empty • automatic • portable

n.

fire extinguisher

distant • approaching • blaring

n.

siren

floating • tethered • uninflated

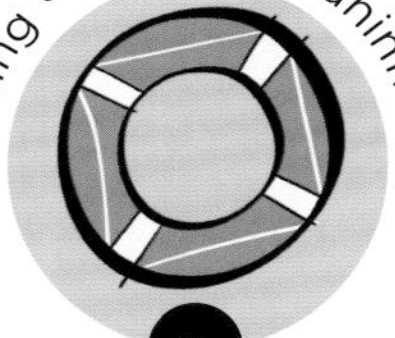

n.

life preserver

basic • complete • essential

n.

first aid kit

sharp • shrill • ear-splitting

n.

whistle

bright • intense • sudden

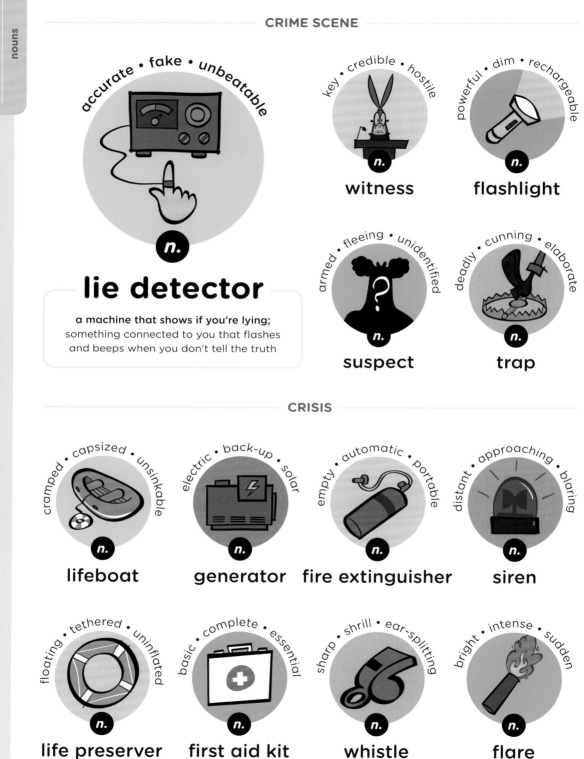

n.

flare

clever • military • khaki

n.

camouflage

concrete • burning • impenetrable

n.

barricade

fearless • exhausted • entire

n.

brigade

secret • underground • windowless

n.

bunker

booming • devastating • rapid-fire

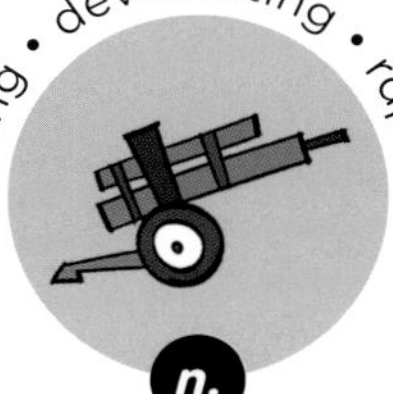

n.

artillery

nuclear • ticking • makeshift

n.

bomb

slow • endless • ambushed

n.

convoy

handmade • flaming • trusty

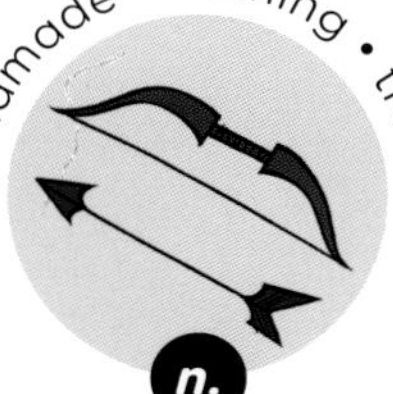

n.

bow and arrow

total • mindless • flaming

n.

mayhem

confusion and violent chaos;
like a situation so out of control that everything gets destroyed

loaded • thundering • belching

n.

cannon

sharp • rusty • electrified

n.

barbed wire

heavy • razor-sharp • blunt

n.

ax

rusty • concealed • ornate

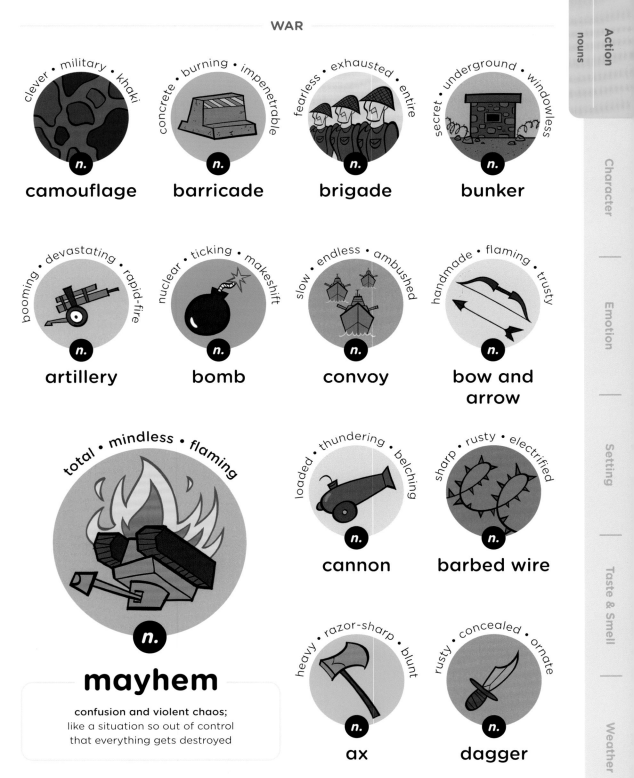

n.

dagger

WAR

giant • homemade • loaded

n.

slingshot

flying • burnt • scattered

n.

debris

historic • celebrated • international

n.

peace treaty

an agreement to end a war;
like a promise by both sides to stop all fighting and decide what to do instead

open • severe • infected

n.

wound

large • protective • impenetrable

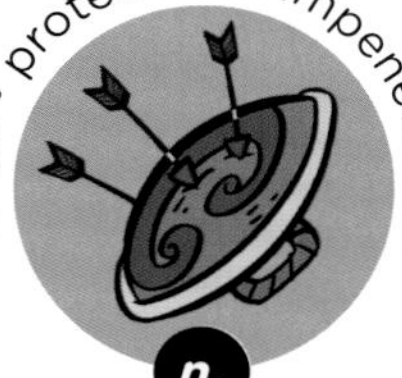

n.

shield

flying • jagged • embedded

n.

shrapnel

rolling • camouflaged • derelict

n.

tank

wooden • abandoned • makeshift

n.

stretcher

dangerous • spiked • twirling

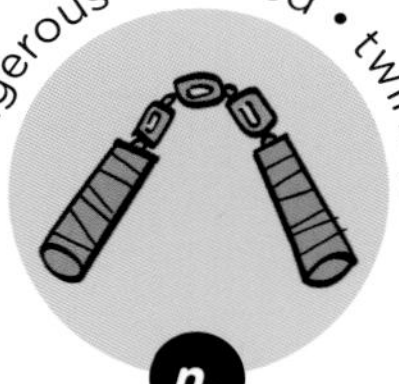

n.

nunchucks

essential • medical • inadequate

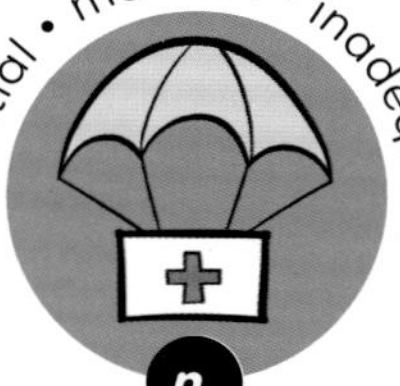

n.

supplies

deep • narrow • captured

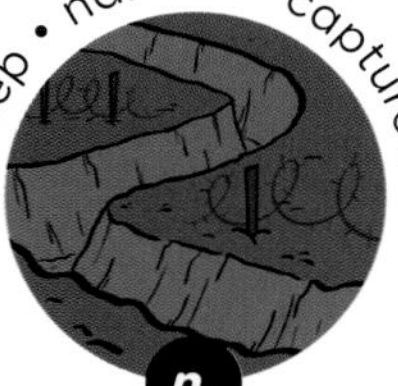

n.

trenches

mighty • legendary • ancient

n.

sword

deep • trampled • viscous

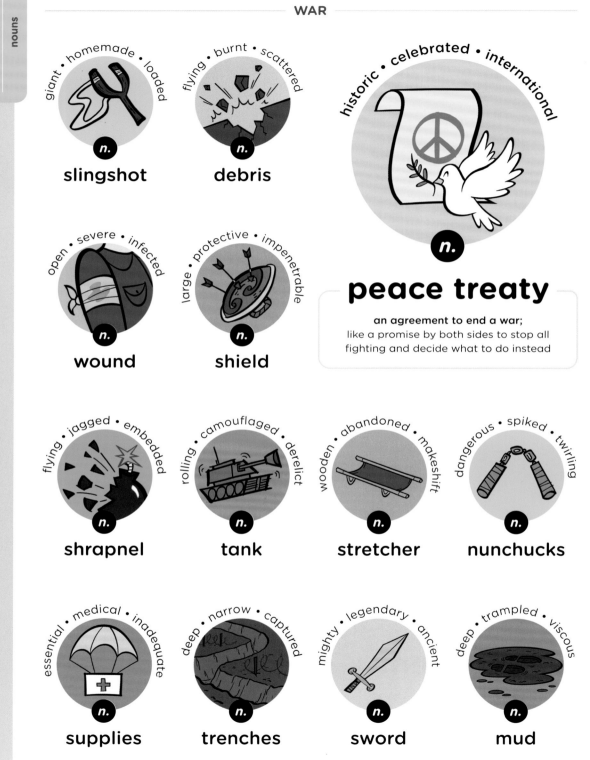

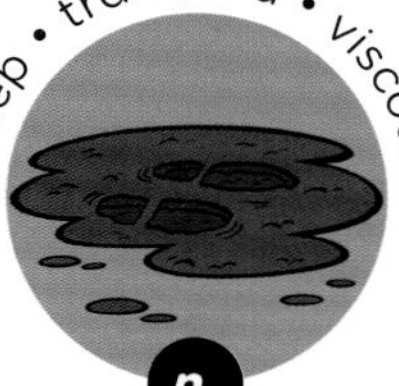

n.

mud

wooden • adjustable • spattered

n.

easel

wet • smudged • treasured

n.

palette

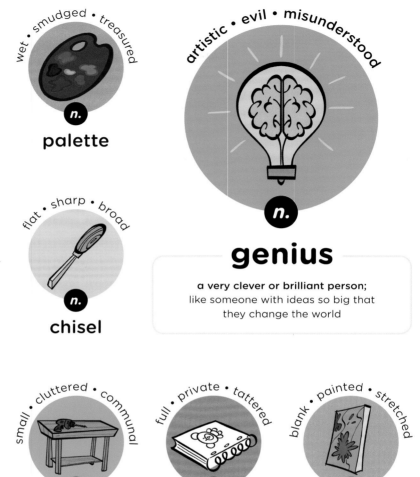

artistic • evil • misunderstood

n.

genius

a very clever or brilliant person;
like someone with ideas so big that they change the world

sharp • heavy-duty • oversized

n.

scissors

flat • sharp • broad

n.

chisel

sticky • hot • super-strong

n.

glue

small • cluttered • communal

n.

worktable

full • private • tattered

n.

sketchbook

blank • painted • stretched

n.

canvas

messy • metallic • fluorescent

n.

spray paint

long • useful • precise

n.

tape measure

cold • baked • moist

n.

clay

fine • wide • misplaced

n.

paintbrush

harsh • chaotic • deafening

n.

cacophony

lots of horrible, loud noises; like terrible singing that's so loud you can't ignore it

famous • strict • expressive

n.

conductor

clear • shrill • mournful

n.

trumpet

sad • screeching • soaring

n.

violin

soft • gentle • shrill

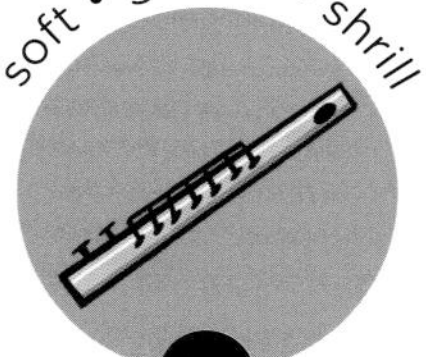

n.

flute

electric • untuned • beloved

n.

piano

loud • mellow • somber

n.

French horn

electric • battered • distorted

n.

guitar

wireless • hidden • crackly

n.

microphone

talented • inspiring • versatile

n.

singer

beating • muffled • thunderous

n.

drums

futuristic • hypnotic • droning

n.

synthesizer

cool • aspiring • legendary

n.

DJ

REST & RELAXATION

bubbling • steamy • moonlit

n.
hot tub

giant • multistory • comfortable

n.
blanket fort

exclusive • therapeutic • indulgent
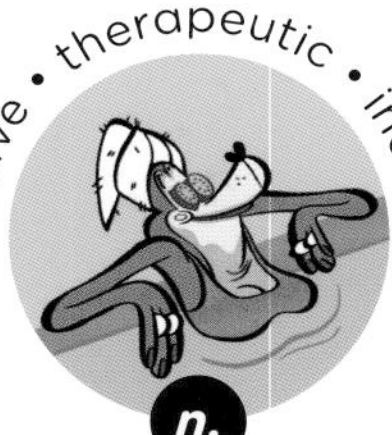
n.
spa

padded • soothing • scented
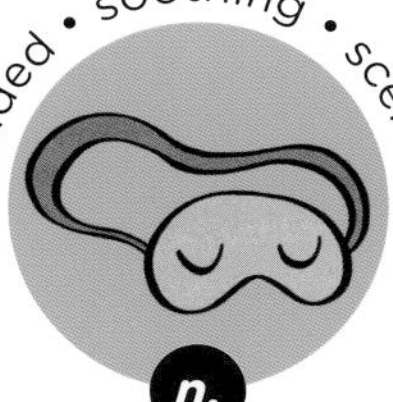
n.
eye mask

deep • ticklish • rejuvenating

n.
massage

thick • rumpled • luxurious

n.
comforter

luxury • rustic • sweltering

n.
sauna

daytime • brief • much-needed
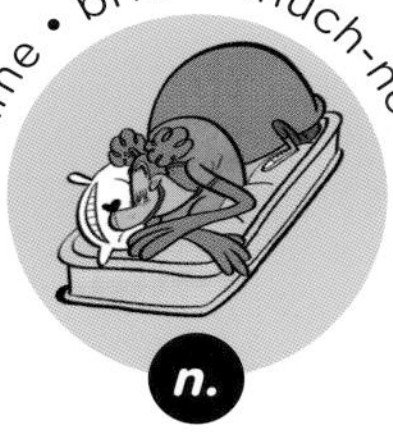
n.
nap

ROMANCE

terrible • devastating • visceral
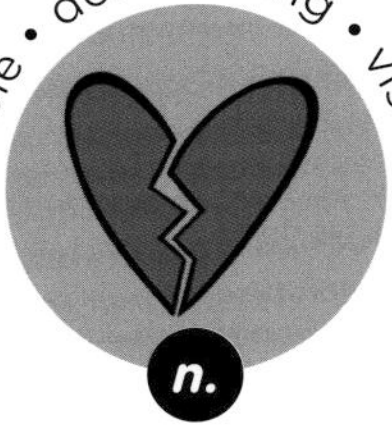
n.
heartbreak

golden • flickering • flattering

n.
candlelight

first • stolen • lingering

n.
kiss

close • trusted • sympathetic

n.
confidant

secret • indecipherable • gossipy

n.
diary

celebrity • teen • brooding

n.
heartthrob

special • strong • unbreakable
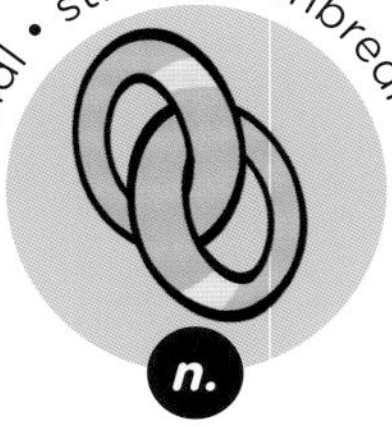
n.
bond

long • handwritten • bittersweet

n.
love letter

ROMANCE

sweet • subtle • intoxicating

n.

perfume

strong • mysterious • magic

n.

love potion

blind • excessive • unwavering

n.

devotion

deep love and commitment;
when you promise your whole heart to something or someone

romantic • bold • unexpected

n.

proposal

painful • precious • fond

n.

memories

FANTASY

enchanted • dusty • billowing

n.

flying carpet

black • bubbling • fiery

n.

cauldron

dreadful • bitter • eternal

n.

curse

magical • ancient • sacred

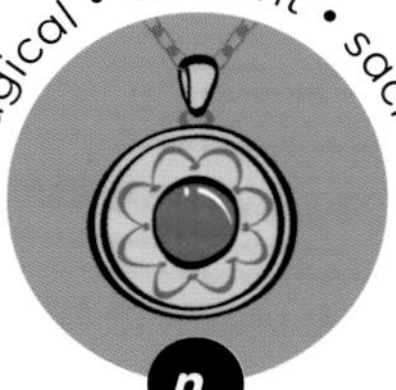

n.

amulet

golden • brimming • poisoned

n.

goblet

magical • stolen • enchanted

n.

invisibility cloak

magic • lucky • powerful

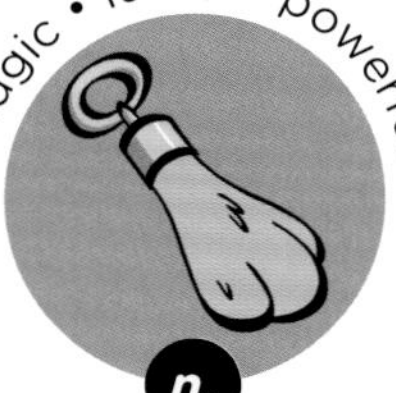

n.

charm

glowing • mysterious • radiant

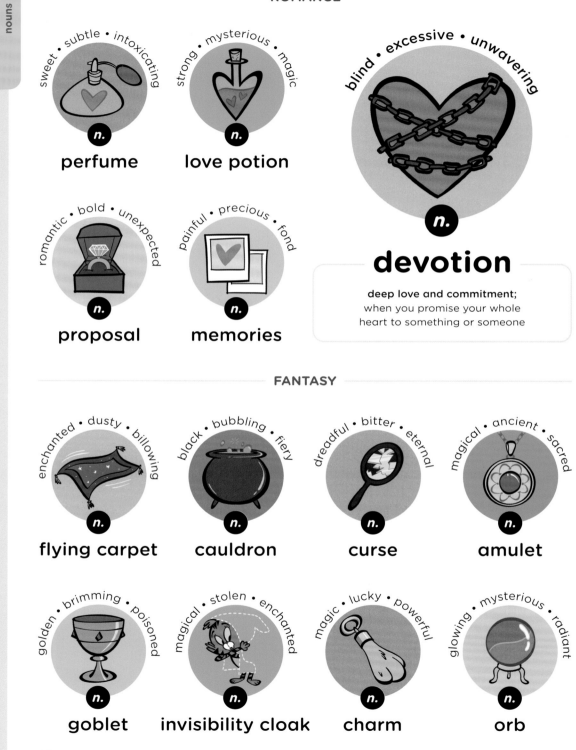

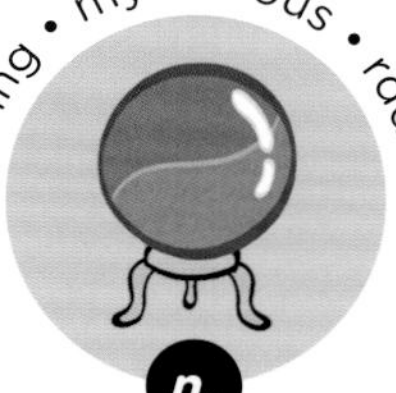

n.

orb

FANTASY

strange • ancient • mysterious

n.

alchemy

a magical kind of chemistry;
like mixing and creating materials
that have magic powers

foolish • perilous • epic

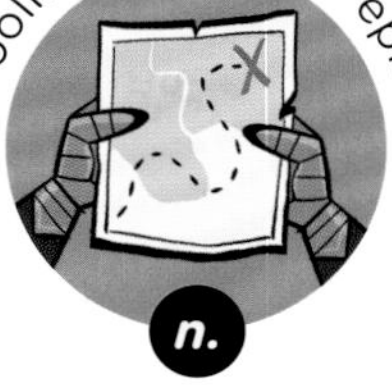

n.

quest

fine • glittering • iridescent

n.

pixie dust

powerful • faulty • gnarled

n.

wand

dusty • ancient • legendary

n.

spell book

CONSTRUCTION

temporary • flimsy • unsightly

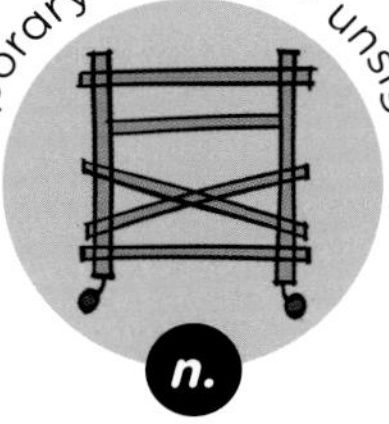

n.

scaffolding

noisy • monstrous • devastating

n.

jackhammer

gigantic • towering • overhead

n.

crane

dirty • heavy • bent

n.

shovel

tiled • solar • corrugated

n.

roofing

high-tech • robotic • precise

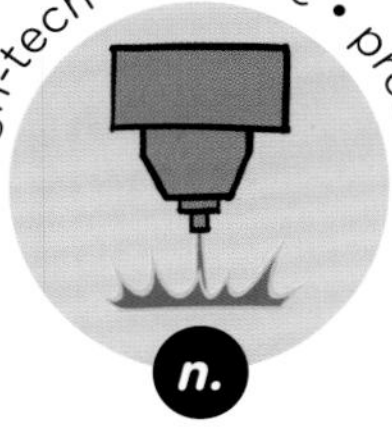

n.

laser cutter

clear • detailed • architectural

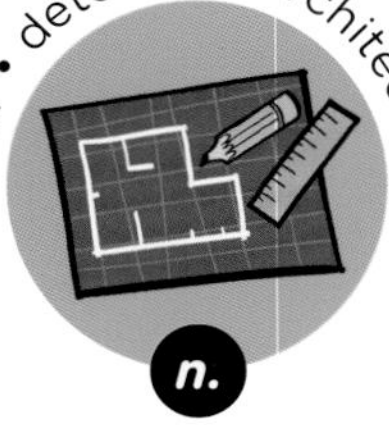

n.

blueprints

handheld • secure • noisy

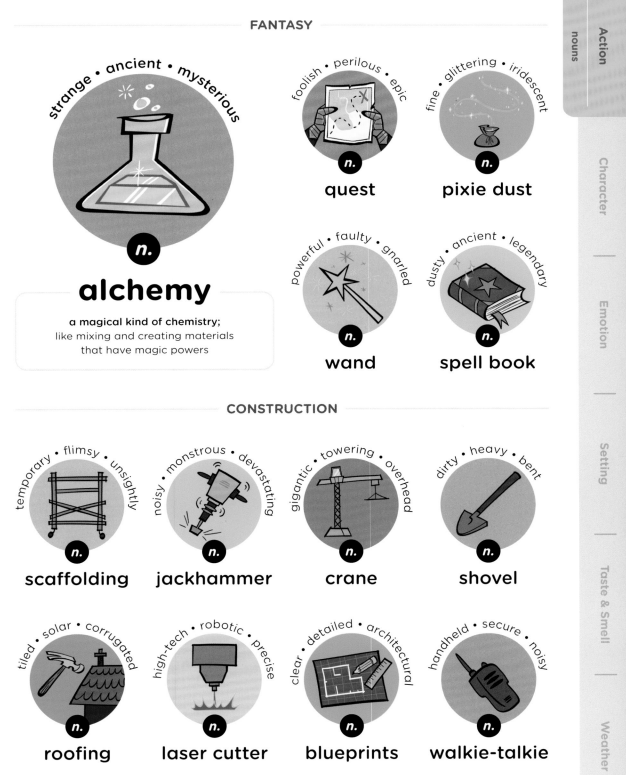

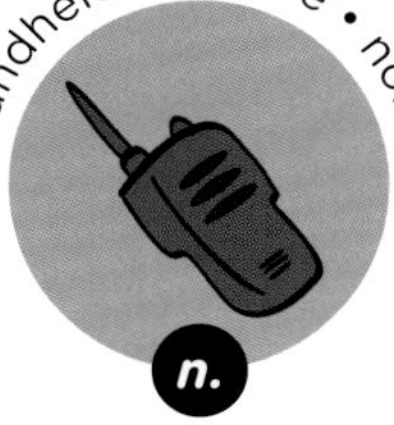

n.

walkie-talkie

EXPERIMENTS

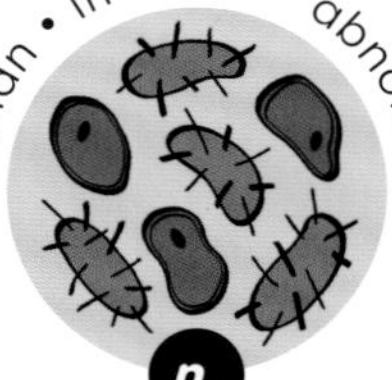

human • immune • abnormal

n.

cells

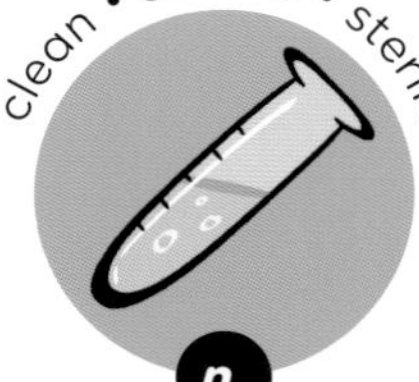

clean • sealed • sterile

n.

test tube

scientific • daring • unsuccessful

n.

experiment

a test, trial, or investigation; like mixing two things to find out what happens

speedy • alleged • miraculous

n.

cure

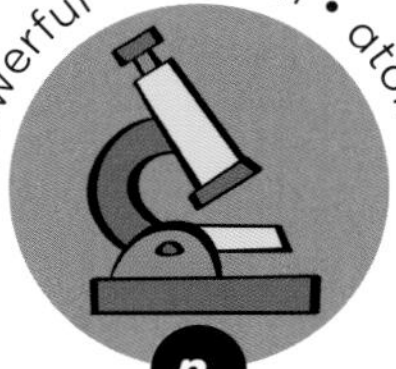

powerful • optical • atomic

n.

microscope

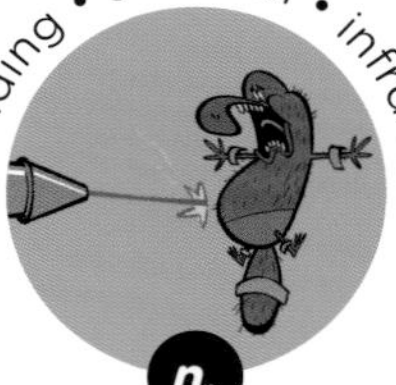

blinding • surgical • infrared

n.

laser

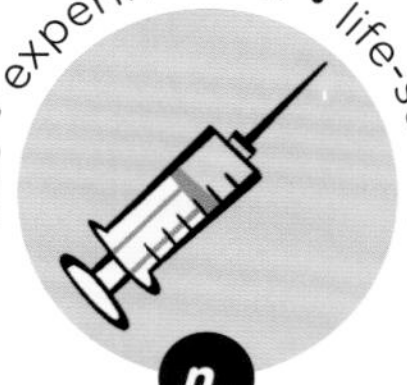

free • experimental • life-saving

n.

vaccine

alien • unique • mutated

n.

DNA

clear • grubby • protective

n.

goggles

harmful • random • genetic

n.

mutation

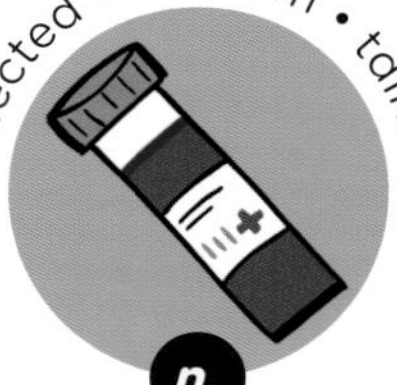

collected • random • tainted

n.

sample

lit • unattended • corroded

n.

Bunsen burner

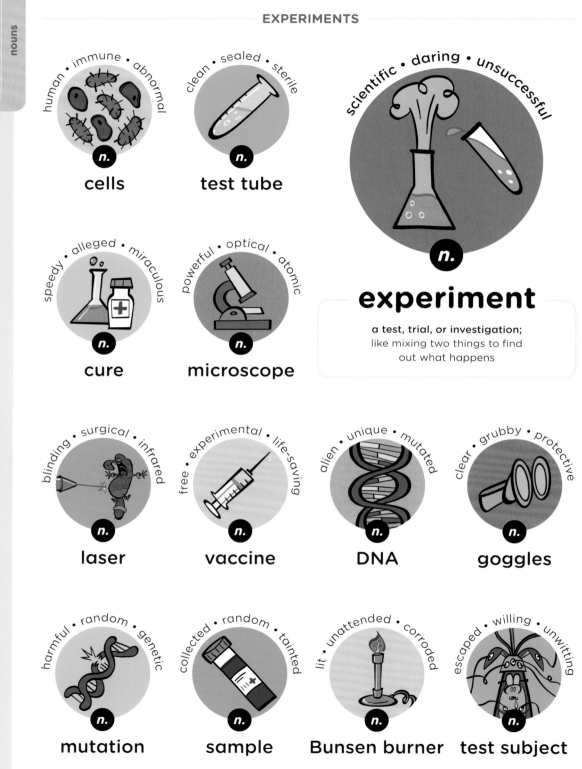

escaped • willing • unwitting

n.

test subject

alien • unmanned • interstellar

n.

probe

dead • drained • long-lasting

n.

battery

powerful • robotic • armored

n.

exosuit

helpful • malfunctioning • annoying

n.

virtual assistant

fiery • unwieldy • mechanical

n.

rocket boots

spare • external • corrupt

n.

hard drive

bulky • expensive • noise-canceling

n.

headphones

personal • sensitive • raw

n.

data

futuristic • hurtling • sky-piercing

n.

space elevator

advanced • amphibious • military

n.

hovercraft

stylish • dependable • life-changing

n.

smartwatch

secret • incorrect • encrypted

n.

password

expensive • latest • revolutionary

n.

smartphone

grubby • wireless • Bluetooth

n.

controller

massive • doomed • orbiting

n.

space shuttle

built-in • reliable • homing

n.

GPS

TECHNOLOGY

simple • user-friendly • streamlined

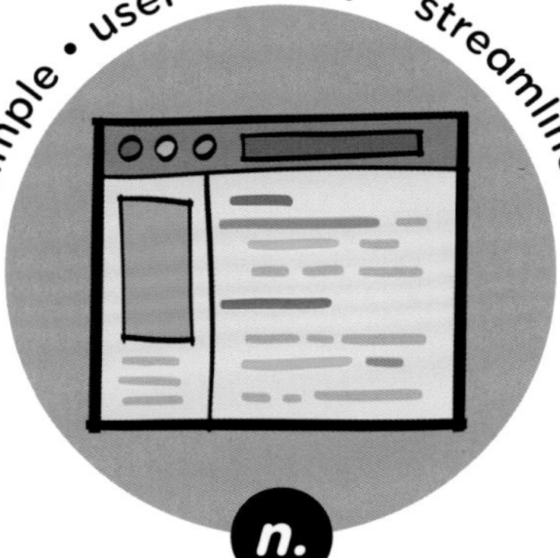

n.

interface

the menus and buttons that you see on a screen; like the tools that help you get around a website

human • broken • interplanetary

n.

teleporter

smart • powerful • innovative

n.

wearables

strange • crashed • hovering

n.

UFO

smashed • glitchy • waterproof

n.

tablet

SPORTS

loyal • die-hard • obsessive

n.

fan

gifted • world-class • retired

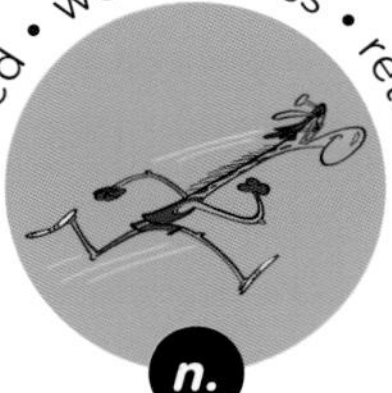

n.

athlete

muscular • talented • aspiring

n.

soccer player

lanky • average • phenomenal

n.

basketball player

respected • livid • legendary

n.

coach

competitive • upcoming • pivotal

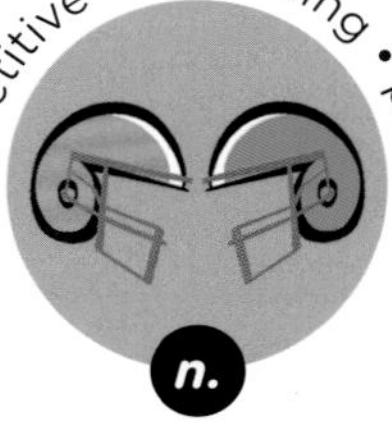

n.

game

tough • trained • heavyweight

n.

boxer

top • avid • accomplished

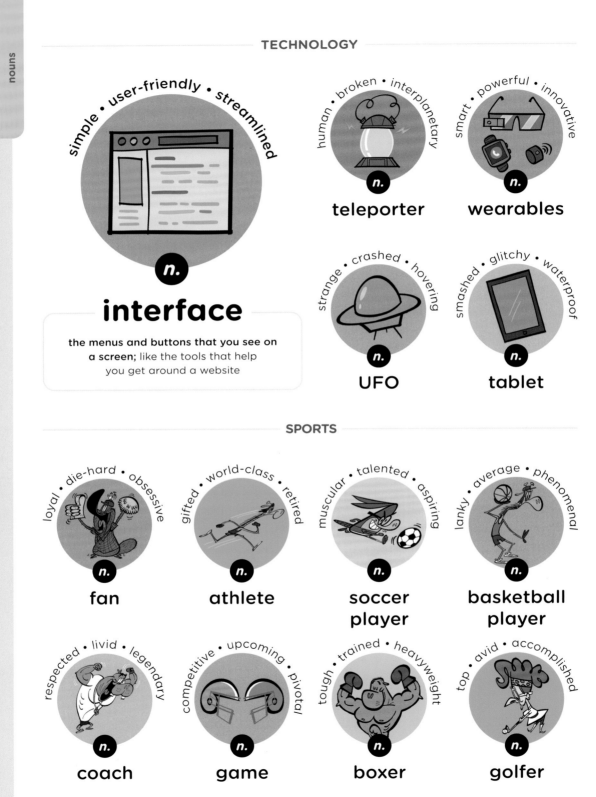

n.

golfer

SPORTS

unlucky • sore • gracious

n.

loser

tight • protective • buoyant

n.

wetsuit

strong • worthy • formidable

n.

opponent

oversized • faulty • retractable

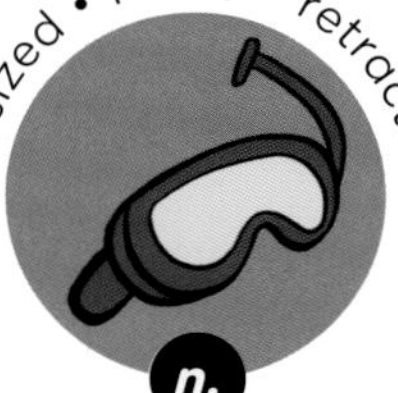

n.

snorkel

smart • accurate • waterproof

n.

fitness tracker

close • hard-fought • televised

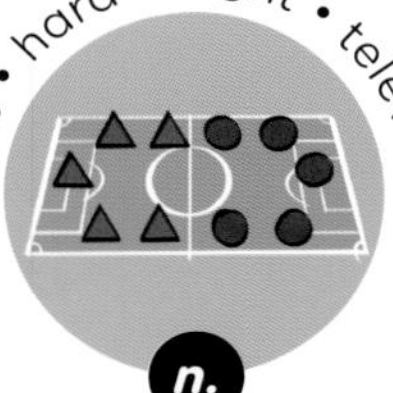

n.

match

graceful • powerful • agile

n.

gymnast

winning • dedicated • undefeated

n.

team

protective • flexible • fitted

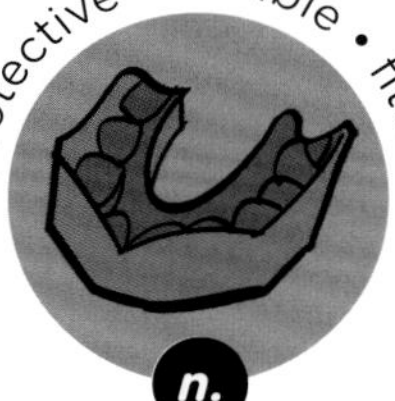

n.

mouthguard

number-one • competitive • avid

n.

tennis player

high • slippery • daunting

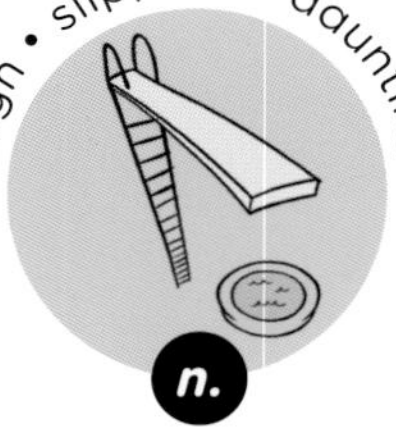

n.

diving board

baggy • comfortable • garish

n.

tracksuit

loose • secure • adjustable

n.

harness

glorious • coveted • prestigious

n.

trophy

huge • portable • ruptured

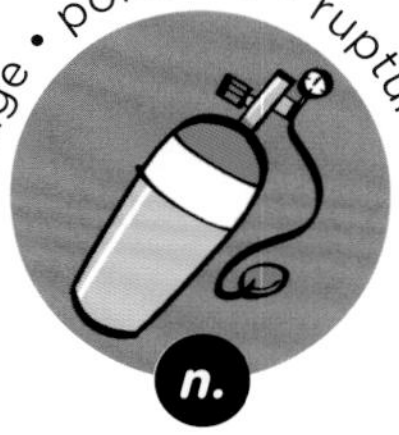

n.

oxygen tank

two-time • worthy • unexpected

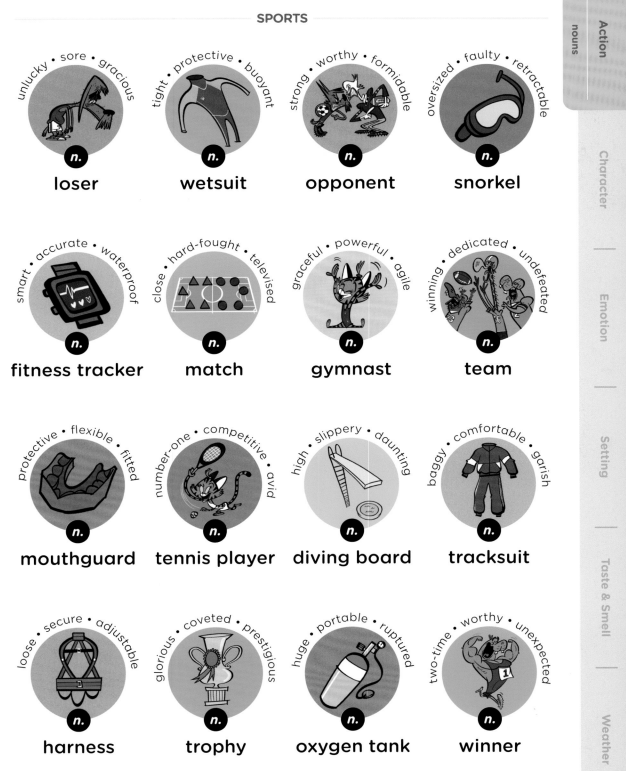

n.

winner

gargantuan

CHARACTER

chiseled *adj*. perfectly carved or sculpted; like the square jaw of a handsome superhero

word pairs: jaw, marble, cheekbones

impeccable *adj*. elegant and perfect; like a well-groomed dog

word pairs: style, reputation, manners

dazzling *adj*. sparkling or amazing; like the glittering lights of a hundred cameras

word pairs: lights, smile, beauty

mesmerizing *adj*. very attractive or bewitching; like something that hypnotizes and distracts you

word pairs: effect, music, spell

flawless *adj*. perfect or impeccable; like a ballet dancer who never makes a single mistake

word pairs: performance, kitchen, logic

---

statuesque *adj*. tall, beautiful, and dignified; like someone who looks as impressive as a statue

word pairs: figure, model, goddess

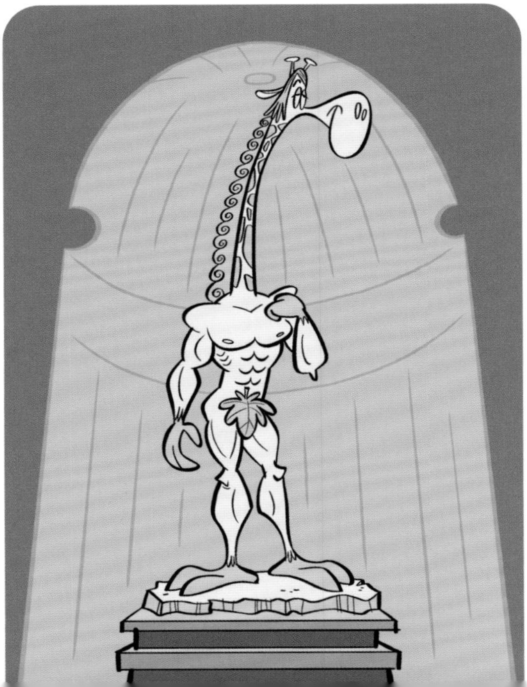

beautiful words

word pair after:

chiseled jaw
dazzling lights
flawless performance
impeccable style
mesmerizing effect
statuesque figure

bulbous *adj*. rounded, bulging, or swollen; like a big head that blocks your view

word pairs: head, nose, eyes

gargantuan *adj*. huge or enormous; like a giant who towers above you

word pairs: monster, appetite, laughter

bulky *adj*. large, heavily built, or stocky; like a big body with chunky muscles

word pairs: sweater, camera, body

robust *adj*. strong and tough; like something so hardy it can't be hurt or broken

word pairs: frame, health, appetite

big & strong words

word pair after:

bulbous head
bulky sweater
colossal statue
gargantuan monster
robust frame
sinewy arm

colossal *adj*. massive or gigantic; like a huge statue that makes you feel tiny in comparison

word pairs: statue, mistake, waste

---

sinewy *adj*. muscly or lean; like a bodybuilder

word pairs: arm, finger, throat

astute *adj*. shrewd or quick-witted; like someone who understands things quickly

word pairs: reader, move, politician

discerning *adj*. showing good judgment; like a judge who can decide on the best cupcake

word pairs: judge, eye, taste

cunning *adj*. sly and crafty; like someone who cleverly gets out of doing their chores

word pairs: plan, fox, disguise

innovative *adj*. creative or inventive; like the genius who carved the first wheel

word pairs: design, idea, technology

devious *adj*. cheating or sly; like someone who is busy making evil plans

word pairs: villain, trick, plan

shrewd *adj*. clever or sharp-witted; like someone who comes up with a plan to get rich quickly

word pairs: businesswoman, question, politician

clever words

word pair after:

astute reader
cunning plan
devious villain
discerning judge
innovative design
shrewd businesswoman

blundering *adj*. goofy or making lots of mistakes; like accidentally dropping your bowling ball

word pairs: fool, politician, buffoon

---

heavy-handed *adj*. overly forceful; like someone who doesn't know their own strength

word pairs: giant, comment, metaphor

bumbling *adj*. awkward or useless; like a fisherman who gets tangled up in his rod

word pairs: fisherman, detective, burglar

---

inept *adj*. unskilled or incompetent; like someone who gets tangled up in their shoelaces

word pairs: handling, scientist, referee

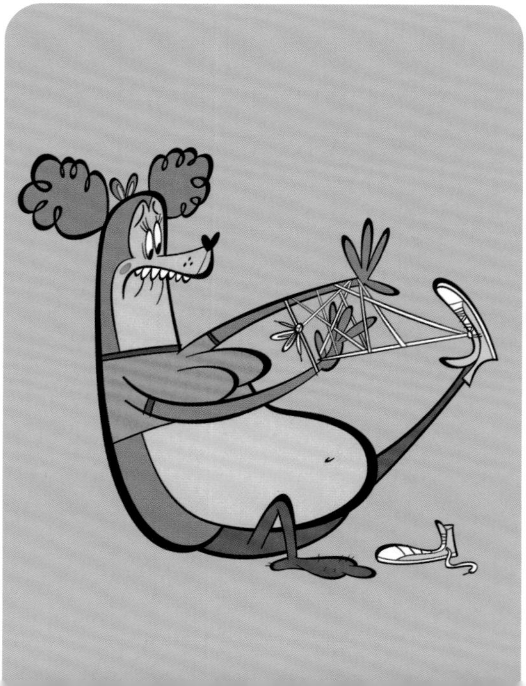

butterfingered *adj*. accident-prone; like someone who constantly drops things

word pairs: cook, waiter, catcher

---

lumbering *adj*. moving in a slow and heavy way; like someone who isn't fully awake yet

word pairs: sleepwalker, bear, oaf

clumsy words

word pair after:

blundering fool
bumbling fisherman
butterfingered cook
heavy-handed giant
inept handling
lumbering sleepwalker

assertive *adj*. forceful or self-confident; like someone who always manages to get their way

word pairs: salesperson, personality, stance

audacious *adj*. bold and daring; like someone brave enough to dive into a pool full of sharks

word pairs: stunt, move, attempt

---

conceited *adj*. vain or proud; like someone who is constantly taking selfies

word pairs: attitude, snob, opinion

presumptuous *adj*. overconfident or arrogant; like thinking a dragon will be happy to see you

word pairs: claim, attitude, idea

confident words

brazen *adj*. bold and shameless; like stealing a police officer's wallet in plain sight

word pairs: thief, lie, defiance

---

unflappable *adj*. cool, calm, or unworried; when you're so chilled out that nothing can upset you

word pairs: calm, confidence, poise

word pair after:

assertive salesperson
audacious stunt
brazen thief
conceited attitude
presumptuous claim
unflappable calm

bloodshot *adj*. red and sore; how your eyes look when you haven't had nearly enough sleep

word pairs: eyes, appearance, glare

bulging *adj*. swollen or sticking out; how your eyes look when you stare at something

word pairs: eyes, biceps, wallet

fiery *adj*. hot-tempered or furious; like the look in someone's eyes when they lose their temper

word pairs: temper, eyes, debate

steely *adj*. cold and determined; like a tough look in someone's eyes

word pairs: expression, sky, determination

expressive *adj*. showing your feelings; like an emotional look in someone's eyes

word pairs: face, eyes, language

---

vacant *adj*. empty or without emotion; like eyes that have a blank and lifeless look

word pairs: stare, streets, expression

eye words

word pair after:

bloodshot eyes
bulging eyes
expressive face
fiery temper
steely expression
vacant stare

diffident *adj*. modest or shy; like someone who doesn't feel confident in their abilities

word pairs: manner, smile, voice

hesitant *adj*. nervous or uncertain; like someone afraid to jump off a diving board

word pairs: step, start, glance

self-conscious *adj*. overly aware of yourself; how you feel when you get the wrong dress code

word pairs: person, teenager, athlete

sheepish *adj*. shy, ashamed, or uncomfortable; like feeling too nervous to go on stage

word pairs: grin, laugh, apology

shy words

reticent *adj*. shy and reserved; like feeling nervous about performing

word pairs: temperament, nature, personality

---

wary *adj*. careful or cautious; like a fly who is afraid of getting zapped

word pairs: distance, glance, animal

word pair after:

diffident manner
hesitant step
reticent temperament
self-conscious person
sheepish grin
wary distance

dainty *adj*. small, delicate, and pretty; like an exquisite tea party

word pairs: finger, flower, sandwich

diminutive *adj*. unusually small; like someone so tiny you almost don't notice them

word pairs: frame, stature, army

---

shriveled *adj*. wrinkled or shrunken; like skin that has been in the bathtub too long

word pairs: skin, apple, flower

squat *adj*. short and stubby; like something that looks as if it has been squashed down

word pairs: figure, building, hut

minuscule *adj*. tiny or microscopic;
like an insect so small you can barely see it

word pairs: insect, detail, particle

---

willowy *adj*. slender and graceful;
like the branches of a drooping willow tree

word pairs: limbs, dancer, branches

small words

word pair after:

dainty finger
diminutive frame
minuscule insect
shriveled skin
squat figure
willowy limbs

abrasive *adj*. harsh and grating; like a horrible noise that makes your hair stand on end

word pairs: shriek, personality, siren

gruff *adj*. rough or husky; like a growling cowboy

word pairs: voice, manner, exterior

nasal *adj*. whiny or from your nose; like a voice that sounds like it comes from your nose

word pairs: singing, twang, accent

shrill *adj*. sharp or high-pitched; like the sound of a giant whistle

word pairs: whistle, scream, laugh

hoarse *adj*. sounding rough and harsh; like a voice that's worn out from too much shouting

word pairs: croak, whisper, voice

---

velvety *adj*. smooth and silky; a voice so lovely it feels like velvet on your ears

word pairs: tone, texture, darkness

voice words

word pair after:

abrasive shriek
gruff voice
hoarse croak
nasal singing
shrill whistle
velvety tone

164

captivating **character** nouns

Use these nouns and word pairs to dress your characters in **custom-made tuxedos**, **knee-high boots**, and **venomous fangs**. This section is sure to leave a lasting impression.

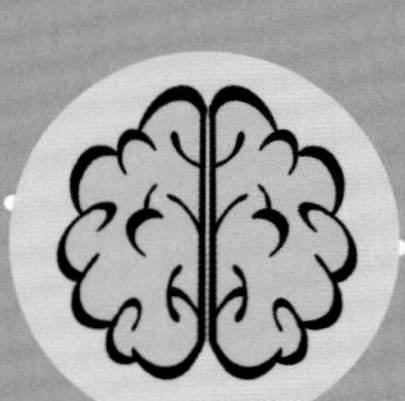

unlikely • unsung • valiant

n.

hero

old • arch • vengeful

n.

nemesis

cowardly • suspected • filthy

n.

traitor

wise • lifelong • spiritual

n.

mentor

bitter • longtime • formidable

n.

rival

sly • charming • lovable

n.

rogue

evil • scheming • treacherous

n.

villain

mighty • corrupt • oppressive

n.

ruler

young • loyal • annoying

n.

sidekick

frightened • innocent • unsuspecting

n.

victim

secret • jealous • faithful

n.

lover

professional • cunning • devious

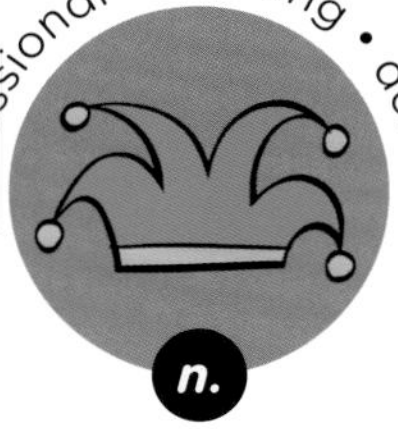

n.

trickster

clear • scrappy • lovable

n.

underdog

someone who isn't expected to win;
like a tiny boxer facing the heavyweight champion

golden • reborn • immortal

n.

phoenix

wounded • savage • ravenous

n.

beast

bloodsucking • charming • rogue

n.

vampire

evil • ancient • vengeful

n.

demon

scaly • hulking • snarling

n.

dinosaur

flying • two-headed • fiery

n.

dragon

howling • prowling • rabid

n.

werewolf

lonely • beady-eyed • loathsome

n.

troll

sleeping • gentle • towering

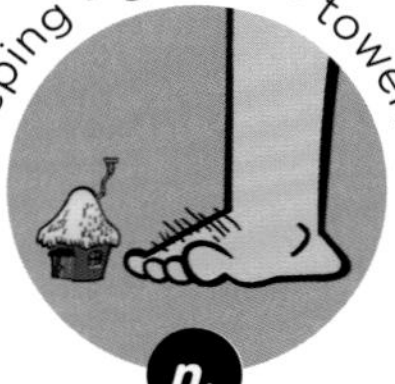

n.

giant

sneaky • angry • cunning

n.

goblin

drooling • mindless • flesh-eating

n.

zombie

ugly • slobbering • savage

n.

ogre

rare • beached • mythical

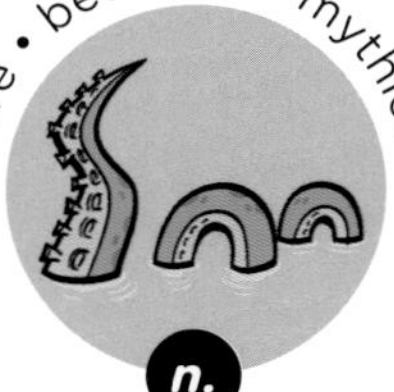

n.

sea creature

wicked • alluring • mesmerizing

n.

siren

greedy • beastly • leering

n.

cyclops

howling • headless • vengeful

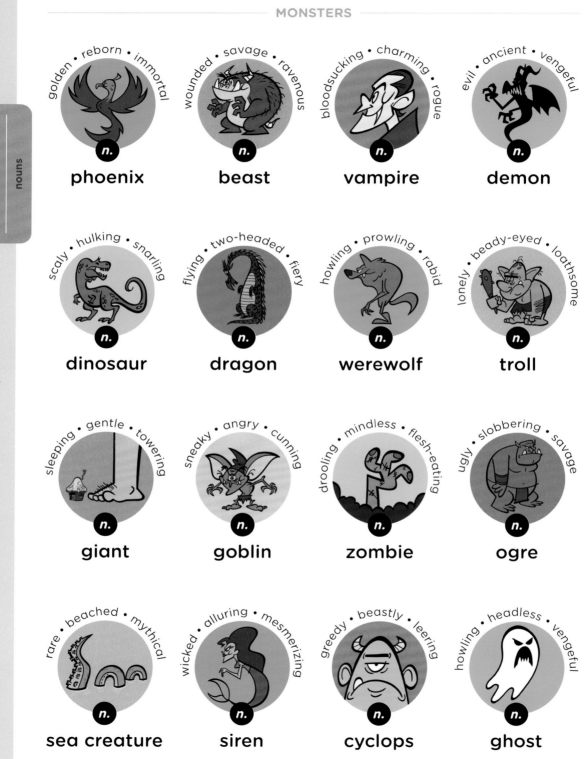

n.

ghost

rare • mistreated • telepathic

n.

mutant

friendly • refurbished • glitching

n.

android

human • futuristic • expensive

n.

cryogenics

deep-freezing human bodies; like freezing yourself so you can wake up thousands of years later

human • evil • genetic

n.

clone

skillful • anonymous • malicious

n.

hacker

evil • unfeeling • indestructible

n.

robot

lifelike • military • advanced

n.

cyborg

young • billionaire • prolific

n.

inventor

brave • pioneering • weightless

n.

astronaut

famous • dangerous • erratic

n.

scientist

peaceful • bug-eyed • hostile

n.

alien

flying • armed • annoying

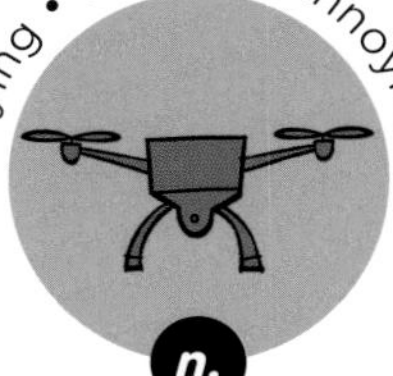

n.

drone

accidental • stranded • meddling

n.

time traveler

DRESSING UP

smart • pressed • frayed

n.

shirt

simple • sparkly • chic

n.

cocktail dress

elbow-length • delicate • satin

n.

evening gloves

tailored • rumpled • pinstripe

n.

suit

loose • silk • dapper

n.

tie

borrowed • elegant • stunning

n.

ballgown

classic • rented • custom-made

n.

tuxedo

lucky • gleaming • engraved

n.

cufflinks

SHOES

sky-high • platform • impractical

n.

heel

sparkly • pointy • towering

n.

stilettos

strappy • chunky • gladiator

n.

sandals

knee-high • cowboy • antigravity

n.

boots

fancy • formal • polished

n.

dress shoes

thick • worn-out • sturdy

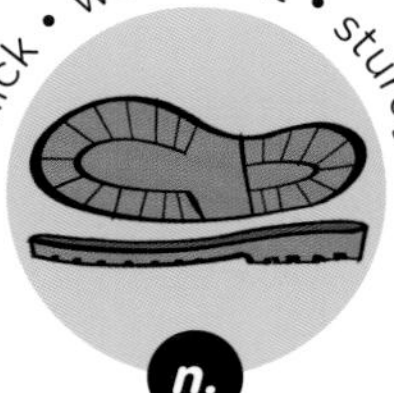

n.

sole

scruffy • running • worn-out

n.

sneakers

scuffed • reinforced • peep

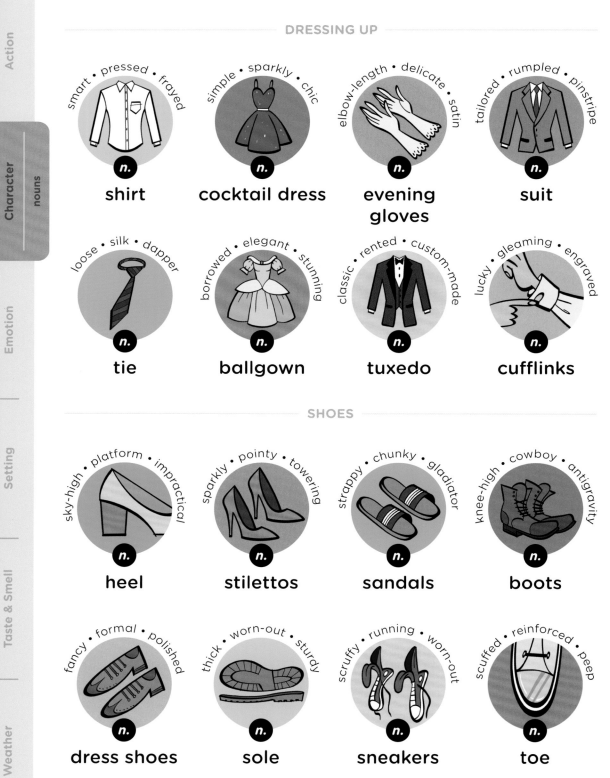

n.

toe

SUMMER CLOTHES

colorful • unbuttoned • garish

n.

Hawaiian shirt

comfy • squeaky • durable

n.

flip-flops

loose • flowing • tie-dyed

n.

sarong

baggy • tailored • khaki

n.

shorts

cheap • mirrored • branded

n.

sunglasses

bright • skimpy • bejeweled

n.

bikini

simple • floral • strapless

n.

sundress

wet • baggy • faded

n.

swim trunks

WINTER CLOTHES

fluffy • knitted • moth-eaten

n.

cardigan

favorite • tattered • faded

n.

denim jacket

leather • fur-lined • protective

n.

gloves

comfy • fuzzy • protective

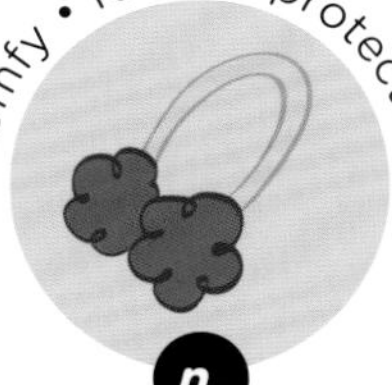

n.

earmuffs

dark • quilted • concealing

n.

hood

toasty • activated • robust

n.

hand warmer

ripped • skinny • well-worn

n.

jeans

woolly • baggy • bulky

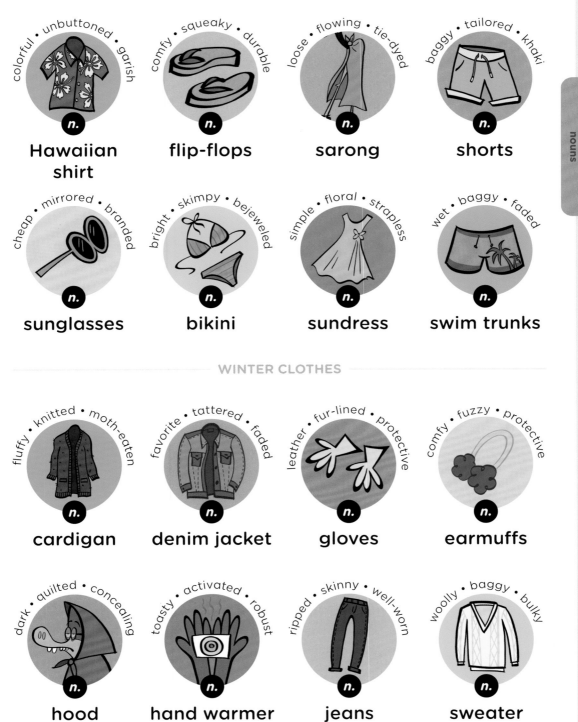

n.

sweater

WINTER CLOTHES

cracked • studded • vintage

n.

leather jacket

oversized • well-cut • nondescript

n.

trench coat

woolly • waterproof • heavy-duty

n.

mittens

furry • bulky • quilted

n.

snowsuit

warm • comfy • neon

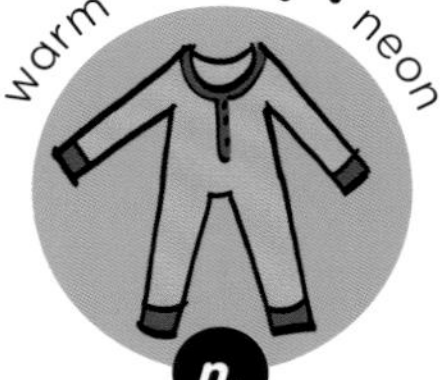

n.

onesie

heavy • trusty • double-breasted

n.

winter coat

knee-high • holey • mismatched

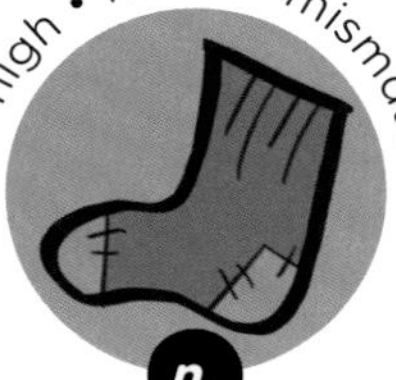

n.

socks

short • dripping • lightweight

n.

raincoat

CREATURE FEATURES

sharp • powerful • retractable

n.

claws

heavy • towering • impressive

n.

antlers

shaggy • glossy • matted

n.

fur

curved • hooked • gaping

n.

beak

sharp • bloody • venomous

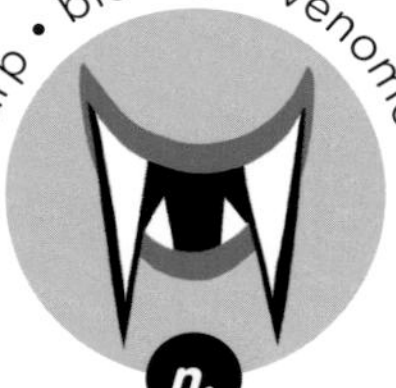

n.

fangs

silvery • delicate • flared

n.

gills

ghostly • gloopy • viscous

n.

ectoplasm

galloping • clattering • trampling

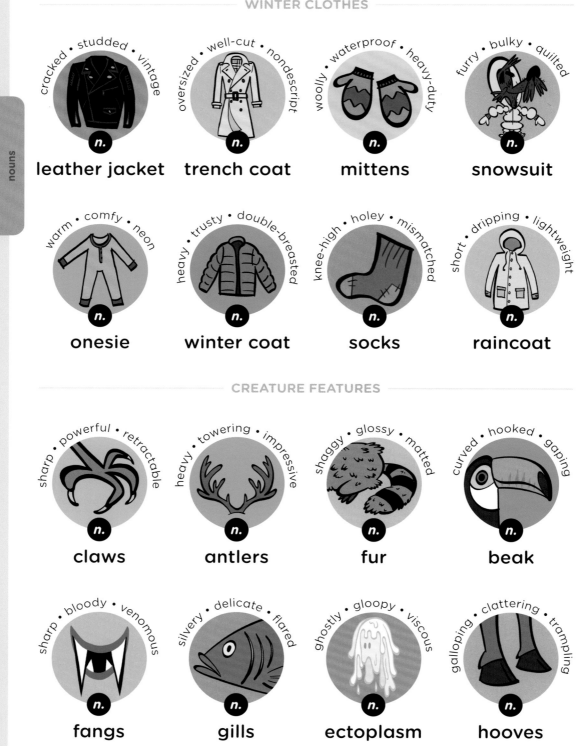

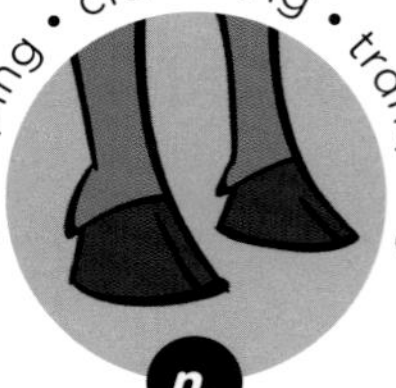

n.

hooves

CREATURE FEATURES

long • writhing • venomous
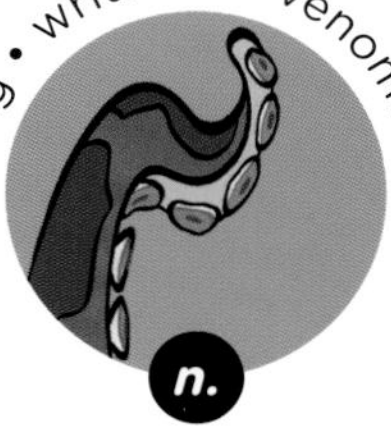
n.
tentacle

sharp • stubby • spiraling

n.
horns

muddy • nimble • oversized

n.
paws

mighty • clenched • gaping

n.
jaws

huge • crushing • unforgiving

n.
pincer

striped • deadly • fearsome

n.
stinger

slimy • coarse • glistening
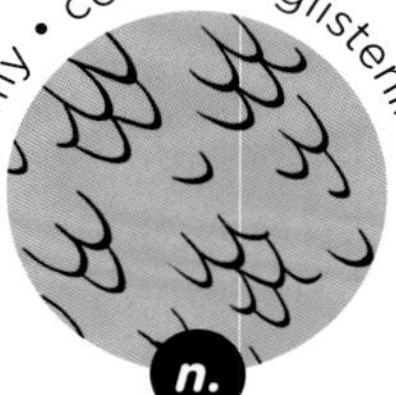
n.
scales

powerful • menacing • fierce

n.
talons

rubbery • greasy • shriveled
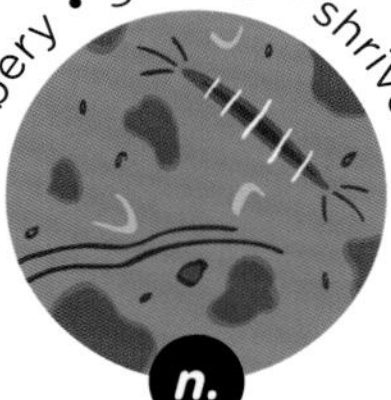
n.
skin

bushy • stumpy • curly
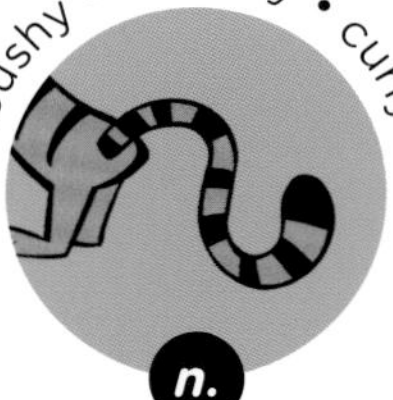
n.
tail

slippery • toxic • oozing
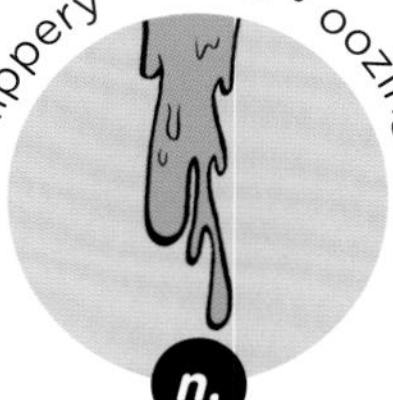
n.
slime

sharp • bristly • bony

n.
spines

protective • outer • fragile

n.
shell

sensitive • bristly • twitching

n.
whiskers

broad • pointed • velvety

n.
muzzle

flapping • outspread • clipped

n.
wings

long • injured • wooden

n.
leg

bony • sturdy • hunched
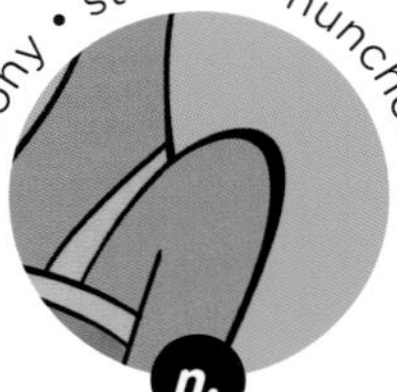
n.
shoulder

bald • bowed • bandaged

n.
head

hairy • aching • strained
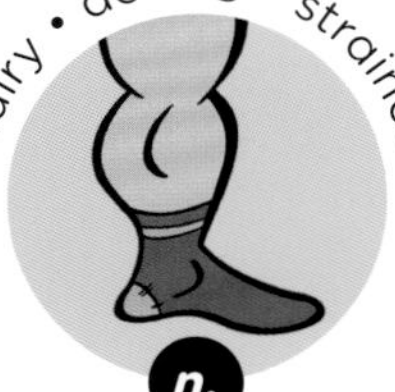
n.
calf

broad • bare • puffed-up
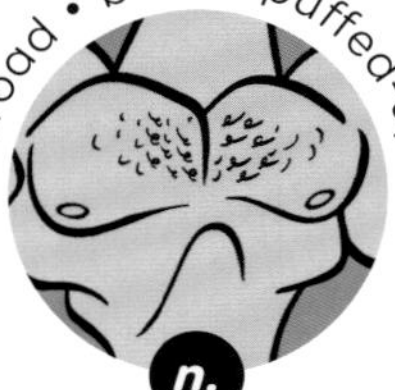
n.
chest

bare • swollen • blistered
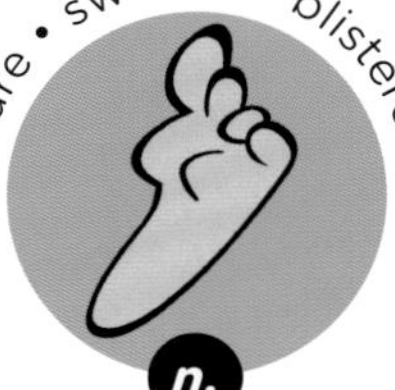
n.
foot

bare • broken • prosthetic

n.
arm

grazed • knobby • quaking

n.
knee

muscular • delicate • athletic

n.
physique

body type or build; like the size and shape of a person's body

empty • bloated • rumbling

n.
belly

stiff • arched • elongated
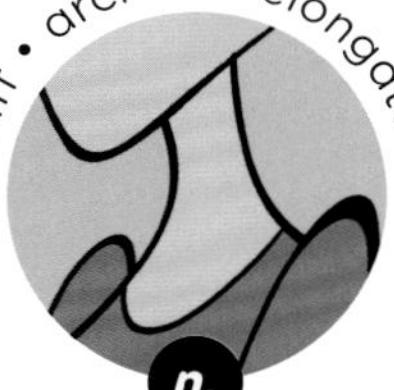
n.
neck

bulging • skinny • bronzed

n.
bicep

muscular • strong • sore
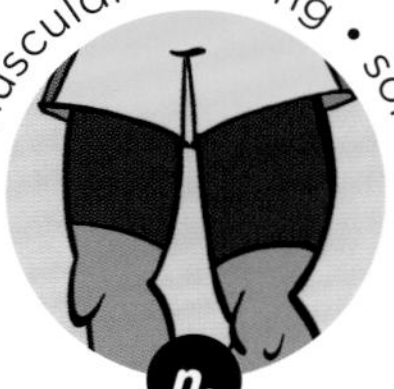
n.
thigh

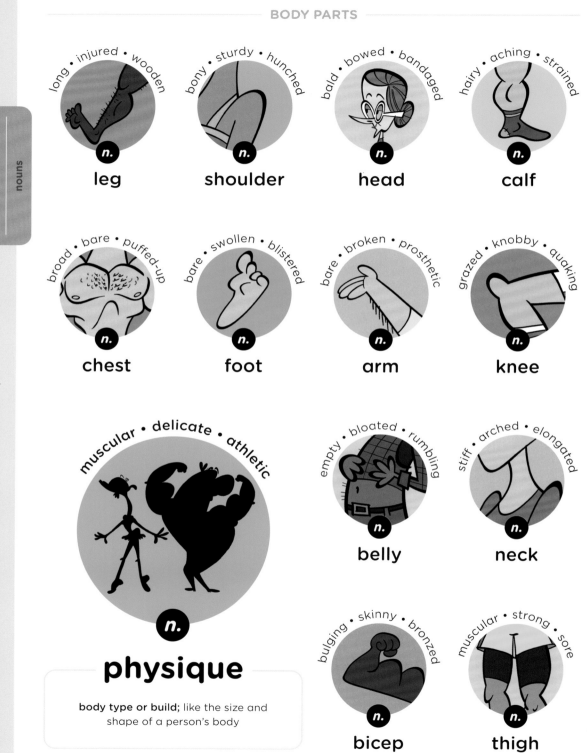

GROSS STUFF

salty • beaded • stale

n.
sweat

thick • gushing • clotted

n.
blood

smelly • steaming • fossilized
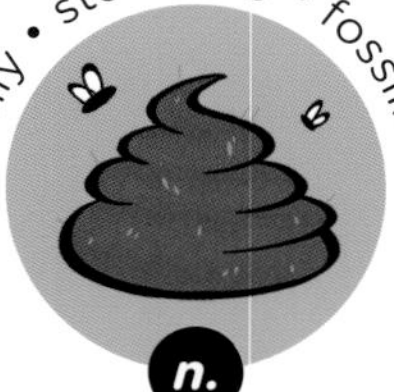
n.
poop

loud • hilarious • fishy

n.
burp

thick • greenish • stubborn

n.
phlegm

sticky • hardened • excessive
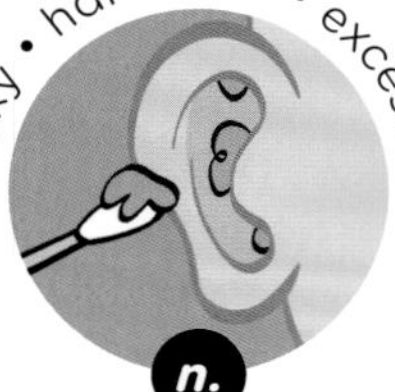
n.
earwax

stinking • chunky • projectile

n.
vomit

sore • swollen • mammoth

n.
boils

HAIR

spiked • fierce • iconic

n.
mohawk

silver • sculpted • voluminous

n.
afro

short • military • bristly

n.
crew cut

high • greasy • sleek

n.
ponytail

short • stylish • flattering

n.
bob

floppy • wispy • feathered
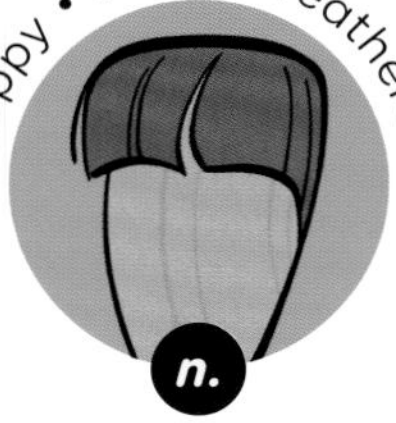
n.
fringe

messy • tight • severe

n.
bun

stylish • obvious • unconvincing

n.
toupee

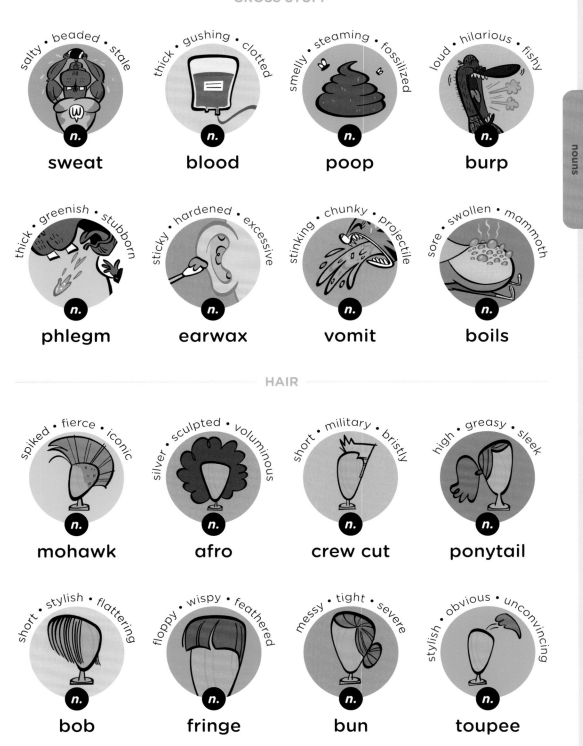

HANDS

open • grimy • clammy
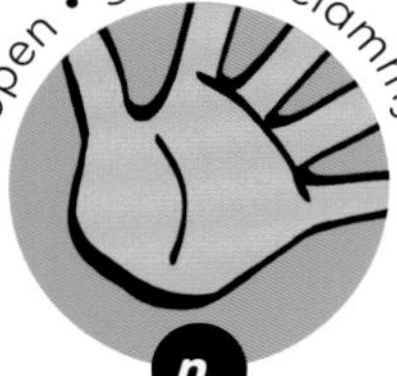
n.
palm

hairy • scraped • callused

n.
knuckle

greasy • unique • unidentified

n.
fingerprint

dirty • wrinkled • trembling

n.
hand

wagging • slender • accusatory

n.
finger

grubby • ingrown • manicured
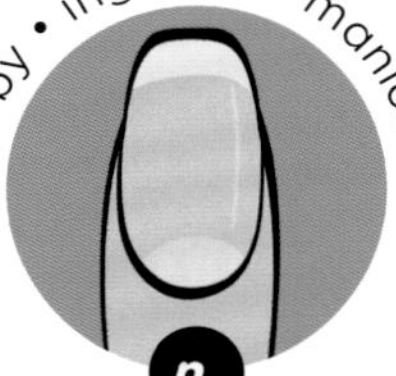
n.
nail

sparkly • chipped • scarlet

n.
nail polish

clenched • menacing • powerful

n.
fist

INSIDES

failing • swollen • transplanted
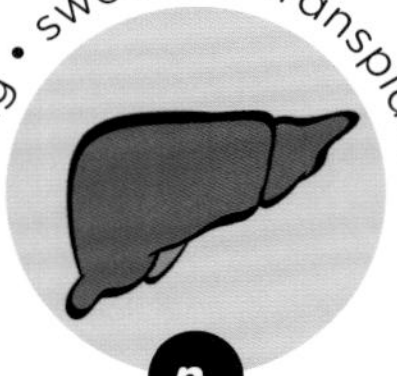
n.
liver

bloodshot • twitching • glistening

n.
eyeballs

broken • pounding • stony
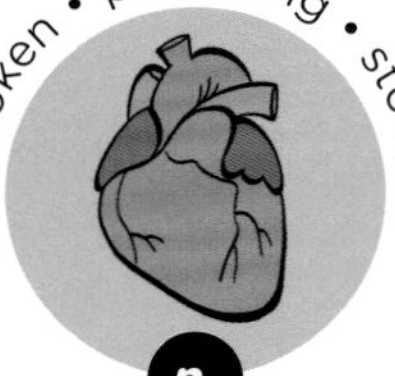
n.
heart

inflated • wheezy • asthmatic
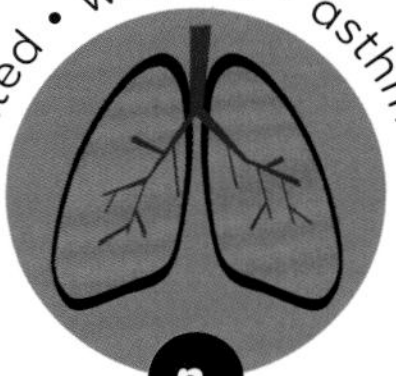
n.
lungs

mushy • muddled • scheming
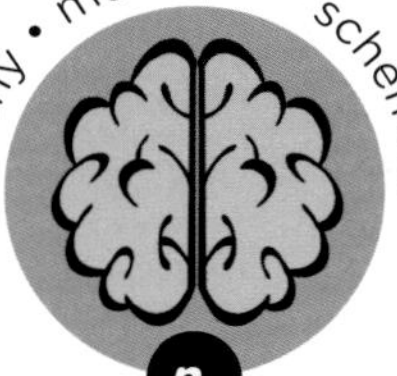
n.
brain

healthy • slimy • twisting
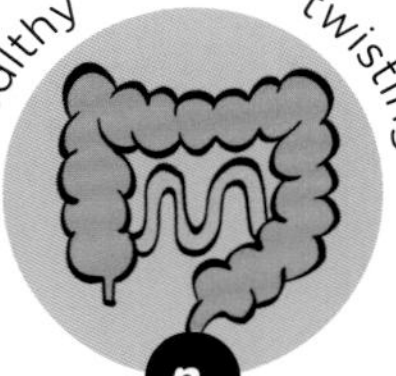
n.
intestines

purple • throbbing • varicose
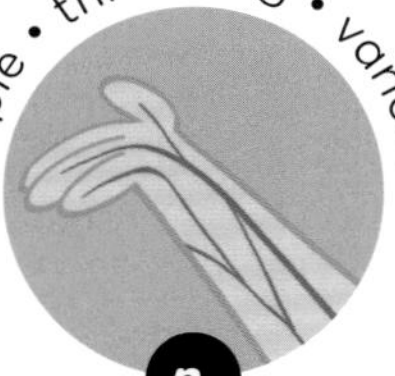
n.
veins

empty • growling • queasy
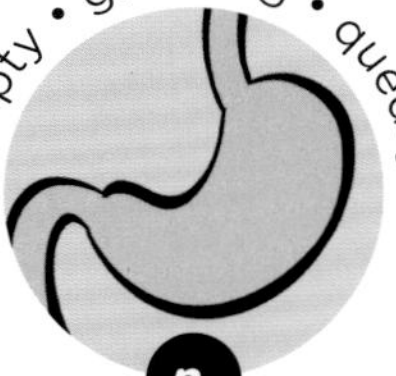
n.
stomach

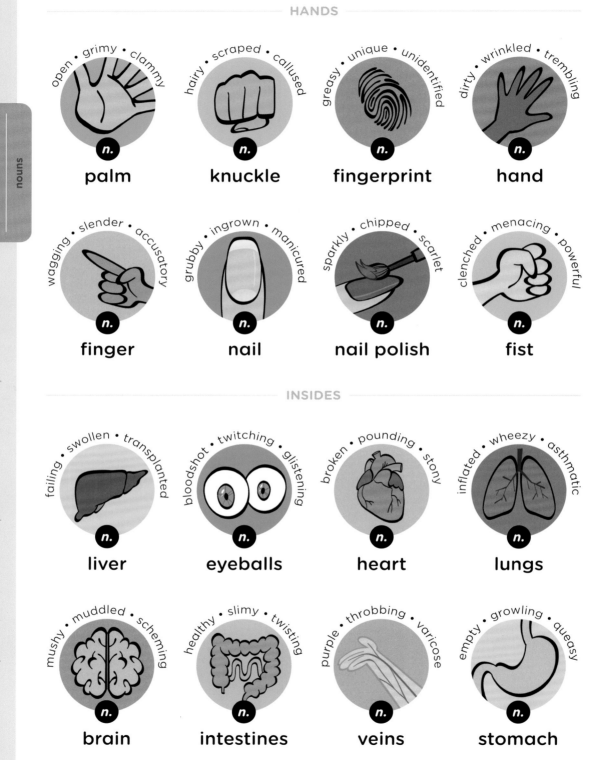

thick • wire-framed • tinted

n.

glasses

bushy • bristly • grizzly

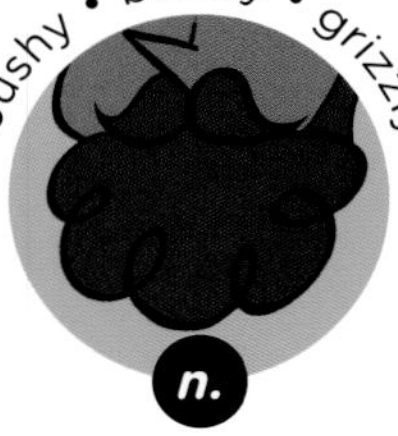

n.

beard

huge • distinctive • green

n.

wart

thick • groomed • drooping

n.

mustache

fresh • severe • first-degree

n.

burn

high • sculpted • defined

n.

cheekbones

strong • rounded • chiseled

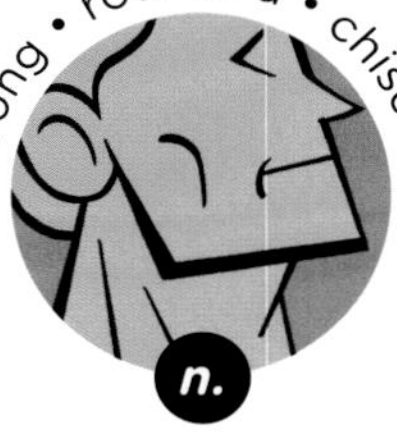

n.

jawline

deep • charming • angelic

n.

dimples

beautiful • unique • blotchy

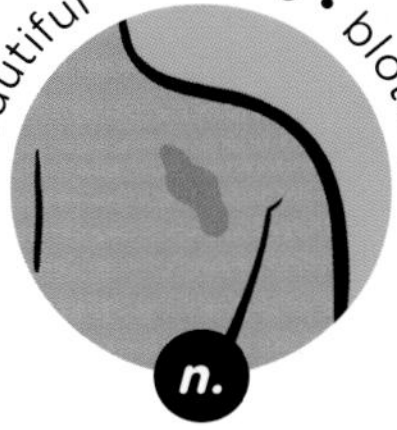

n.

birthmark

fresh • jagged • prominent

n.

scar

stiff • upright • slouchy

n.

posture

position or stance;
the way a person holds themselves when they're standing or sitting

kind • faint • deep-set

n.

wrinkles

dark • distinctive • fake

n.

mole

wistful

EMOTION

furious *adj*. angry or enraged; how you feel when tickets for your favorite band sell out

word pairs: reaction, pace, debate

livid *adj*. raging or furious; how you feel when you lose in a video game

word pairs: face, glare, bruise

grudge *n*. hatred or bitterness; when you stay angry with someone and won't forgive them

word pairs: hold a, settle a, harbor a

raging *adj*. furious or fuming; like an angry bull on a rampage

word pairs: bull, fire, debate

irritated *adj*. annoyed or peeved; how you feel when you fall into a patch of stinging nettles

word pairs: skin, tone, glance

---

spiteful *adj*. hateful or mean; like purposefully spilling paint on someone's work to ruin it

word pairs: action, remark, gossip

angry words

word pair before:

hold a **grudge**

word pair after:

furious reaction
irritated skin
livid face
raging bull
spiteful action

contented *adj*. satisfied and comfortable; like feeling so calm and happy that you sleep well

word pairs: smile, heart, silence

ecstatic *adj*. blissful or thrilled; how you would feel if you won an award

word pairs: joy, crowd, celebration

gleeful *adj*. cheerful or merry; when you feel full of joy

word pairs: smile, laughter, grin

lighthearted *adj*. carefree and happy; so pleased that you could jump for joy

word pairs: mood, fun, comedy

exhilarated *adj.* excited or thrilled; like the feeling of riding a rollercoaster

word pairs: gasp, feeling, spirit

overjoyed *adj.* delighted and gleeful; like when you feel like partying

word pairs: reaction, parent, crowd

happy words

word pair after:

contented smile
ecstatic joy
exhilarated gasp
gleeful smile
lighthearted mood
overjoyed reaction

auspicious *adj*. hopeful or encouraging; like getting a sign that everything will go well

word pairs: sign, occasion, feeling

encouraging *adj*. positive or motivating; like someone who cheers you on

word pairs: smile, news, response

---

optimistic *adj*. hopeful and positive; like being certain that the weather is going to get better

word pairs: attitude, view, outlook

promising *adj*. hopeful or encouraging; like a baby rocket scientist

word pairs: youngster, student, future

idealistic *adj*. very optimistic and unrealistic; like someone who dreams of a perfect world

word pairs: goal, vision, philosophy

sanguine *adj*. optimistic and cheery; like feeling happy even when things go wrong

word pairs: expectations, prediction, attitude

hopeful words

word pair after:

auspicious sign
encouraging smile
idealistic goal
optimistic attitude
promising youngster
sanguine expectations

admire *v.* to respect or look up to; like the feeling you get when you're impressed by somebody

word pairs: deeply, warmly, professionally

cherish *v.* to care for lovingly; like a pirate who'll do anything to protect his treasure

word pairs: dearly, fondly, secretly

fixated *adj.* obsessed or focused; like a hungry tiger cub staring at her next meal

word pairs: mind, interest, desire

infatuated *adj.* in love and obsessed; like falling for a dreamy singer

word pairs: admirer, fan, fool

devoted *adj*. loving or loyal; like being there through the bad times as well as the good

word pairs: fan, dog, friend

---

respect *n*. thoughtfulness and appreciation; like consideration for people's feelings and traditions

word pairs: deep, utmost, profound

love words

word pair before:

deep **respect**

word pair after:

admire deeply
cherish dearly
devoted fan
fixated mind
infatuated admirer

deflated *adj.* hopeless or let down; like when you feel as empty as a ball with the air let out

word pairs: ball, mood, ego

desolate *adj.* miserable, depressed, and lonely; how you would feel if you lost everything

word pairs: situation, sadness, wasteland

envious *adj.* jealous or resentful; when you want something that someone else has

word pairs: neighbor, rival, glance

glum *adj.* sad or gloomy; when you feel like you're walking around under a black cloud

word pairs: mood, silence, expression

sad words

disheartened *adj.* sad, crushed, or disappointed; how you feel when you drop your ice cream

word pairs: expression, fans, voice

---

humiliated *adj.* ashamed or embarrassed; how you feel if someone pulls a mean prank on you

word pairs: classmate, politician, candidate

word pair after:

deflated ball
desolate situation
disheartened expression
envious neighbor
glum mood
humiliated classmate

inconsolable *adj*. very unhappy or brokenhearted; like being impossible to cheer up

word pairs: despair, infant, sorrow

melancholy *adj*. depressed or gloomy; like someone who feels sad about everything

word pairs: thoughts, smile, song

snubbed *adj*. ignored or rejected; how you feel if someone rudely ignores you

word pairs: friend, admirer, expression

wistful *adj*. sad, longing, or nostalgic; like the sad feeling you get from some memories

word pairs: sigh, smile, memory

regretful *adj.* wishing you'd done things differently; like someone who parked under the wrong tree

word pairs: sigh, smile, tone

---

yearning *n.* a strong desire or longing; like a prisoner who misses her friends

word pairs: deep, desperate, passionate

sad words

word pair before:

deep **yearning**

word pair after:

inconsolable despair
melancholy thoughts
regretful sigh
snubbed friend
wistful sigh

alarmed *adj*. frightened, startled, or disturbed; how you feel when you're woken suddenly

word pairs: look, voice, expression

astonished *adj*. surprised or amazed; how you feel when you can't believe what you're seeing

word pairs: eyes, silence, spectator

speechless *adj*. lost for words; how you feel when someone hangs up on you

word pairs: shock, moment, rage

startled *adj*. surprised or frightened; like the feeling you get when someone jumps out at you

word pairs: expression, cry, deer

flabbergasted *adj*. shocked or amazed; how you would feel if you won the lottery

word pairs: reaction, audience, onlooker

---

stunned *adj*. amazed or stupefied; like being so surprised you instantly freeze

word pairs: silence, surprise, disbelief

surprised words

word pair after:

alarmed look
astonished eyes
flabbergasted reaction
speechless shock
startled expression
stunned silence

ambitious *adj*. determined to achieve big things; like someone who plans to rule the world

word pairs: goal, student, project

committed *adj*. loyal and dedicated; like a protester fighting for a cause they believe in

word pairs: protester, relationship, performance

determined *adj*. driven or completely set on; like working extra hard to get what you want

word pairs: effort, expression, opponent

persevere *v*. to keep going or carry on; like running all the way to the end of a marathon

word pairs: steadily, somehow, resolutely

dedicated *adj*. eager or devoted; when you care so much that nothing else matters

word pairs: employee, teacher, volunteer

tenacious *adj*. determined or strong-willed; like refusing to let go of something

word pairs: grip, interviewer, spirit

trying-hard words

word pair after:

ambitious goal
committed protester
dedicated employee
determined effort
persevere steadily
tenacious grip

anxious *adj*. worried or nervous; how you might feel if you panic about a test at school

word pairs: glance, thoughts, moment

apprehensive *adj*. nervous or afraid; like when you feel worried about a big decision

word pairs: feeling, face, glance

exasperated *adj*. annoyed or frustrated; when you feel like nothing is going your way

word pairs: groan, sigh, grimace

flustered *adj*. nervous, muddled, and unsettled; how you act when you forget your homework

word pairs: student, latecomer, performance

distressed *adj.* worried and upset; like feeling so worried you start to bite your nails

word pairs: witness, patient, community

---

petrified *adj.* terrified or horrified; like being so frightened that you turn into stone

word pairs: expression, face, astonishment

worried words

word pair after:

anxious glance
apprehensive feeling
distressed witness
exasperated groan
flustered student
petrified expression

secluded

SETTING

affluent *adj.* rich or wealthy; like a neighborhood where everyone lives in fancy houses

word pairs: area, neighborhood, lifestyle

bustling *adj.* crowded or lively; like a busy market full of shoppers

word pairs: market, port, metropolis

---

hectic *adj.* very busy or manic; how your day is when you have to do everything quickly

word pairs: schedule, day, lifestyle

imposing *adj.* grand or impressive; like a building so big it towers over you

word pairs: mansion, figure, presence

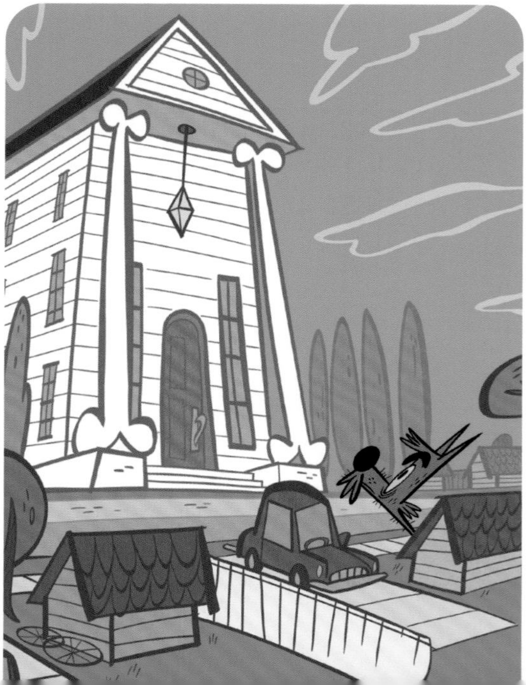

diverse *adj.* mixed or varied; like a group of people who are all different from each other

word pairs: community, team, culture

---

polluted *adj.* dirty or contaminated; like smelly air that you try not to breathe in

word pairs: air, city, environment

city words

word pair after:

affluent area
bustling market
diverse community
hectic schedule
imposing mansion
polluted air

idyllic *adj*. ideal or perfect; like a beautiful place where you can relax in the sun

word pairs: countryside, town, childhood

lush *adj*. rich, flourishing, or overgrown; like a garden full of big, healthy plants

word pairs: greenery, garden, rainforest

rural *adj*. rustic or natural; like being in the countryside

word pairs: life, landscape, community

scenic *adj*. beautiful and picturesque; like a postcard of the countryside

word pairs: route, walk, view

countryside words

word pair after:

idyllic countryside
lush greenery
rolling hills
rural life
scenic route
verdant valley

rolling *adj*. rippling, wavy, or tumbling; like gentle hills that rise and fall like waves

word pairs: hills, waves, mist

---

verdant *adj*. green and leafy; like a lush valley where sheep graze on the grass

word pairs: valley, lawn, landscape

cluttered *adj.* messy or littered; like a room with toys thrown all over the place

word pairs: room, office, desk

palatial *adj.* vast or splendid; like a mansion where you live in luxury

word pairs: mansion, villa, surroundings

dilapidated *adj.* run-down or shabby; like a house with broken windows and leaky ceilings

word pairs: house, school, mansion

cramped *adj.* tiny or stuffy; like a cupboard under the stairs where there is no room to sit

word pairs: cupboard, room, apartment

immaculate *adj*. perfect or spotless; like a house that is so clean it shines and glitters

word pairs: hallway, lawn, appearance

sparse *adj*. scarce or few; like a big, empty room with hardly any furniture

word pairs: furniture, crowd, vegetation

house words

word pair after:

cluttered room
dilapidated house
immaculate hallway
palatial mansion
cramped cupboard
sparse furniture

crevasse *n.* a crack or chasm; like a deep hole that you could never climb out of

word pairs: deep, hidden, narrow

steep *adj.* sharp and vertical; like the big, snowy drop beneath a ski lift

word pairs: drop, path, stairs

precipitous *adj.* steep or dangerously high; like the edge of a very scary mountain

word pairs: cliff, slope, descent

summit *n.* top or peak; the very highest point of a mountain where you can plant your flag

word pairs: snowy, jagged, inaccessible

rugged *adj*. rough, uneven, or craggy; like a coastline covered with big, jagged rocks

word pairs: coastline, terrain, beauty

---

towering *adj*. extremely tall; like a mountain looming over you

word pairs: peak, trees, rage

mountain words

word pair before:

deep **crevasse**
snowy **summit**

word pair after:

precipitous cliff
rugged coastline
steep drop
towering peak

dusk *n.* twilight or nightfall; the time before the sun goes down, when the sky glows

word pairs: falling, soft, deepening

eerie *adj.* weird, ghostly, or creepy; like a room full of skeletons and cobwebs

word pairs: silence, music, glow

---

nocturnal *adj.* nightly or active at night; like animals that come out to hunt in the dark

word pairs: creature, hunter, adventure

sleepless *adj.* wide awake and disturbed; like one of those nights when you can't sleep

word pairs: hour, night, soul

moonlit *adj*. lit up by the moon; like a bright night sky

word pairs: night, stroll, sea

twilight *n*. dusk or early evening; the soft light of evening that is too dim to read by

word pairs: dim, fading, perpetual

night words

word pair before:

falling **dusk**
dim **twilight**

word pair after:

eerie silence
moonlit night
nocturnal creature
sleepless hour

blaring *adj*. loud or booming; like speakers pumping out music so loud that they shake

word pairs: speaker, alarm, headline

deafening *adj*. very loud or noisy; like the sound of an airplane taking off

word pairs: roar, noise, silence

---

grating *adj*. harsh and annoying; like the sound of sharp nails scraping a blackboard

word pairs: screech, sound, personality

muffled *adj*. hushed or stifled; like the sound made when you speak into a pillow

word pairs: sound, thud, scream

ear-splitting *adj.* loud or piercing; like someone playing a flute right into your ear

word pairs: music, siren, screech

---

reverberating *adj.* echoing and vibrating; like crashing cymbals that shake your whole body

word pairs: crash, echo, explosion

noise words

word pair after:

blaring speaker
deafening roar
ear-splitting music
grating screech
muffled sound
reverberating crash

barren *adj*. empty or bare; like a lonely desert where nothing can grow

word pairs: desert, landscape, wasteland

tangled *adj*. twisted or knotted; like a fly trapped in a spiderweb

word pairs: web, hair, undergrowth

impenetrable *adj*. dense and inaccessible; like a thick forest that you can't get through

word pairs: forest, darkness, mystery

teeming *adj*. full or crowded; like a park that is overflowing with birds, insects, and animals

word pairs: jungle, city, station

overgrown *adj*. wild or tangled; like a jungle with plants growing on top of each other

word pairs: wilderness, garden, ruin

---

withered *adj*. wilted and drooping; like a dying tree that doesn't grow leaves anymore

word pairs: tree, flower, root

outdoor words

word pair after:

barren desert
impenetrable forest
overgrown wilderness
tangled web
teeming jungle
withered tree

bucolic *adj*. pleasantly rural or idyllic; like a day out in the countryside

word pairs: countryside, landscape, bliss

---

quaint *adj*. charming or picturesque; like a pretty, old-fashioned cottage

word pairs: cottage, street, village

coastal *adj*. on the coast or beside the sea; like a road winding past beautiful beaches

word pairs: road, resort, scenery

---

remote *adj*. far away and alone; like an island where one person lives all by himself

word pairs: island, village, chance

picturesque *adj.* attractive or scenic; like a village so pretty it could be on a postcard

word pairs: village, scene, beauty

---

secluded *adj.* quiet or remote; like a place where you can be completely alone

word pairs: spot, beach, corner

village words

word pair after:

bucolic countryside
coastal road
picturesque village
quaint cottage
remote island
secluded spot

choppy *adj*. rough or stormy; like the sea when it is full of small, bumpy waves

word pairs: sea, waves, weather

perilous *adj*. dangerous or unsafe; like terrifying rapids that throw your boat around

word pairs: journey, water, road

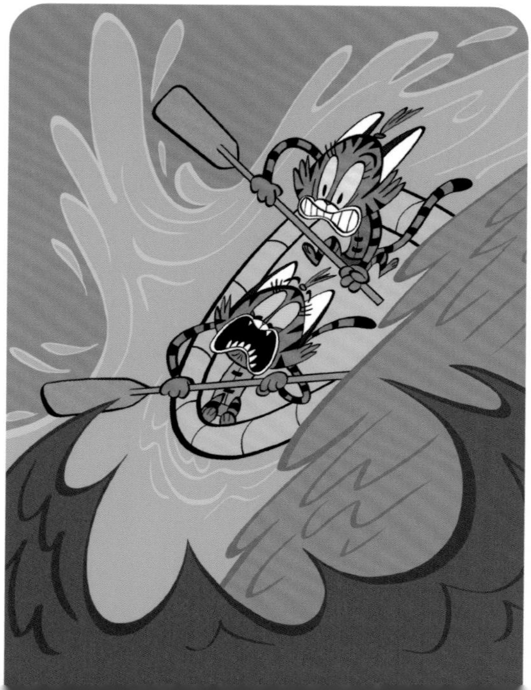

frothy *adj*. foaming or bubbly; like a coffee covered in whipped cream

word pairs: cappuccino, water, foam

shimmering *adj*. gleaming or glistening; like a precious pearl when it catches the light

word pairs: beauty, water, surface

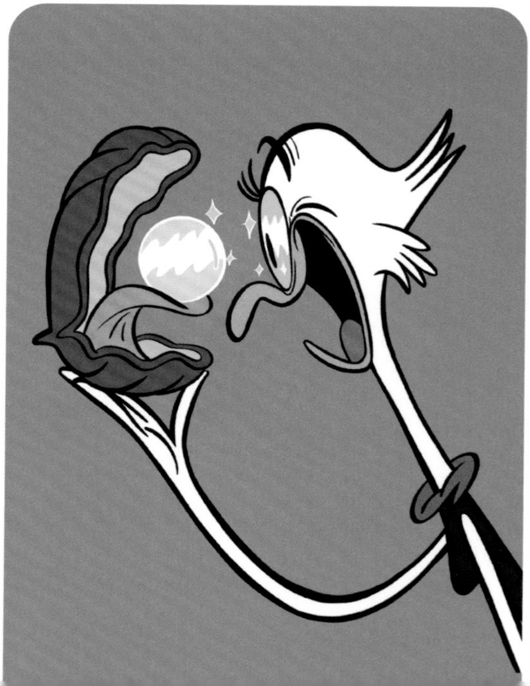

water words

murky *adj*. dark, muddy, or cloudy; like water that's so dirty you can barely see through it

word pairs: water, sky, past

---

stagnant *adj*. stale or motionless; like a dirty pond where nothing is living or moving

word pairs: pond, swamp, sewage

word pair after:

choppy sea
frothy cappuccino
murky water
perilous journey
shimmering beauty
stagnant pond

373

serene setting nouns

Take a tour of the ENTIRE UNIVERSE with these setting nouns and word pairs. Does your story take place in a **medieval fortress** or aboard an **international space station**? This section is for intrepid explorers!

friendly • handy • late-night

n.

convenience store

colorful • spray-painted • rude

n.

graffiti

uneven • slippery • littered

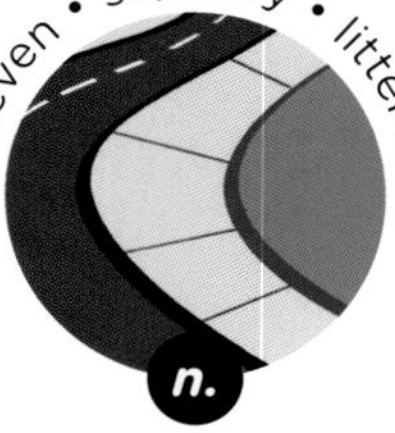

n.

pavement

dark • narrow • winding

n.

alley

local • family-owned • artisan

n.

bakery

digital • interactive • garish

n.

billboard

local • organic • award-winning

n.

butcher shop

passing • honking • available

n.

cab

noisy • dense • bustling

n.

crowd

well-run • reputable • profitable

n.

bank

five-star • trendy • charming

n.

hotel

flashing • blinking • buzzing

n.

neon sign

busy • congested • international

n.

airport

clean • overcrowded • private

n.

hospital

deep • dangerous • gaping

n.

pothole

run-down • automated

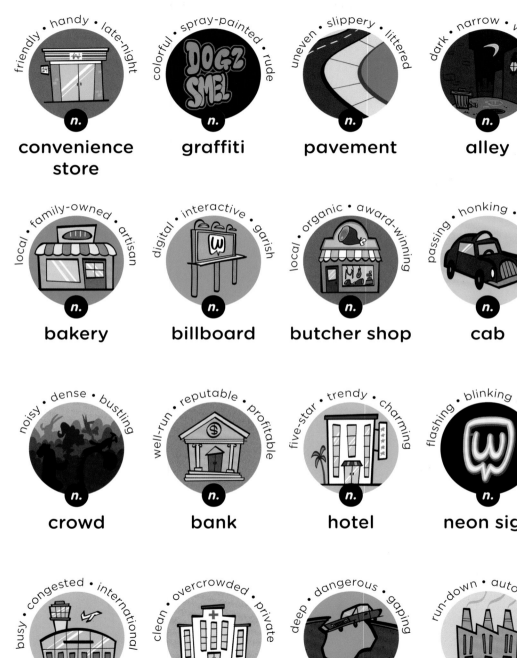

n.

factory

icy • narrow • coastal

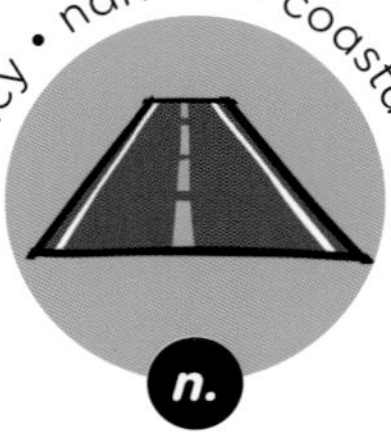

n.

road

bright • flickering • dim

n.

street light

important • confusing • well-lit

n.

road sign

crowded • high-end • abandoned

n.

shopping center

local • self-service • ransacked

n.

supermarket

eager • countless • stranded

n.

tourists

famous • life-size • headless

n.

statue

noisy • bustling • underground

n.

train station

general • excited • big-city

n.

hubbub

a lot of noise caused by people talking over each other; like two basketball teams arguing with the referee

towering • iconic • futuristic

n.

skyscraper

heavy • slow-moving • oncoming

n.

traffic

wide • faded • unlit

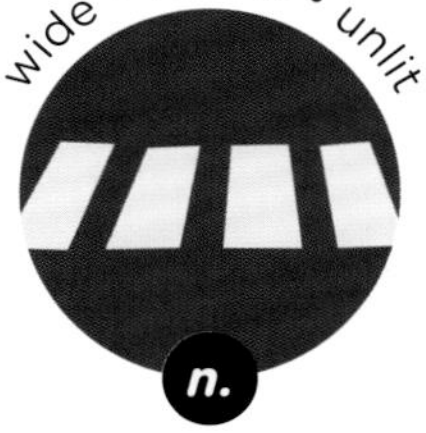

n.

crosswalk

stinking • blocked • overflowing

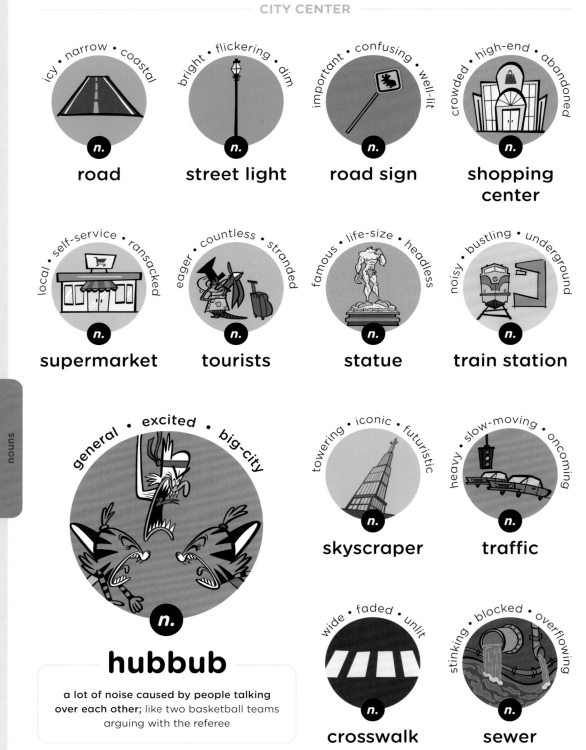

n.

sewer

JUNKYARD

powerful • thunderous • rusty

n.

car crusher

rotting • stinking • accumulated

n.

trash

plastic • toxic • biodegradable

n.

waste

filthy • dented • overflowing

n.

dumpster

parked • speeding • enormous

n.

garbage truck

giant • disgusting • crushed

n.

cockroaches

steaming • hazardous • industrial

n.

landfill

useless • unwanted • salvaged

n.

junk

PARK

wooden • shaded • rickety

n.

bench

flightless • odd-looking • rubber

n.

duck

tame • faithful • stray

n.

dog

fresh • pungent • unscooped

n.

dog poop

narrow • arched • crumbling

n.

bridge

public • ornate • contaminated

n.

drinking fountain

wild • common • wilting

n.

daisy

dewy • overgrown • trampled

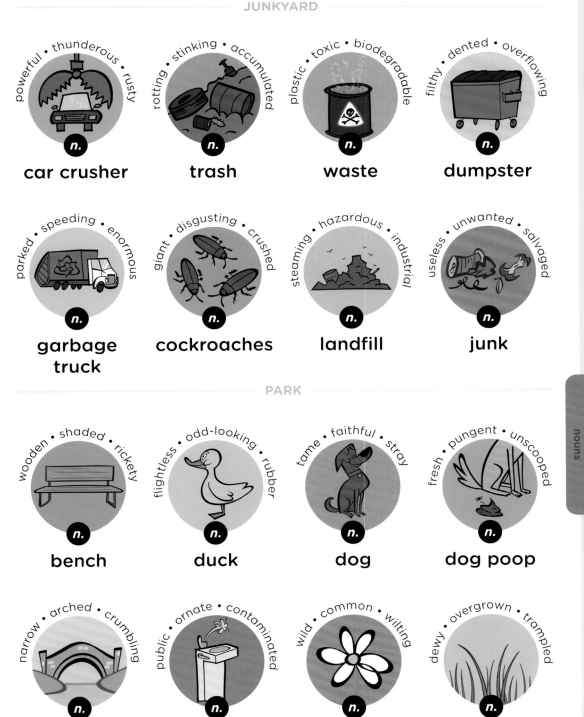

n.

grass

PARK

scruffy • cooing • dim-witted

n.
pigeon

fallen • hollow • lush

n.
trees

fluffy • nimble • inquisitive

n.
squirrel

flowering • overgrown • potted

n.
plants

beloved • fenced-in • deserted

n.
playground

steep • slippery • spiraling

n.
slide

shallow • serene • polluted

n.
lake

rusty • squeaky • perilous
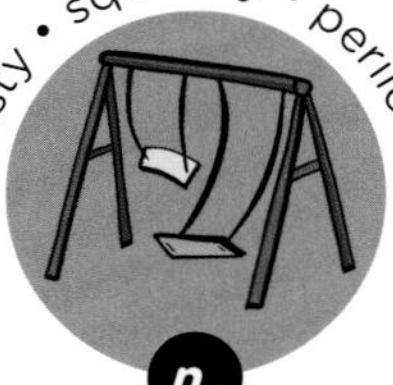
n.
swing set

DANGER ZONE

secret • dismal • imposing
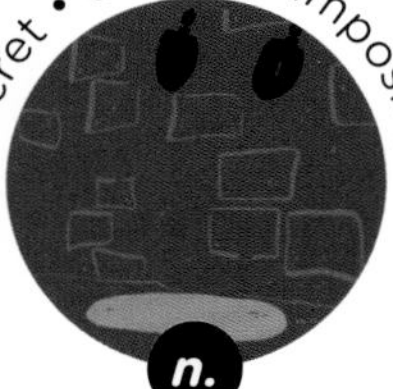
n.
dungeon

brutal • fierce • dangerous

n.
battleground

dark • windowless • dingy

n.
basement

creepy • ghostly • mysterious

n.
abandoned house

dusty • abandoned • hazardous

n.
building site

dangerous • lethal • unswept

n.
minefield

crowded • dreary • high-security

n.
prison

dark • disused • automated

n.
warehouse

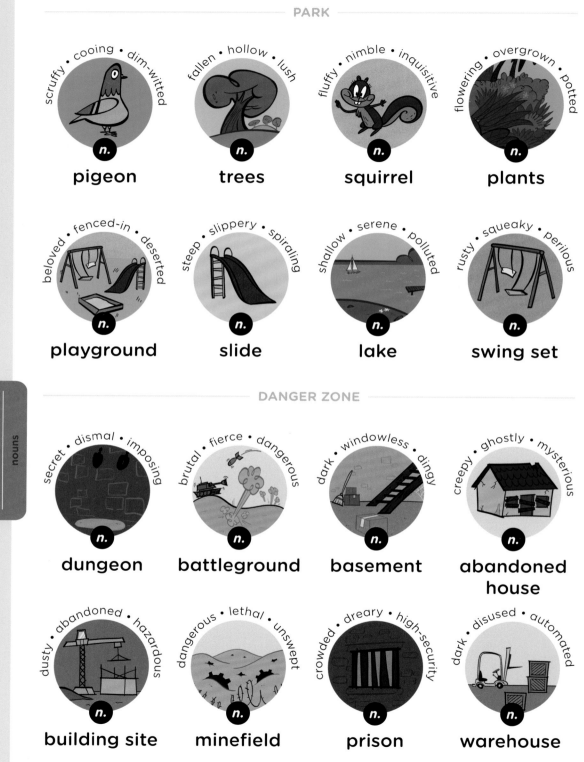

SAFE HAVEN

public • disused • abandoned

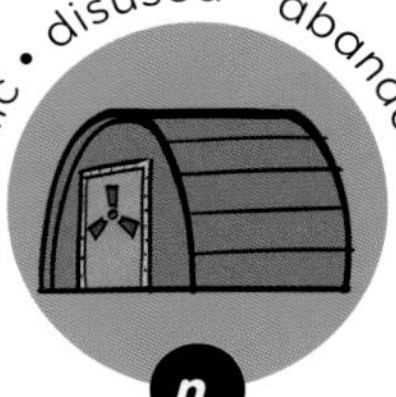

n.

bomb shelter

locked • fireproof • secure

n.

vault

local • isolated • cramped

n.

safe house

mighty • medieval • impregnable

n.

fortress

dark • secret • underground

n.

cave

hidden • secure • soundproofed

n.

panic room

grand • haunted • deserted

n.

castle

futuristic • high-tech • sterile

n.

laboratory

FARM ANIMALS

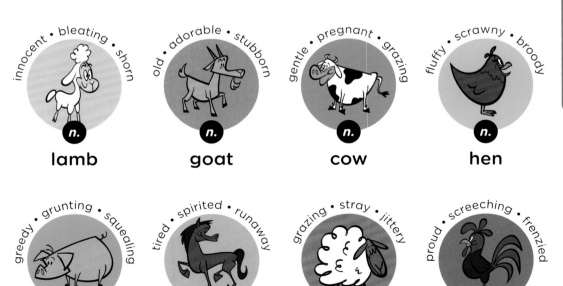

innocent • bleating • shorn

n.

lamb

old • adorable • stubborn

n.

goat

gentle • pregnant • grazing

n.

cow

fluffy • scrawny • broody

n.

hen

greedy • grunting • squealing

n.

pig

tired • spirited • runaway

n.

horse

grazing • stray • jittery

n.

sheep

proud • screeching • frenzied

n.

cockerel

FARMLAND

haunted • drafty • dilapidated

barn

tiny • annoying • gigantic

molehill

run-down • thatched • remote

farmhouse

muddy • filthy • disgusting

pigsty

smelly • natural • chemical

fertilizer

fresh • stacked • prickly
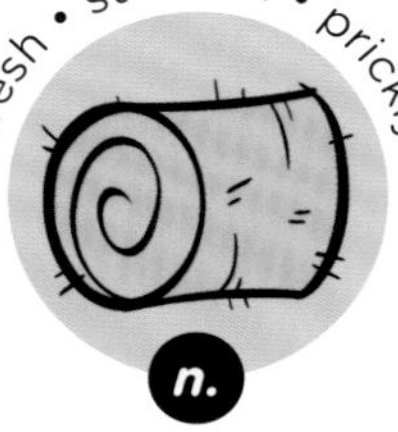
hay bale

muddy • plowed • fertile

field

dried • moist • stinking

dung

GARDEN

lucky • flying • squashed

ladybug

sturdy • barbed-wire • rickety
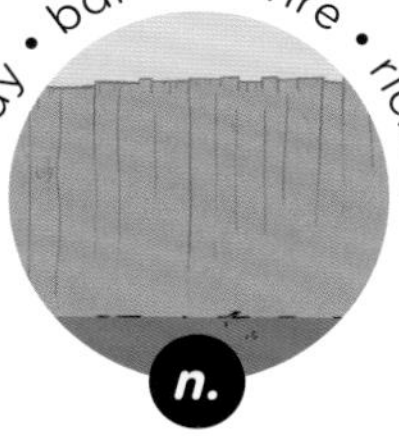
fence

rich • organic • homemade

compost

singing • caged • wary

bird

thick • overgrown • pruned

hedge

brilliant • fluttering • exotic

butterflies

harmless • slimy • poisonous

frog

wild • fragrant • drooping

flower

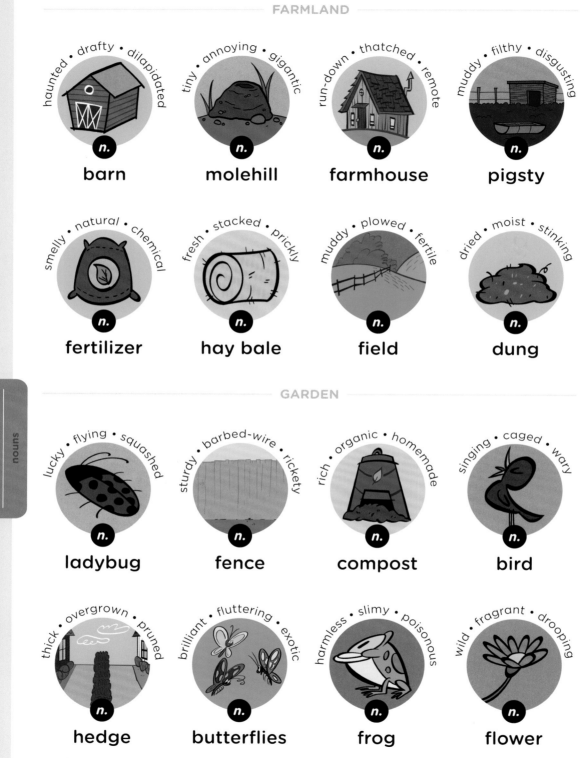

GARDEN

prized • enviable • trampled

n.

vegetable patch

lush • unkempt • immaculate

n.

lawn

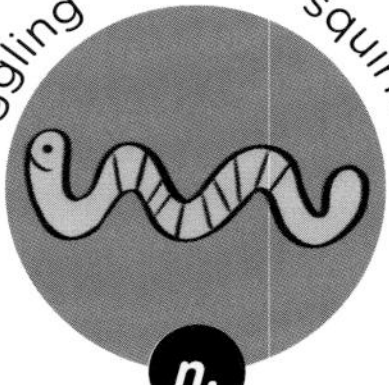

wriggling • slimy • squirming

n.

worm

sunny • spacious • secluded

n.

patio

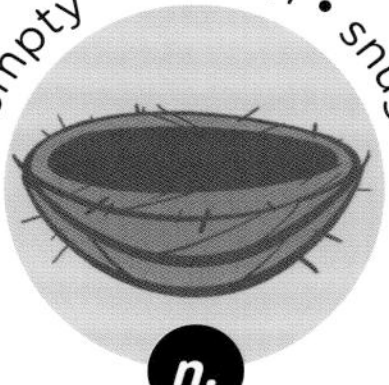

empty • hidden • snug

n.

nest

tiny • fragile • promising

n.

seedlings

shallow • man-made • stagnant

n.

pond

grassy • stubborn • invasive

n.

weeds

INVENTOR'S DEN

broken • advanced • innovative

n.

3D printer

a machine that prints physical objects;
something that can print you a teddy bear

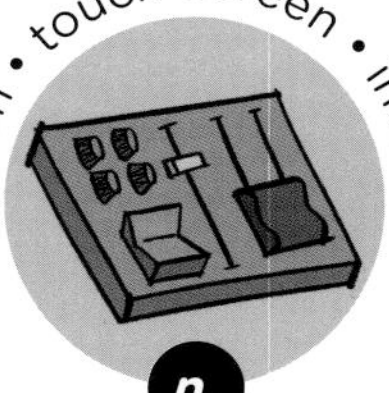

hidden • touch-screen • intuitive

n.

control panel

intelligent • high-tech • secure

n.

biometric system

flying • experimental • defective

n.

hoverboard

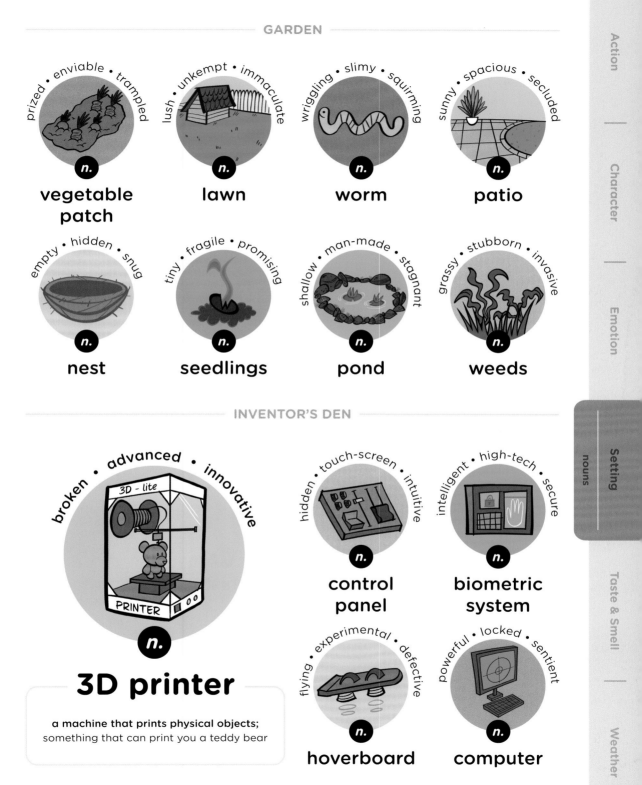

powerful • locked • sentient

n.

computer

INVENTOR'S DEN

zooming • malfunctioning

n. **jetpack**

magical • malfunctioning

n. **x-ray glasses**

bulky • high-tech • infrared

n. **night vision goggles**

cracked • curved • high-definition

n. **monitor**

mobile • bulky • immersive

n. **VR headset**

booming • cutting-edge

n. **sound system**

flickering • flat-screen

n. **television**

stolen • compact • high-speed

n. **laptop**

AT HOME

steaming • porcelain • overflowing

n. **bathtub**

dark • musty • cramped

n. **attic**

wooden • slippery • rickety

n. **banister**

steamy • filthy • spotless

n. **bathroom**

warm • unmade • uncomfortable

n. **bed**

comfy • shabby • reclining

n. **armchair**

untidy • immaculate • ransacked

n. **bedroom**

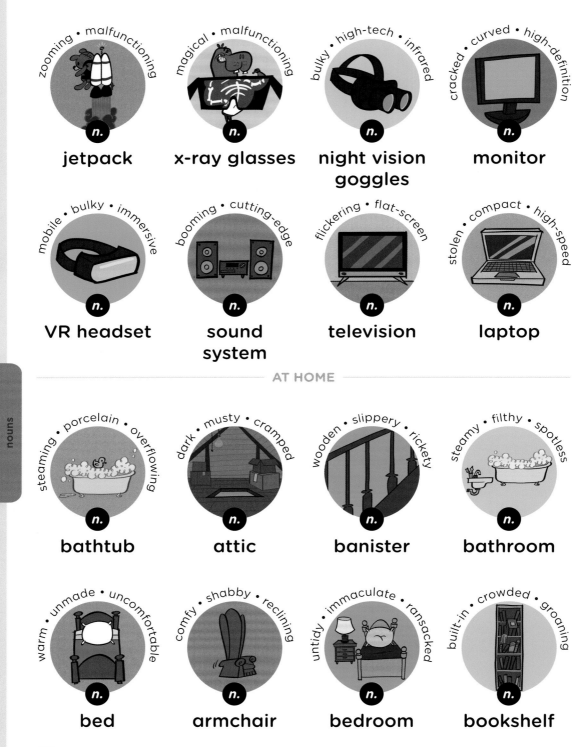

built-in • crowded • groaning

n. **bookshelf**

solid • crumbling • exposed

n.

bricks

thick • stained • threadbare

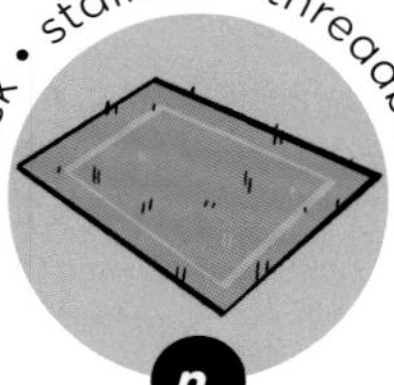

n.

carpet

secret • damp • vast

n.

cellar

dusty • roaring • wood-burning

n.

fireplace

glittering • antique • ornate

n.

chandelier

glass • stylish • antique

n.

coffee table

filthy • underground • cluttered

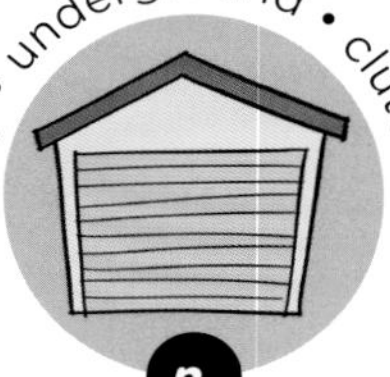

n.

garage

heavy • drawn • gaudy

n.

curtains

spacious • welcoming • elegant

n.

dining room

open • creaky • revolving

n.

door

smoky • blackened • crooked

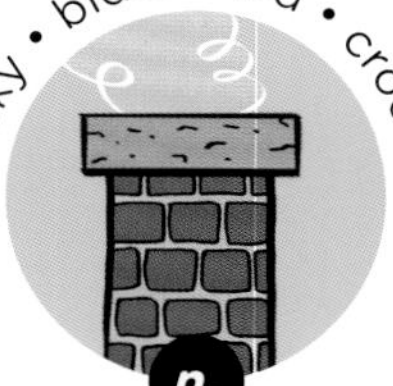

n.

chimney

empty • enormous • saltwater

n.

fish tank

formal • elegant • communal

n.

dining table

wooden • carpeted • creaky

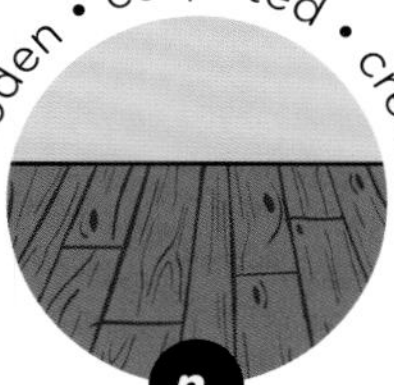

n.

floor

unlocked • cast-iron • imposing

n.

gate

locked • trophy • overhead

n.

cabinet

AT HOME

expensive • luxury • immersive

n.

home theater

empty • adorable • chaotic

n.

nursery

open • walk-in • overstocked

n.

pantry

front • shady • ivy-covered

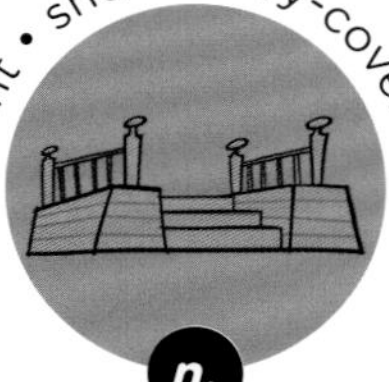

n.

porch

basic • open-plan • immaculate

n.

kitchen

firm • lumpy • stained

n.

mattress

cozy • inviting • contemporary

n.

living room

rusty • clogged • burst

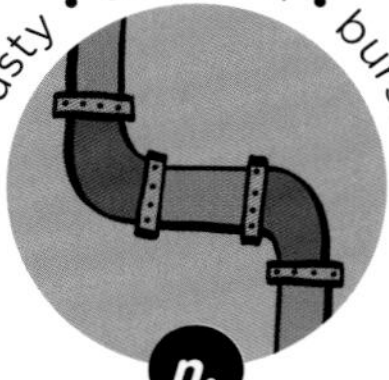

n.

pipes

locked • rusty • stuffed

n.

mail slot

hard • plump • soft

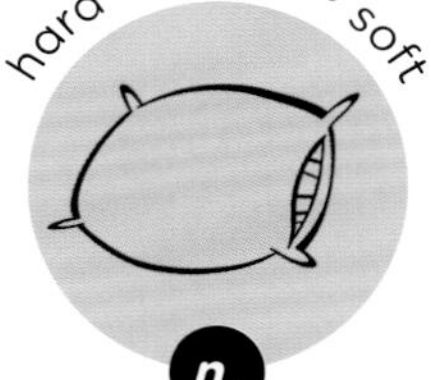

n.

pillow

quiet • private • disorganized

n.

home office

messy • beloved • high-tech

n.

playroom

polished • full-length • shattered

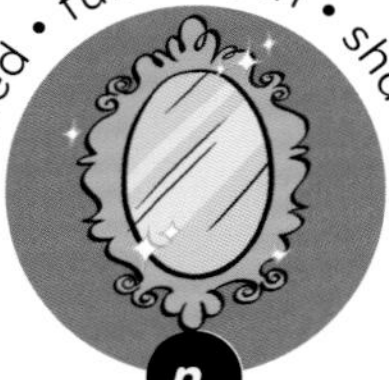

n.

mirror

famous • abstract • exquisite

n.

painting

hanging • dimmed • ornamental

n.

lamp

leaky • tiled • thatched

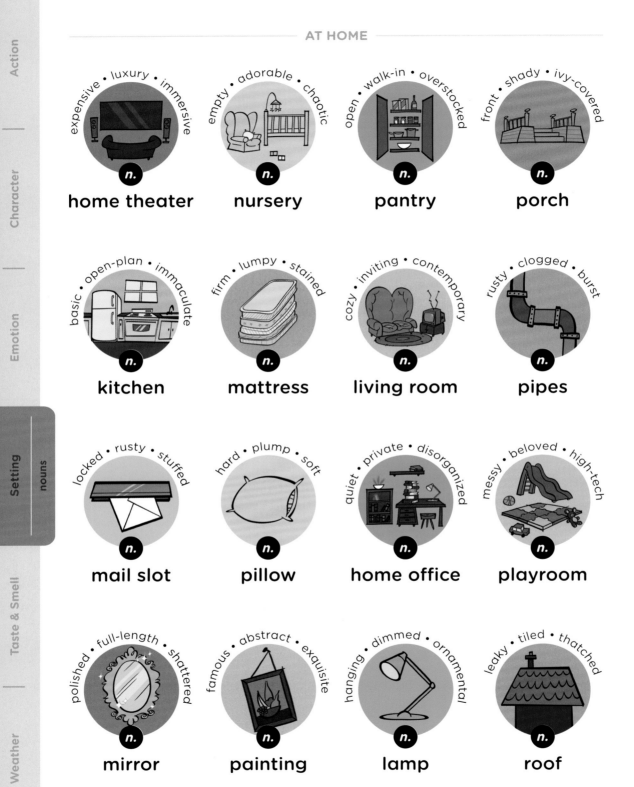

n.

roof

thick • woven • shaggy

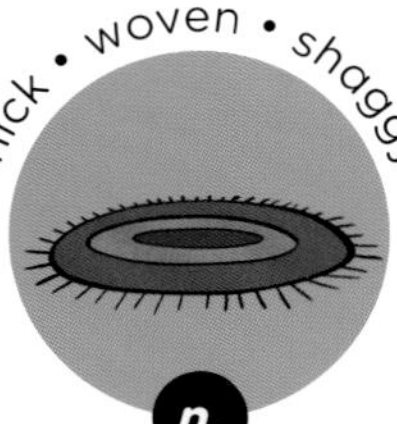

n.

rug

ice-cold • steamy • invigorating

n.

shower

modern • built-in • roof-mounted

n.

solar panels

secret • spiraling • creaky

n.

staircase

plush • sagging • threadbare

n.

couch

three-legged • sturdy • wobbly

n.

stool

stinking • outdoor • unflushed

n.

toilet

patterned • floral • peeling

n.

wallpaper

dated • quirky • opulent

n.

decor

the things in a room that make it comfortable and attractive; like furniture, pictures, wallpaper, and ornaments

locked • oak • overstuffed

n.

wardrobe

bright • airy • modern

n.

solarium

square • hand-painted • cracked

n.

tiles

broken • grimy • shuttered

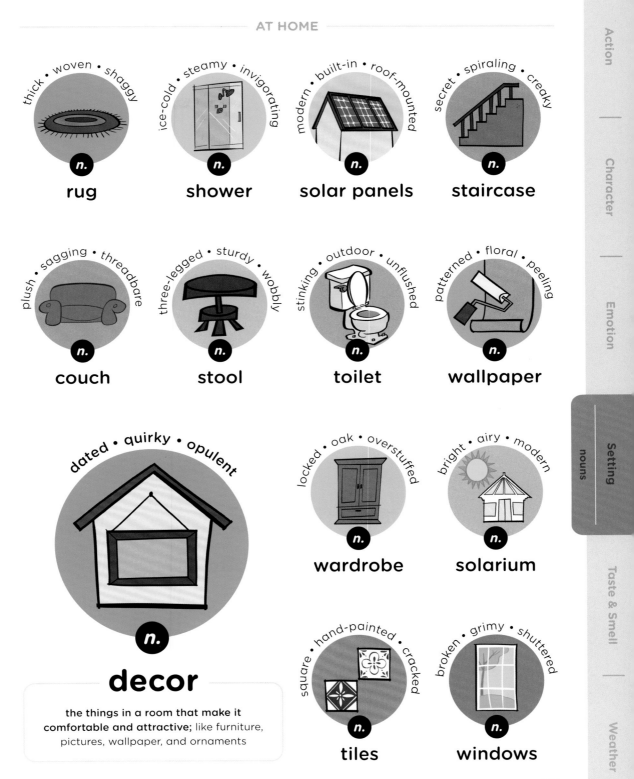

n.

windows

TYPES OF HOUSES

new • humble • temporary

n.
abode

romantic • alpine • luxurious

n.
chalet

stylish • luxurious • sprawling

n.
penthouse

wooden • safari • exclusive

n.
lodge

large • communal • unpatrolled

n.
dormitory

dark • lakeside • remote

n.
cabin

mud • beachside • primitive

n.
hut

floating • moored • ramshackle

n.
houseboat

charming • detached • squat

n.
bungalow

red-brick • grand • restored

n.
manor

seaside • quaint • whitewashed

n.
cottage

elegant • aristocratic • opulent

n.
mansion

grand • vacant • dilapidated

n.
house

royal • vast • enchanted

n.
palace

private • princely • spacious

n.
residence

empty • high-rise • cramped

n.
apartment

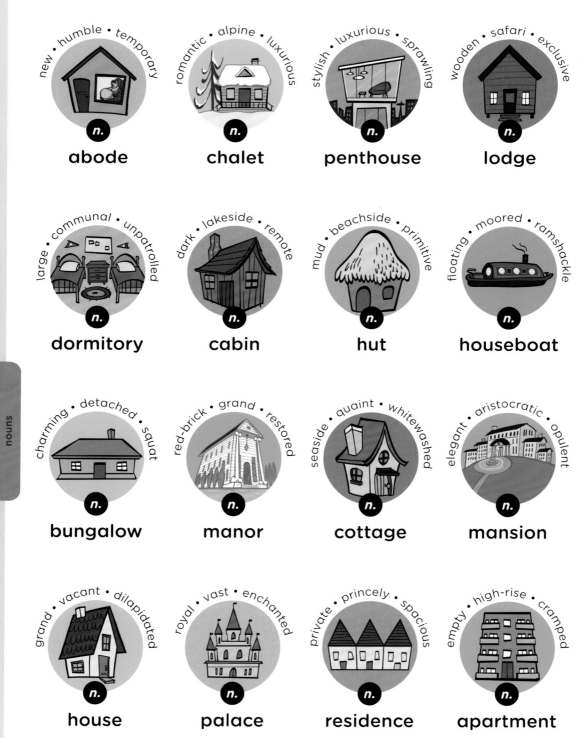

TYPES OF HOUSES

modern • beachfront • detached

n.
villa

rough • makeshift • dilapidated

n.
shanty

stunning • futuristic • ornate
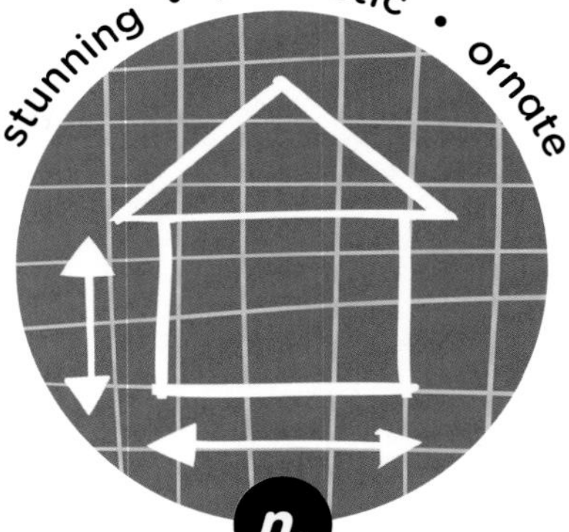
n.
architecture

the design of buildings;
like the planning that goes into getting something built

quiet • serene • immaculate

n.
retirement home

tiny • sturdy • half-finished

n.
tree house

COUNTRYSIDE

wooden • rusty • modern

n.
windmill

shady • secluded • ancient

n.
grove

hilly • scenic • desolate

n.
landscape

steep • rolling • distant
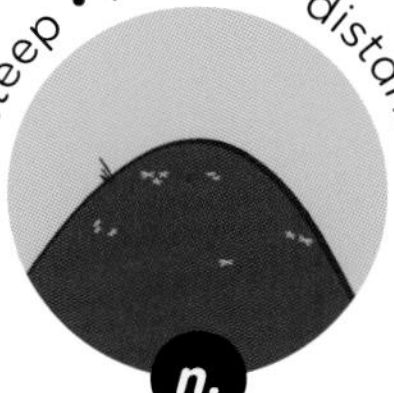
n.
hills

local • organic • seasonal

n.
crops

steep • coastal • scenic

n.
hiking trail

quiet • deserted • neglected

n.
churchyard

weekly • open-air • bustling

n.
market

COUNTRYSIDE

ankle-deep • sticky • pungent

n.
mud

wooden • heavy • horse-drawn

n.
plow

muddy • narrow • dead-end

n.
path

deep • beautiful • grassy

n.
valley

green • lush • abundant
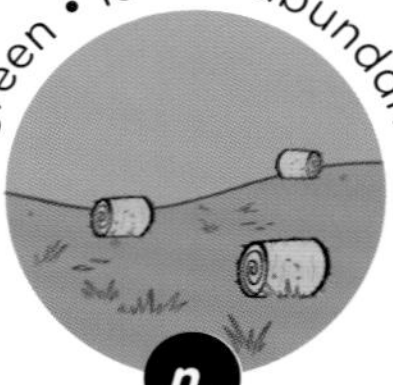
n.
pasture

rusty • powerful • heavy-duty

n.
tractor

grassy • snowy • moonlit
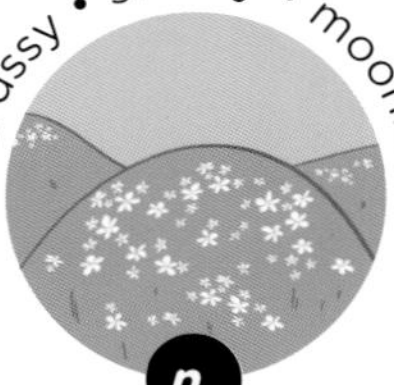
n.
meadow

beautiful • overgrown • fragrant

n.
orchard

DESERT

cute • curious • sharp-eyed

n.
meerkat

giant • wild • prickly

n.
cactus

fine • volcanic • atmospheric

n.
dust

peaceful • distant • fertile

n.
oasis

thirsty • overloaded • tethered

n.
camel

endless • barren • arid
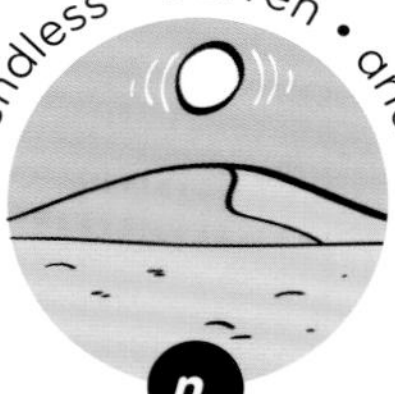
n.
desert

deadly • venomous • monstrous

n.
scorpion

rare • harmless • venomous

n.
lizard

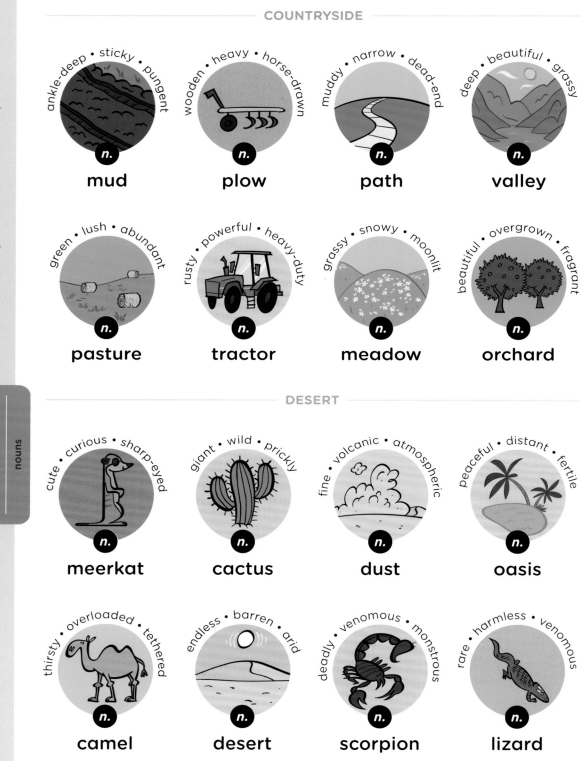

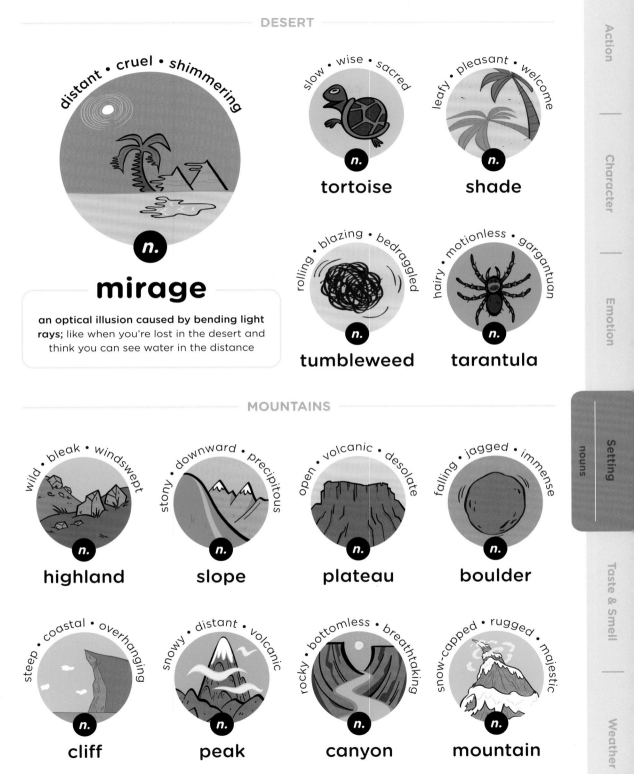

DESERT

distant • cruel • shimmering

n.

mirage

an optical illusion caused by bending light rays; like when you're lost in the desert and think you can see water in the distance

slow • wise • sacred

n.

tortoise

leafy • pleasant • welcome

n.

shade

rolling • blazing • bedraggled

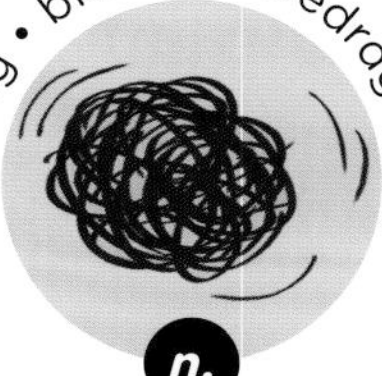

n.

tumbleweed

hairy • motionless • gargantuan

n.

tarantula

MOUNTAINS

wild • bleak • windswept

n.

highland

stony • downward • precipitous

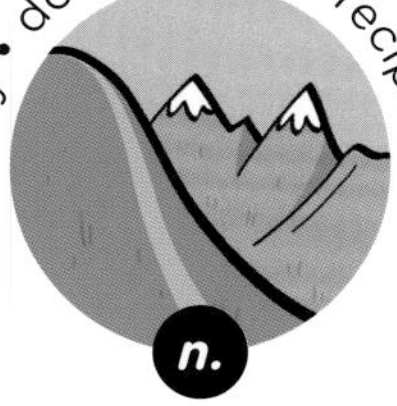

n.

slope

open • volcanic • desolate

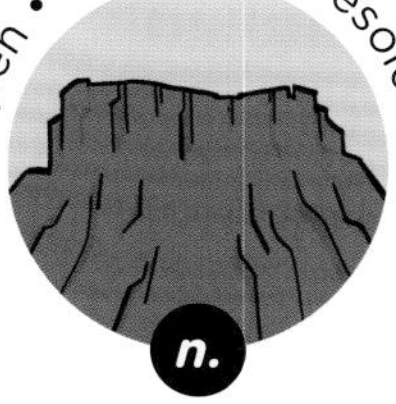

n.

plateau

falling • jagged • immense

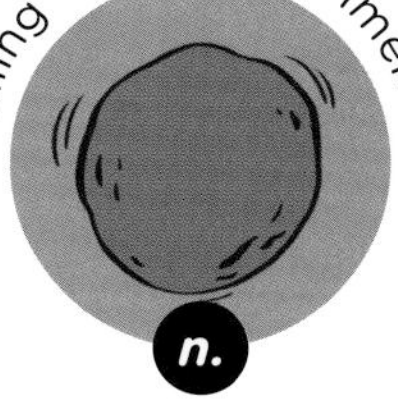

n.

boulder

steep • coastal • overhanging

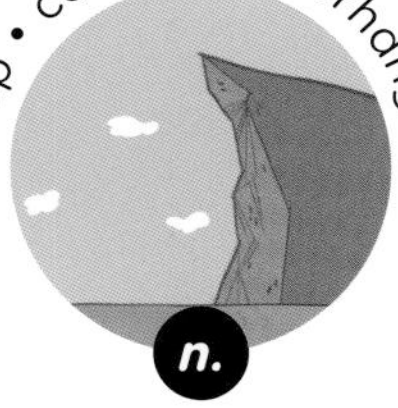

n.

cliff

snowy • distant • volcanic

n.

peak

rocky • bottomless • breathtaking

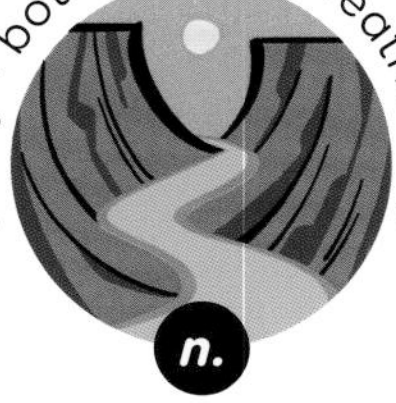

n.

canyon

snow-capped • rugged • majestic

n.

mountain

mighty • playful • endangered

n.

polar bear

friendly • waddling • comical

n.

penguin

melting • immense • advancing

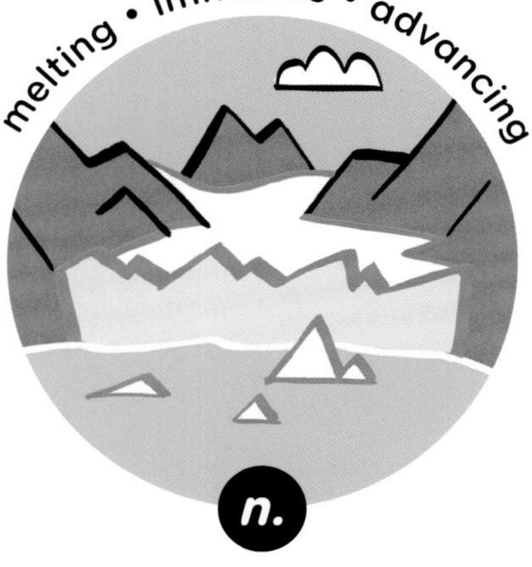

n.

glacier

a huge mass of moving ice;
like a slow-moving, frozen river

floating • enormous • submerged

n.

iceberg

horned • gigantic • mysterious

n.

narwhal

howling • shaggy • gaunt

n.

husky

swimming • curious • lovable

n.

puffin

hungry • enormous • beached

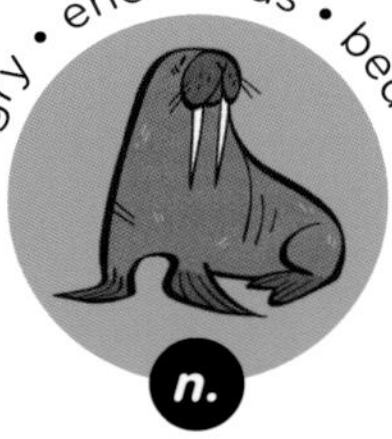

n.

walrus

playful • majestic • elusive

n.

Arctic fox

polar • thawing • colossal

n.

icecap

wooden • loaded • overturned

n.

sled

cozy • hidden • abandoned

n.

igloo

stray • harnessed • timid

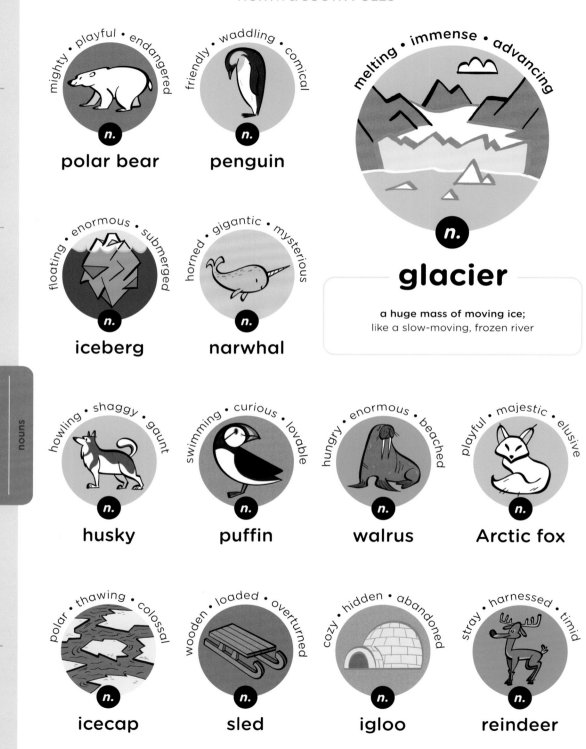

n.

reindeer

shallow • secluded • picturesque

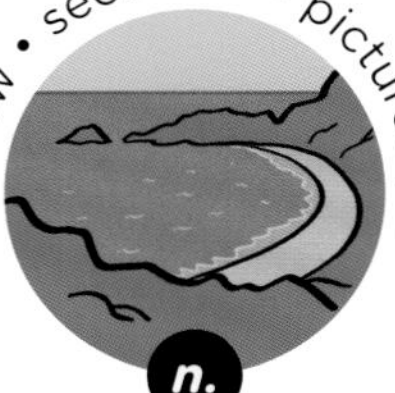

n.

bay

seaside • crowded • rickety

n.

pier

trained • muscular • responsible

n.

lifeguard

colorful • bouncing • deflated

n.

beach ball

tall • collapsed • elaborate

n.

sandcastle

deep-water • jagged • precious

n.

coral

inflatable • drifting • upturned

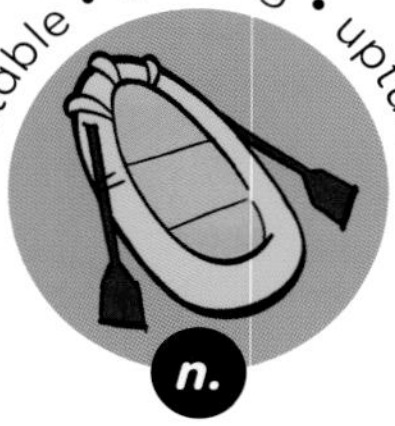

n.

dinghy

soaked • faded • garish

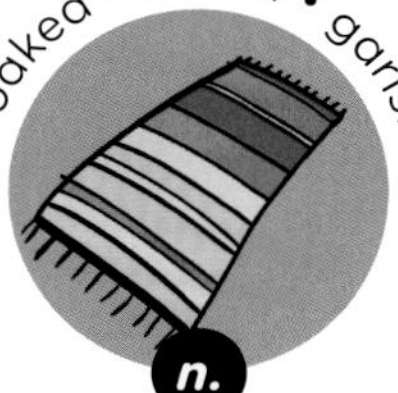

n.

beach towel

spiral • fragile • brittle

n.

seashells

calm • choppy • tempestuous

n.

ocean

golden • damp • scorching

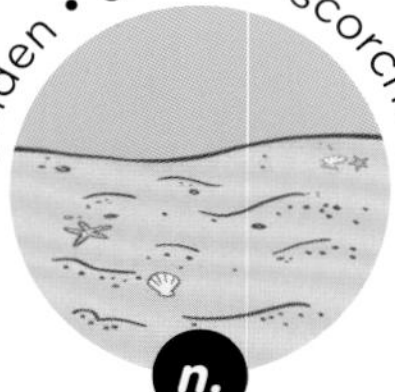

n.

sand

sandy • pebbly • pristine

n.

beach

rocky • sunken • treacherous

n.

reef

hungry • squawking • thieving

n.

seagulls

friendly • beady-eyed • scuttling

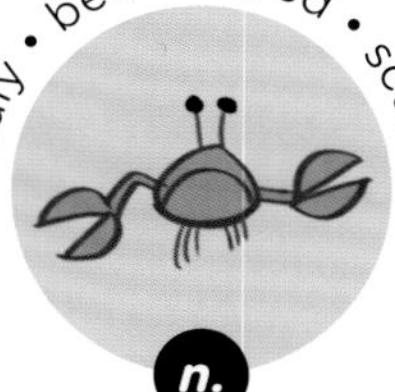

n.

crab

plastic • gleaming • custom-made

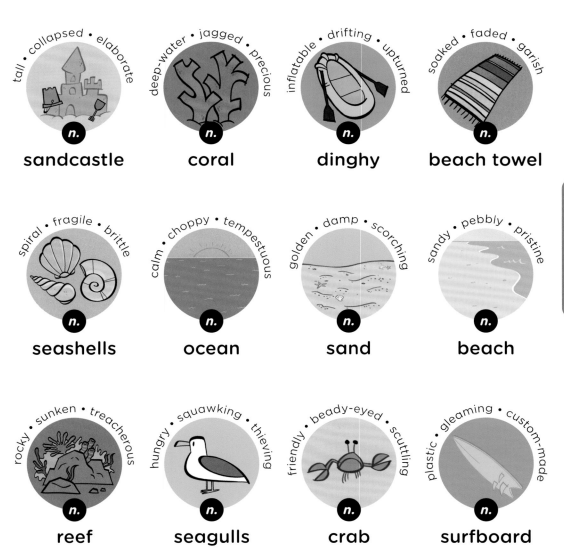

n.

surfboard

TROPICAL

leafy • sheltering • magnificent

n.
canopy

tall • hollow • sharpened

n.
bamboo

tropical • swaying • towering

n.
palm tree

lush • tropical • humid

n.
rainforest

thick • dense • tangled

n.
undergrowth

thorny • tangled • creeping
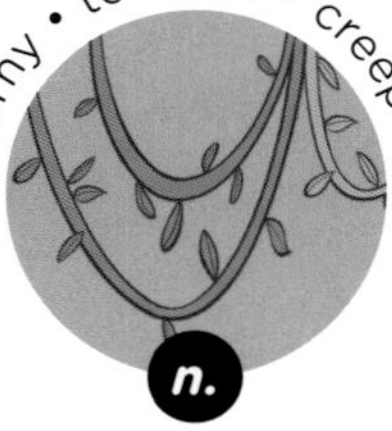
n.
vines

tangled • remote • dense

n.
jungle

distant • fertile • idyllic

n.
island

UNDER THE SEA

floating • slippery • washed-up

n.
seaweed

glowing • deadly • venomous

n.
jellyfish

gigantic • intelligent • sprawling

n.
octopus

sinking • lurking • undetectable

n.
submarine

scaly • silvery • predatory

n.
fish

circling • man-eating • ravenous

n.
shark

lonely • spouting • migrating
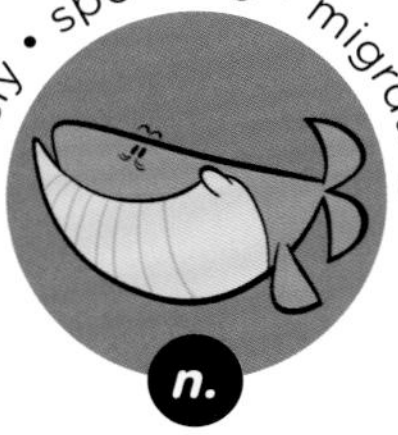
n.
whale

harmless • chubby • stranded

n.
starfish

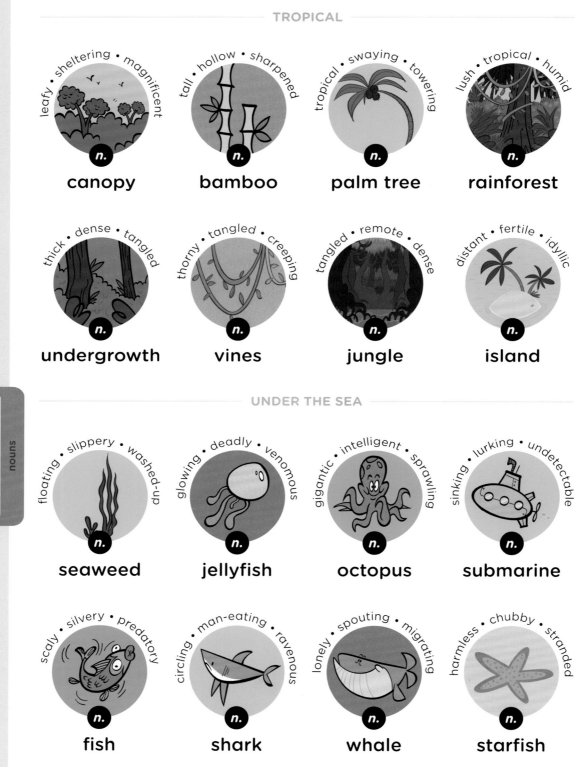

rich • marshy • flooded

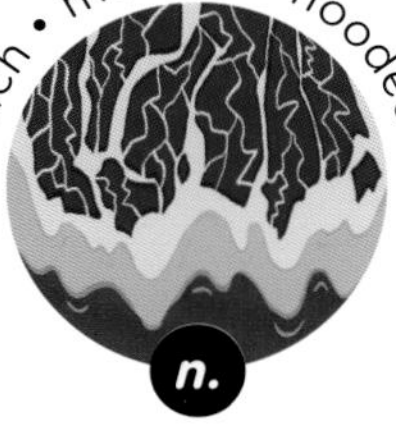

n.

delta

shallow • sleepy • tranquil

n.

lagoon

clear • babbling • sparkling

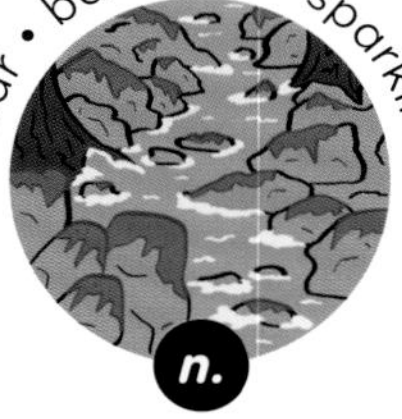

n.

brook

hot • natural • sulfurous

n.

spring

narrow • swollen • meandering

n.

creek

deadly • raging • unstoppable

n.

riptide

powerful • foaming • cascading

n.

waterfall

winding • mighty • turbulent

n.

river

wild • frothy • challenging

n.

rapids

a very fast-moving and rough part of a river; like a terrifying stretch of white water that throws you from your canoe

winding • polluted • sluggish

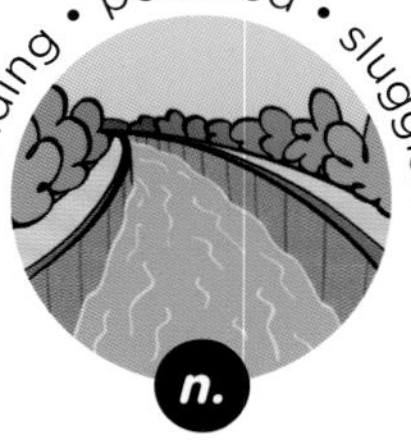

n.

canal

shallow • sparkling • meandering

n.

stream

muddy • slippery • marshy

n.

bank

crashing • lapping • choppy

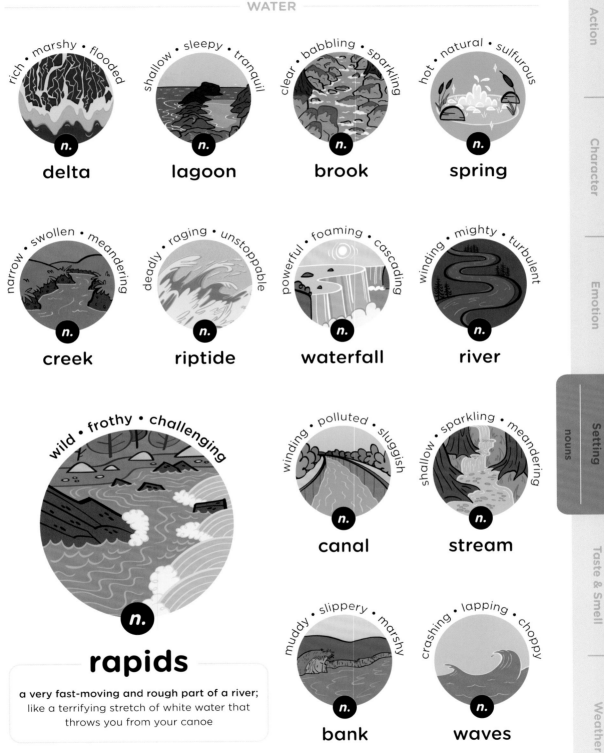

n.

waves

WETLAND

foul • deadly • bottomless

n.
quagmire

broad • natural • fertile
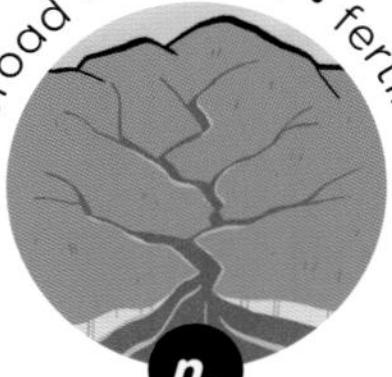
n.
basin

dark • dismal • stagnant
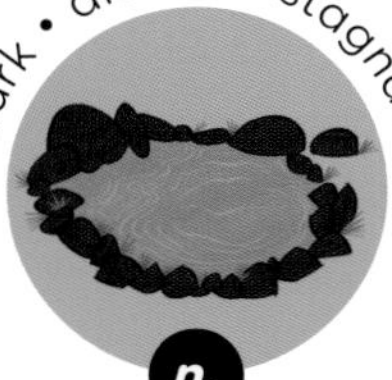
n.
swamp

oozing • reedy • sodden

n.
marsh

deep • stinking • treacherous
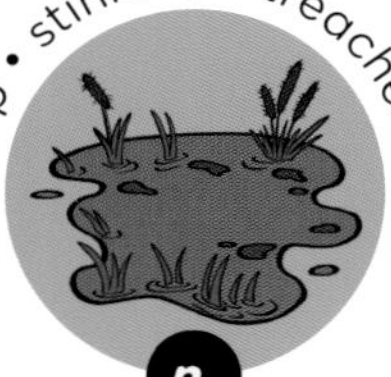
n.
bog

hidden • dangerous • shifting

n.
quicksand

tall • slender • feathery

n.
reeds

high • bursting • hydroelectric

n.
dam

WOODLAND

fresh • mysterious • obscure
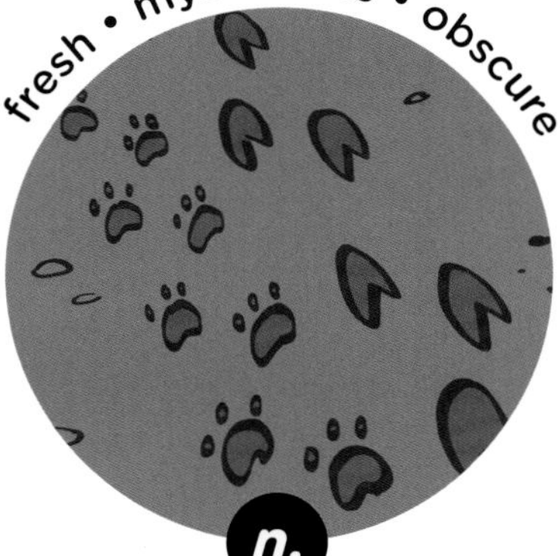
n.
animal tracks

prints that creatures leave behind when they move; like the imprints of hooves and paws in wet sand

fallen • leafless • withered

n.
branch

hovering • killer • industrious

n.
bee

deep • underground • deserted
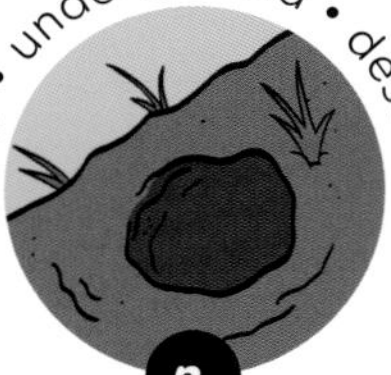
n.
burrow

enormous • swarming • thriving

n.
beehive

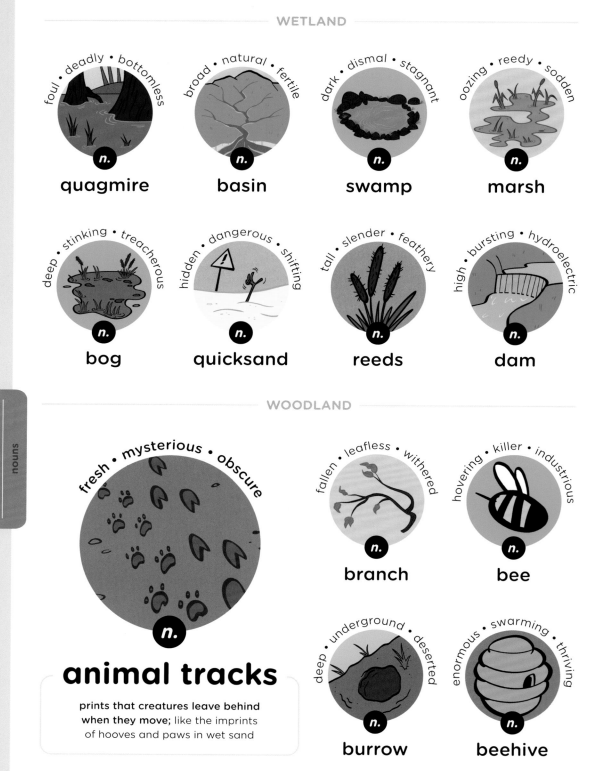

WOODLAND

crackling • blazing • dwindling

n.

campfire

thorny • tangled • impenetrable

n.

thicket

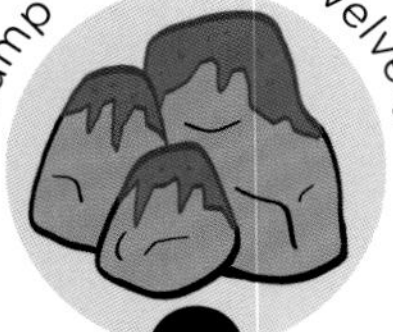

damp • springy • velvety

n.

moss

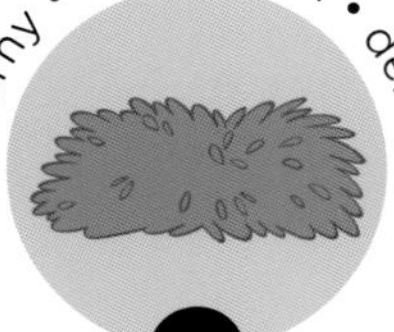

thorny • overgrown • dense

n.

bush

dark • protected • impenetrable

n.

forest

stinging • prickly • overgrown

n.

nettles

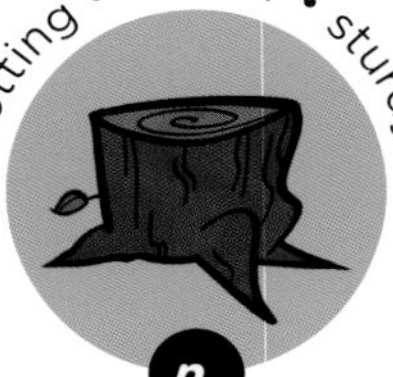

rotting • hollow • sturdy

n.

tree stump

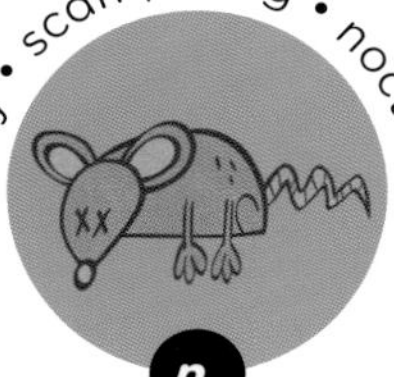

pesky • scampering • nocturnal

n.

rodent

DAYTIME

fine • radiant • crisp

n.

morning

bright • approaching • glorious

n.

midday

direct • dazzling • dappled

n.

sunlight

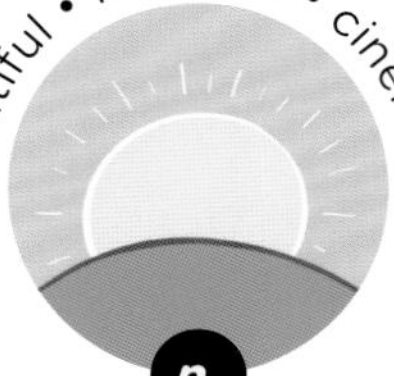

beautiful • magical • cinematic

n.

sunrise

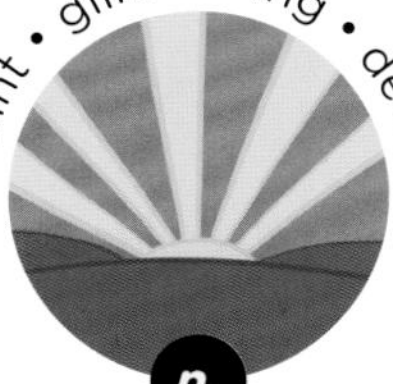

faint • glimmering • dewy

n.

dawn

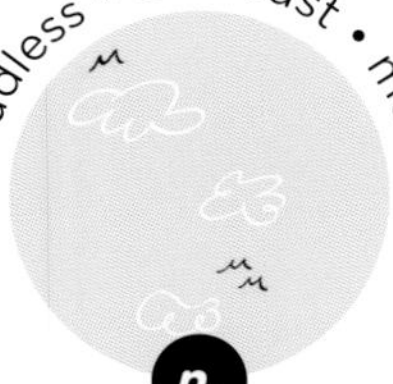

cloudless • overcast • murky

n.

sky

lazy • balmy • gloomy

n.

afternoon

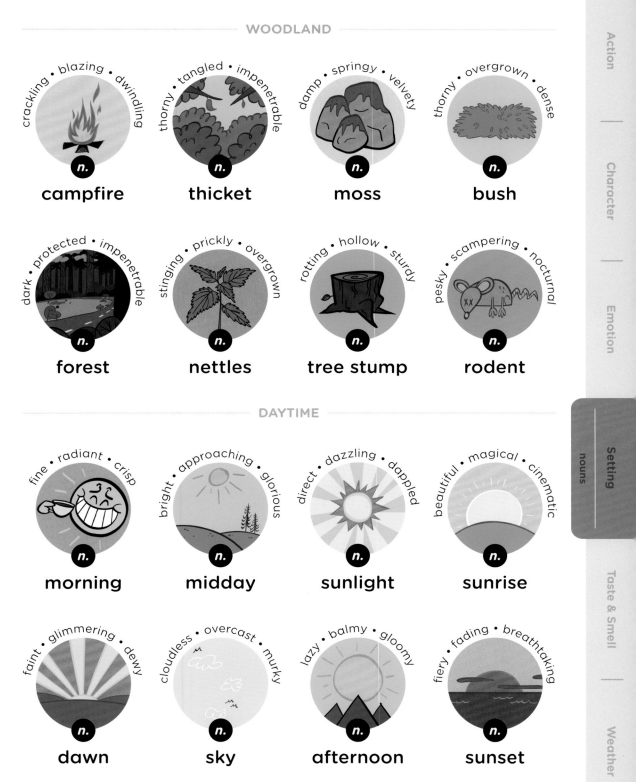

fiery • fading • breathtaking

n.

sunset

NIGHTTIME

strict • sensible • regular

n.
bedtime

shooting • faint • twinkling

n.
stars

stormy • frosty • balmy

n.
evening

long • eerie • deafening

n.
silence

long • gloomy • mysterious

n.
shadow

total • velvety • impenetrable

n.
darkness

ghostly • mysterious • distinctive

n.
silhouette

full • crescent • eclipsed

n.
moon

SPACE

beautiful • fragile • teeming

n.
Earth

giant • distant • uninhabitable

n.
Jupiter

dusty • mysterious • colonized
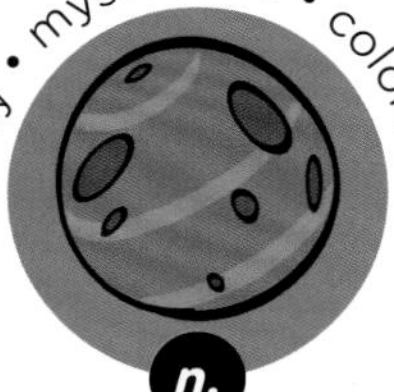
n.
Mars

strange • faraway • uncharted
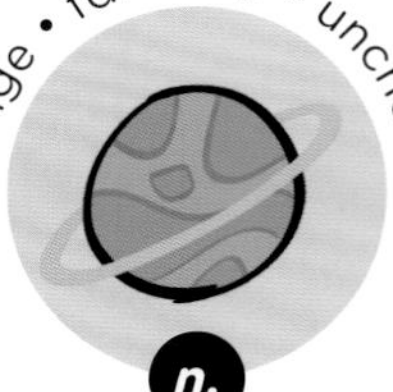
n.
planet

dark • vast • infinite
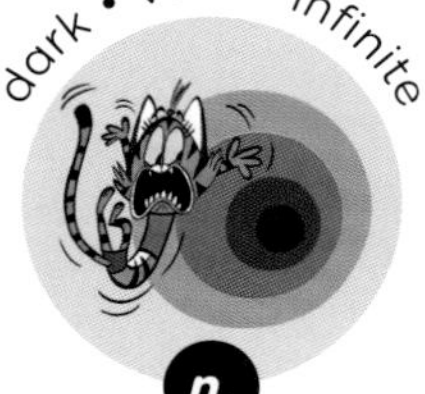
n.
abyss

bright • incoming • hurtling
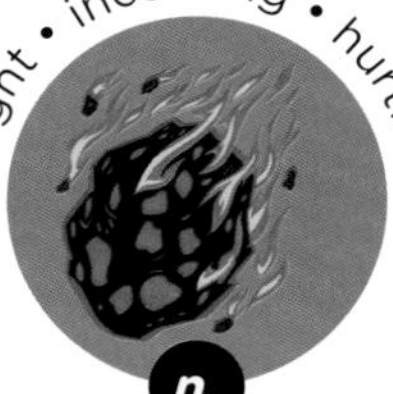
n.
asteroid

deep • volcanic • sulfurous
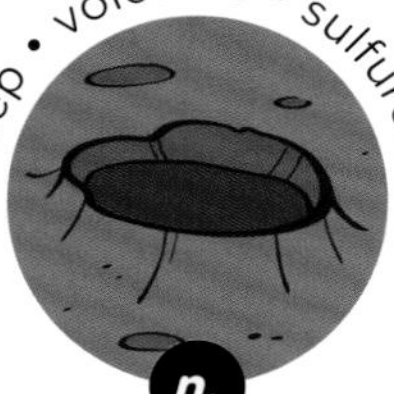
n.
crater

powerful • crashed • sabotaged

n.
rocket

SPACE

lost • stranded • unidentified

n.

spaceship

tiny • orbiting • malfunctioning

n.

satellite

vast • boundless • unknowable

n.

universe

all of space, time, and everything else; all the planets, galaxies, and things you can and can't see

alien • international • derelict

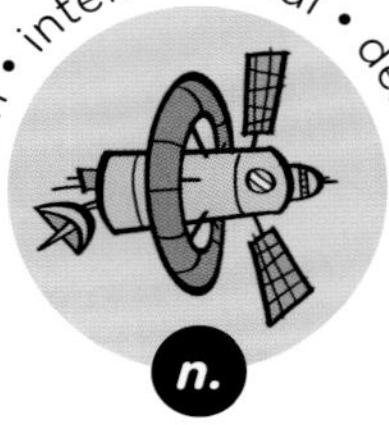

n.

space station

icy • distant • majestic

n.

Saturn

WILD ANIMALS

prowling • cunning • rabid

n.

fox

mighty • enraged • captive

n.

elephant

flying • bloodsucking

n.

bat

startled • timid • nimble

n.

deer

hungry • stealthy • endangered

n.

crocodile

busy • trapped • industrious

n.

beaver

gentle • graceful • colossal

n.

giraffe

huge • cuddly • ferocious

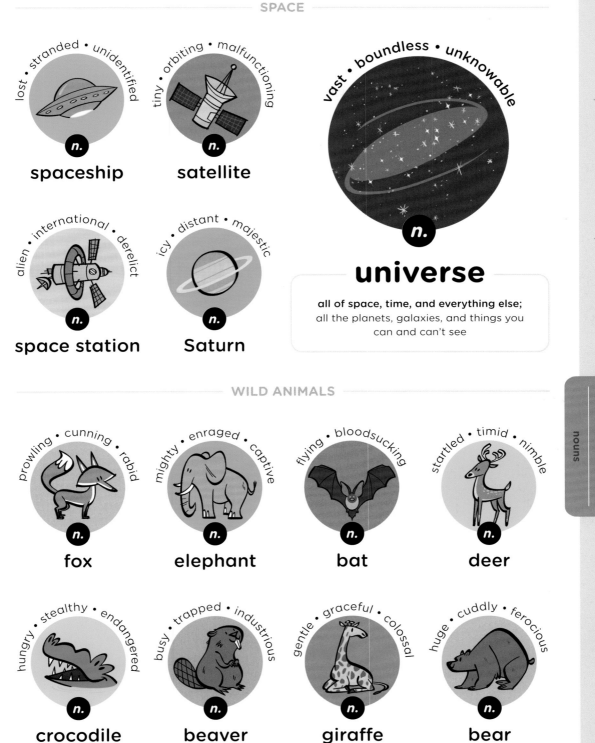

n.

bear

WILD ANIMALS

striped • man-eating • tranquilized

n.

tiger

rescued • orphaned • solitary

n.

orangutan

rare • raging • endangered

n.

rhinoceros

roaring • caged • magnificent

n.

lion

hungry • howling • lone

n.

wolf

hopping • frightened • tame

n.

hare

hissing • slithering • venomous

n.

snake

cute • sleek • playful

n.

otter

BIRDS

soaring • watchful • majestic

n.

eagle

little • speckled • hovering

n.

hummingbird

pink • beautiful • fabulous

n.

flamingo

clever • thieving • mischievous

n.

magpie

young • mechanical • intrusive

n.

cuckoo

hungry • fierce • marauding

n.

hawk

huge • strutting • rapid

n.

ostrich

slender • elegant • solitary

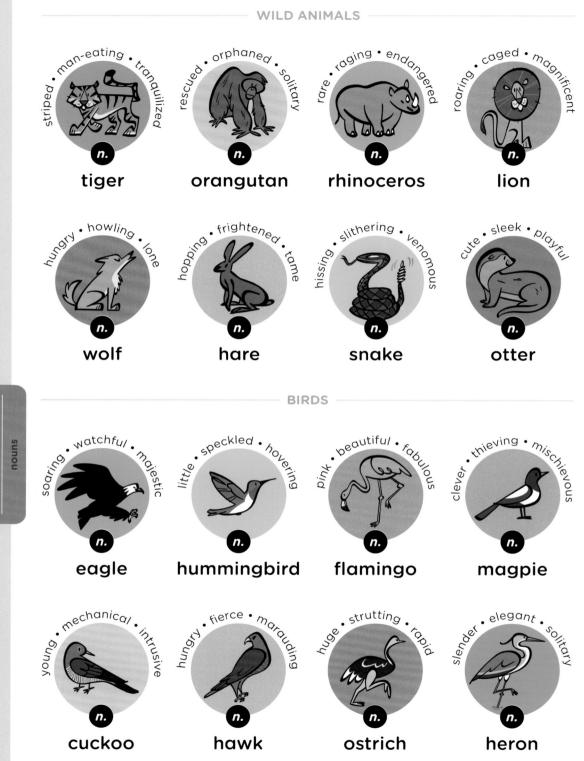

n.

heron

BIRDS

swooping • nesting • soaring

n. **pelican**

wise • swooping • solemn

n. **owl**

noisy • proud • industrious

n. **woodpecker**

proud • splendid • preening

n. **peacock**

talkative • screeching • tame

n. **parrot**

dark • grim • ominous

n. **raven**

bright • exotic • rainbow-billed

n. **toucan**

singing • jolly • scarlet

n. **robin**

COLLECTIVE ANIMAL NOUNS

grazing • bleating • scattered

n. **flock**

massive • healthy • stampeding

n. **herd**

healthy • unwanted • stray

n. **litter**

wild • snarling • ravenous

n. **pack**

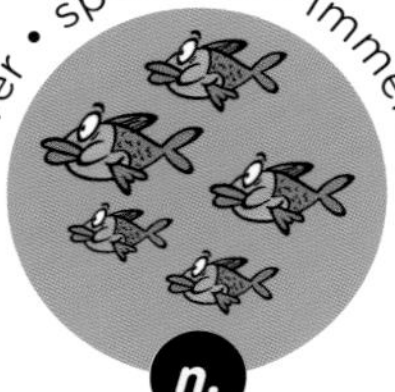
silver • spooked • immense

n. **shoal**

playful • passing • surfacing

n. **pod**

dark • buzzing • endless

n. **swarm**

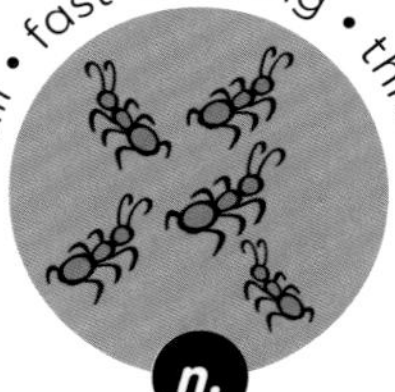
small • fast-growing • thriving

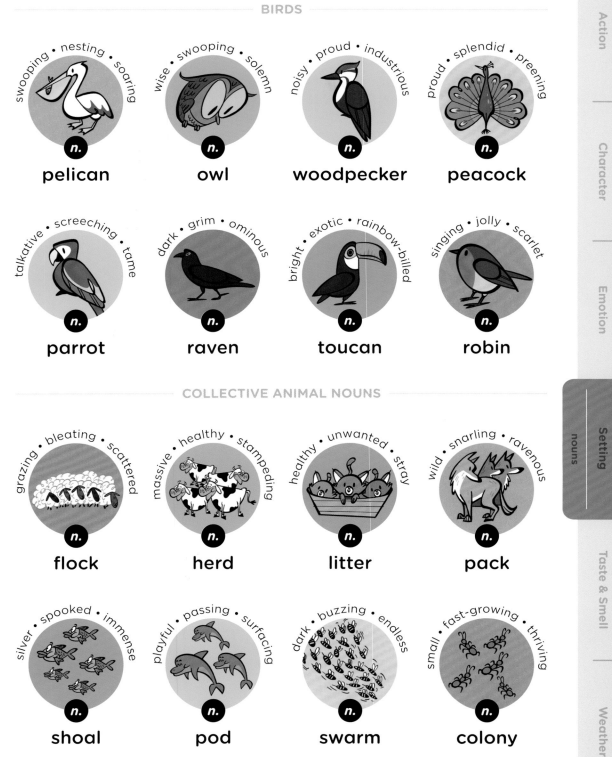

n. **colony**

savor

TASTE & SMELL

irresistible *adj.* appealing and inviting; like something you can't help reaching for

word pairs: temptation, craving, urge

scrumptious *adj.* tasty or delicious; like a fancy selection of cakes

word pairs: cakes, dessert, feast

moist *adj.* damp or not dry; like a fluffy chocolate cake that oozes chocolate syrup

word pairs: cake, soil, towel

succulent *adj.* juicy and fresh; like perfectly ripe peaches that are full of delicious juice

word pairs: peaches, lobster, steak

delicious words

mouthwatering *adj*. looking or smelling delicious; like something that makes you drool

word pairs: treat, smell, recipe

tantalizing *adj*. tempting and tormenting; like delicious doughnuts that you can't reach

word pairs: food, possibility, glimpse

word pair after:

irresistible temptation
moist cake
mouthwatering treat
scrumptious cakes
succulent peaches
tantalizing food

inedible *adj*. not fit for eating; like a pizza covered in nuts and bolts

word pairs: meal, mushroom, leaves

nauseating *adj*. sickening or disgusting; like a rotten sandwich

word pairs: stench, fear, opinions

repulsive *adj*. disgusting or gross; like an ugly gargoyle that makes you feel sick

word pairs: creature, odor, manners

stale *adj*. old, hard, and crusty; like bread that has become hard because you left it out

word pairs: bread, air, sweat

rancid *adj*. foul or rotten; like milk that has been left out for days and gone sour

word pairs: milk, meat, smell

---

unpalatable *adj*. unappealing or off-putting; like a can of gross, brown dog food

word pairs: food, mush, truth

disgusting words

word pair after:

inedible meal
nauseating stench
rancid milk
repulsive creature
stale bread
unpalatable food

demolish *v.* to destroy or eat up; when you gobble something up until there's nothing left

word pairs: your lunch, a cake, a house

---

guzzle *v.* to gobble or devour; like gulping down a huge carton of milk all at once

word pairs: gallons, water, gas

devour *v.* to eat hungrily or gobble up; when you swallow your dinner quickly and hungrily

word pairs: a meal, a steak, a book

---

inhale *v.* to breathe in or eat quickly; like vacuuming up your food in one breath

word pairs: food, gas, fumes

eating words

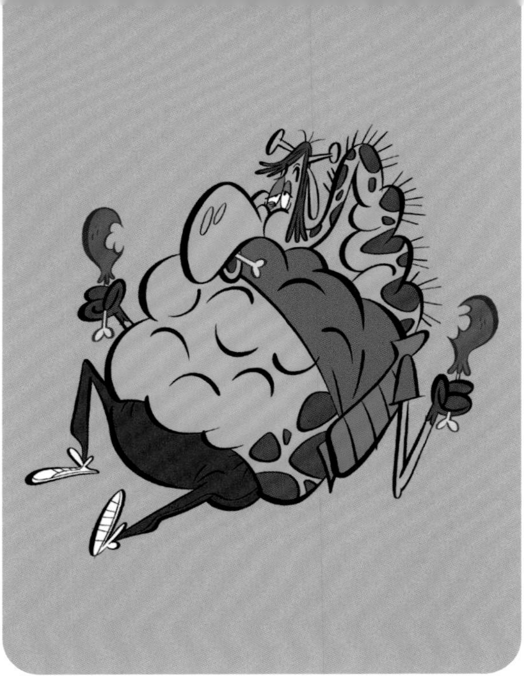

gorge *v*. to stuff yourself or overeat; when you eat a giant mountain of food and feel sick

word pairs: shamelessly, greedily, completely

---

savor *v*. to enjoy or appreciate; when you eat very slowly so you can enjoy every bite

word pairs: the taste, a mouthful, a moment

word pair after:

demolish your lunch
devour a meal
gorge shamelessly
guzzle gallons
inhale food
savor the taste

bland *adj*. plain or flavorless; like boring food that doesn't taste like anything

word pairs: food, smile, statement

peppery *adj*. spicy or fiery; like food that makes your face turn red and your eyes water

word pairs: taste, sauce, aftertaste

sugary *adj*. very sweet; like a bath full of doughnuts

word pairs: doughnuts, cereal, drink

tangy *adj*. flavorful and sharp; like the sour taste of a grapefruit

word pairs: fruit, jam, sauce

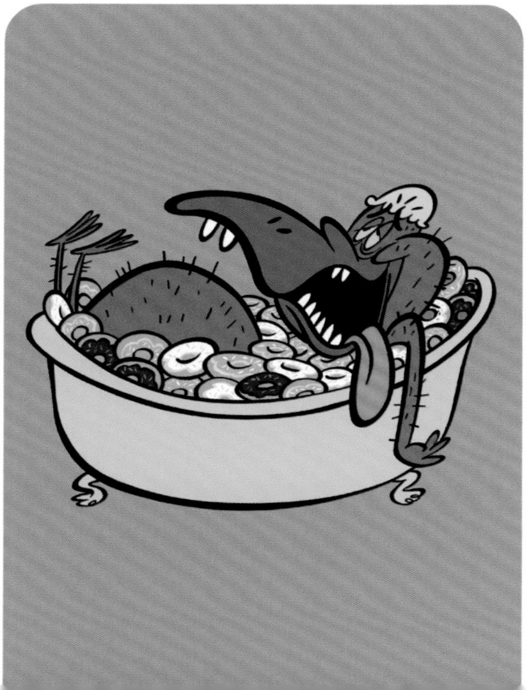

savory *adj*. salty or spicy but not sweet; like pizza sauce or a peppery steak

word pairs: steak, stew, snack

---

tart *adj*. sharp and sour; like the taste of freshly squeezed lemonade

word pairs: flavor, apple, reply

flavor words

word pair after:

bland food
peppery taste
savory steak
sugary doughnuts
tangy fruit
tart flavor

crave *v.* to long for or desire; when you want something so much it's all you think about

word pairs: coffee, power, attention

famished *adj.* very hungry or ravenous; how you feel when you're wild with hunger

word pairs: beast, lion, traveler

parched *adj.* dry or thirsty; how your throat feels if you run out of water in the desert

word pairs: throat, lips, desert

ravenous *adj.* hungry or starving; like you could eat an entire dinner in one bite

word pairs: dog, appetite, shark

insatiable *adj*. greedy or impossible to satisfy; so hungry you never fill up

word pairs: appetite, greed, curiosity

voracious *adj*. greedy or very hungry; like having a never-ending hunger for hamburgers

word pairs: appetite, predator, reader

hungry & thirsty words

word pair after:

crave coffee
famished beast
insatiable appetite
parched throat
ravenous dog
voracious appetite

hearty *adj*. filling and wholesome; like a healthy bowl of stew on a winter's day

word pairs: stew, breakfast, welcome

meager *adj*. small, limited, or not enough; like a meal made up of a single bean

word pairs: portion, meal, wage

humble *adj*. modest, plain, and simple; like a bowl of simple soup for dinner

word pairs: meal, offering, home

sumptuous *adj*. lavish and luxurious; like a banquet made up of the finest food and drink

word pairs: dinner, breakfast, feast

lavish *adj*. sumptuous and luxurious; like a huge banquet for just one person

word pairs: banquet, gift, lifestyle

---

wholesome *adj*. healthy or good for you; like a bag of fresh fruit and vegetables

word pairs: meal, diet, fun

meal words

word pair after:

hearty stew
humble meal
lavish banquet
meager portion
sumptuous dinner
wholesome meal

faint *adj*. barely noticeable or slight; like the trace of a smell carried on a breeze

word pairs: perfume, smell, smile

fragrance *n*. a sweet smell or perfume; like the odor of delicious herbs or exotic flowers

word pairs: floral, sweet, subtle

odor *n*. a smell or stink; like the fumes from someone's armpits

word pairs: unpleasant, strong, offensive

overpowering *adj*. overwhelming or unbearable; like a smell that knocks you over

word pairs: smell, force, urge

musty *adj*. stuffy and stale; like the smell of a stinky sweater that has never been washed

word pairs: clothes, smell, attic

pungent *adj*. very strong and smelly; like the stench of sweaty sneakers after a day of sports

word pairs: feet, smell, sauce

smell words

word pair before:

floral **fragrance**
unpleasant **odor**

word pair after:

faint perfume
musty clothes
overpowering smell
pungent feet

putrid *adj.* rotten and decayed; like a stinky, old sandwich

word pairs: food, smell, meat

stench *n.* an odor or stink; like the smell of someone who hasn't showered for months

word pairs: unbearable, foul, overpowering

reek *v.* to stink or smell; like someone's breath after eating a raw onion

word pairs: of onions, of fish, of sweat

toxic *adj.* poisonous or harmful; like dangerous radioactive waste

word pairs: waste, chemicals, gas

scent *n.* a smell or aroma; like the particular smell that someone leaves behind

word pairs: strong, lingering, unmistakable

whiff *n.* a sniff or trace; like the smell of your favorite pie wafting through the air

word pairs: faint, distinct, delicious

smell words

word pair before:

strong **scent**
unbearable **stench**
faint **whiff**

word pair after:

putrid food
reek of onions
toxic waste

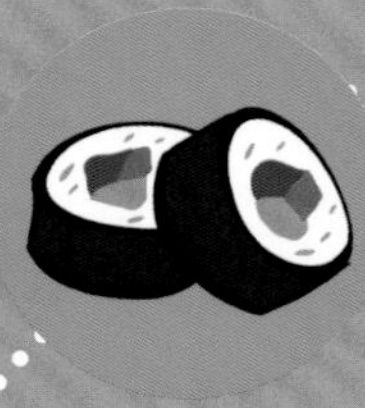

167

decadent **taste** & **smell nouns**

Enhance the flavors of your story with some **fiery hot sauce** and a drizzle of **golden honey**. This section is a feast for the eyes.

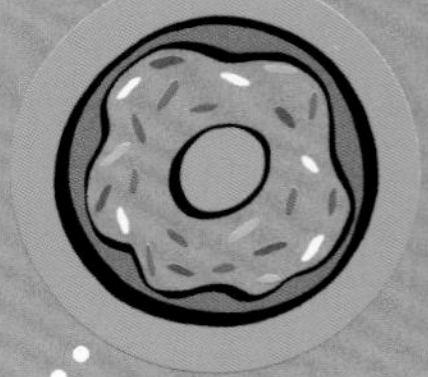

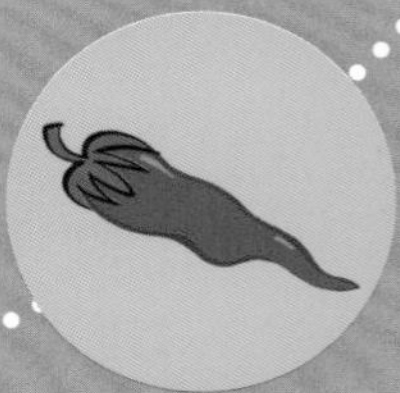

spiced • decorated • fragrant

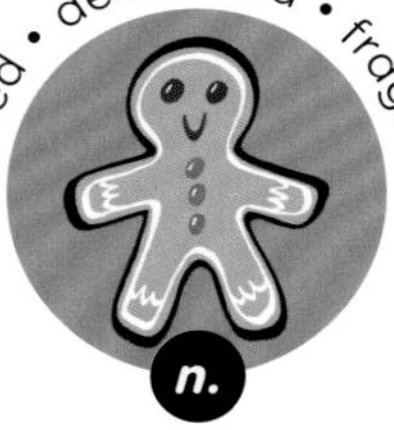

n.

gingerbread

handheld • buzzing • electric

n.

blender

broken • accurate • precise

n.

scales

towering • tiered • toppling

n.

cake stand

rich • melted • homemade

n.

ice cream

piped • whipped • slathered

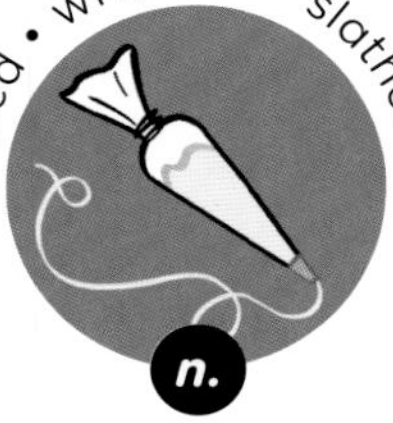

n.

icing

melted • rich • bittersweet

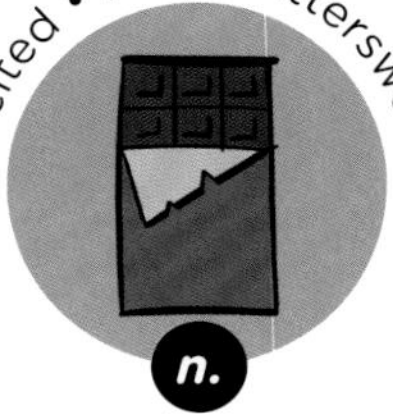

n.

chocolate

blueberry • half-eaten • mini

n.

muffin

gooey • dense • decadent

n.

brownie

moist • iced • scrumptious

n.

cake

whipped • clotted • curdled

n.

cream

floured • heavy • wooden

n.

rolling pin

sugary • crushed • tempting

n.

macarons

warm • freshly baked • fortune

n.

cookie

iced • gluten-free • decorated

n.

cupcakes

glazed • deep-fried • stale

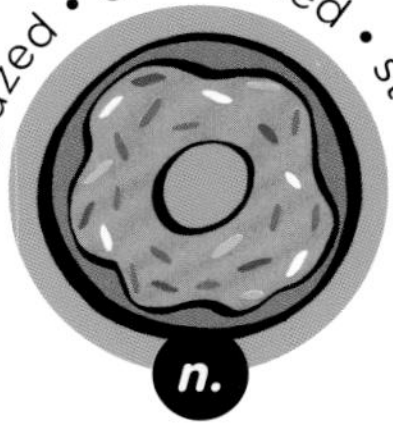

n.

doughnut

BAKING

fluffy • thick • blueberry

n.

waffles

brown • burnt • caramelized

n.

sugar

electric • sturdy • metal

n.

mixer

colorful • heart-shaped • extra

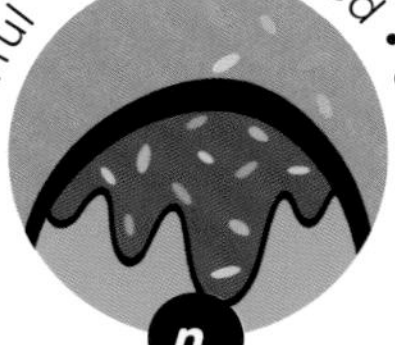

n.

sprinkles

huge • raging • incurable

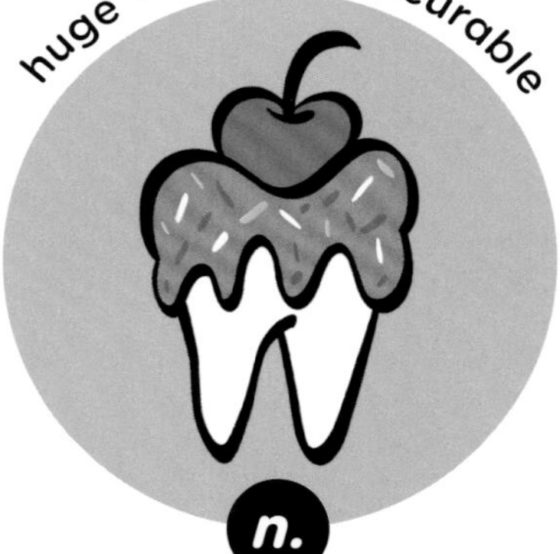

n.

sweet tooth

a taste for sugary food;
like a person who is always ready for dessert

BREAKFAST

fried • beaten • free-range

n.

eggs

buttery • warm • flaky

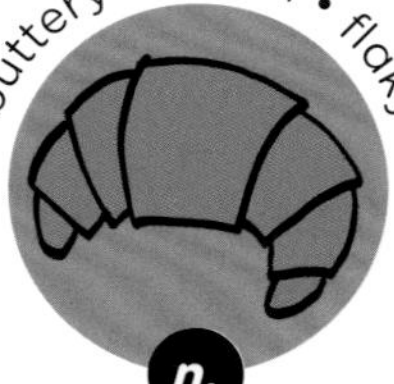

n.

croissant

streaky • crispy • sizzling

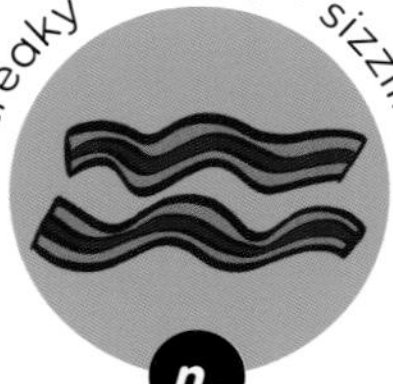

n.

bacon

toasted • chewy • stale

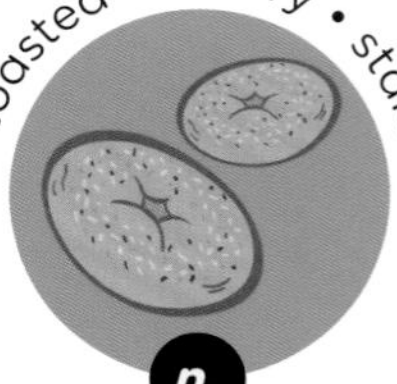

n.

bagel

sweetened • soggy • crunchy

n.

cereal

raw • whole-grain • oaty

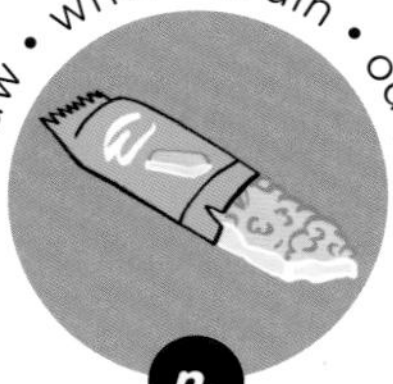

n.

cereal bar

wild • steamed • smoked

n.

fish

soft • rich • low-fat

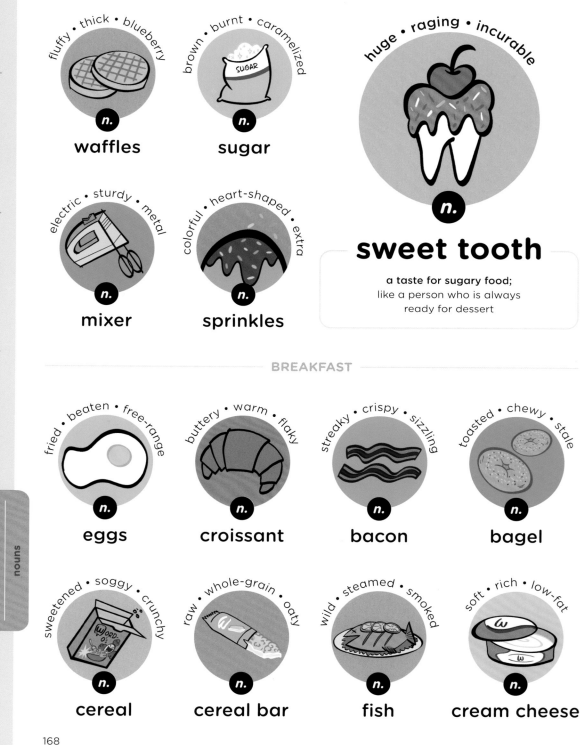

n.

cream cheese

BREAKFAST

healthy • nutty • crunchy

n.
granola

warm • creamy • hearty

n.
oatmeal

natural • dairy-free • frozen

n.
yogurt

fluffy • stacked • homemade

n.
pancakes

juicy • spicy • gristly

n.
sausage

golden • runny • raw
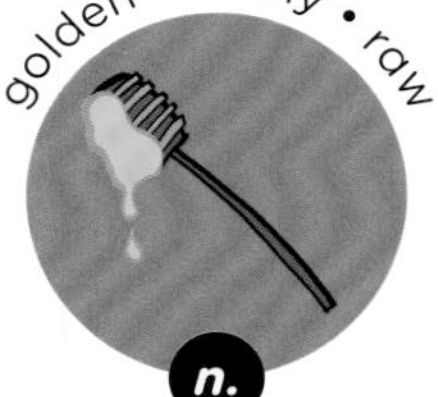
n.
honey

wild • finest • exquisite
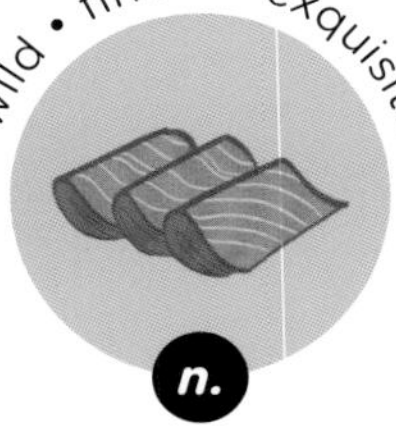
n.
smoked salmon

buttered • well-done • avocado

n.
toast

COOKING

blunt • steak • serrated

n.
knife

fine • dirty • heavy
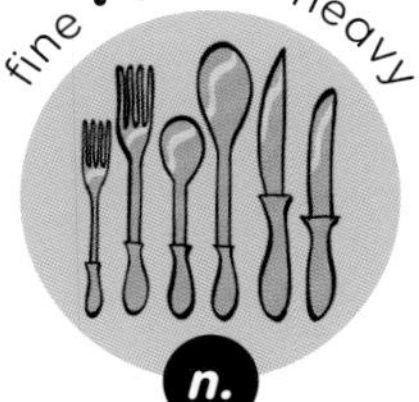
n.
cutlery

huge • two-pronged • loaded

n.
fork

imported • fancy • noisy

n.
espresso machine

sizzling • hot • electric
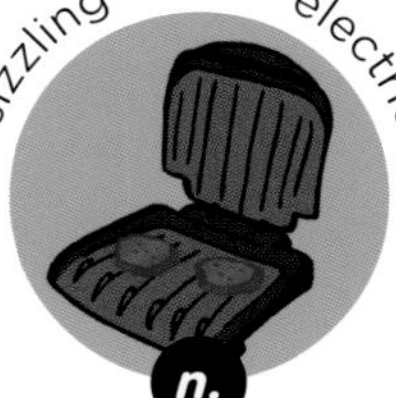
n.
grill

wooden • floured • plastic

n.
cutting board

dirty • high-powered • humming

n.
microwave

wooden • disposable • fancy

n.
chopsticks

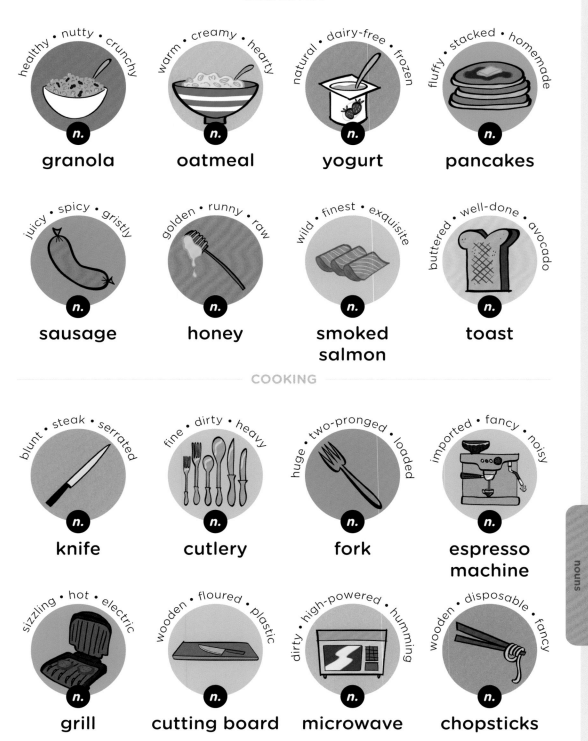

COOKING

preheated • blazing • wood-fired

n. **oven**

rubber • plastic • greasy

n. **spatula**

heavy • dented • flaming
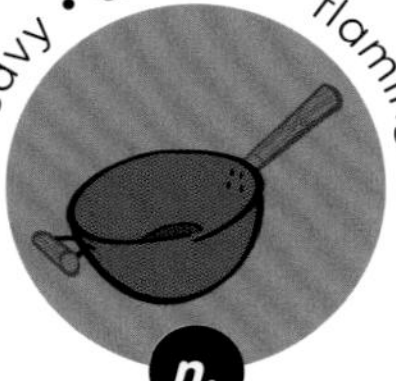
n. **wok**

dull • sharp • industrial

n. **peeler**

nonstick • cast-iron • roasting

n. **pan**

heaped • serving • metal

n. **spoon**

pop-up • faulty • electric

n. **toaster**

red-hot • bamboo • rotating

n. **skewer**

DRINKS

sweet • refreshing • legendary

n. **iced tea**

iced • frothy • lukewarm

n. **cappuccino**

sugary • addictive • delicious
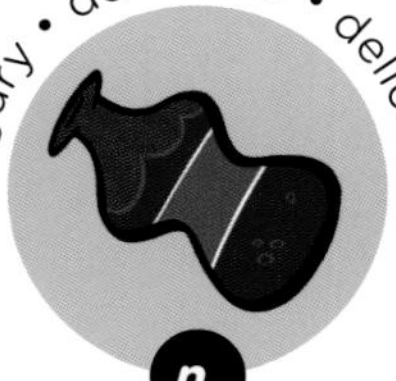
n. **soft drink**

fruit • freshly squeezed • spilled
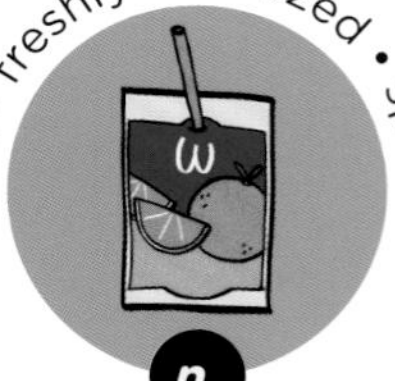
n. **juice**

rich • steaming • decadent

n. **hot chocolate**

fruity • powerful • caffeinated

n. **energy drink**

strong • steaming • undrinkable

n. **coffee**

mint • spiced • chilled

n. **lassi**

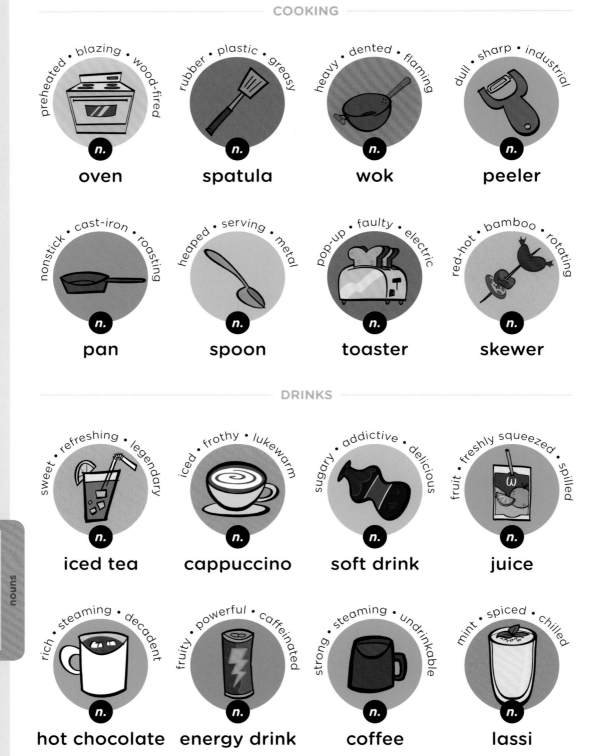

DRINKS

ice-cold • homemade • tart

n.

lemonade

healthy • tropical • disgusting

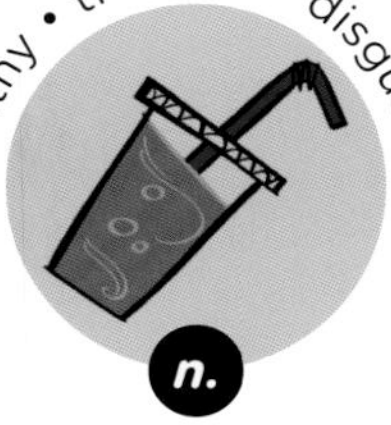

n.

smoothie

herbal • loose-leaf • weak

n.

tea

thick • frothy • chocolate

n.

milkshake

fruity • fancy • tasty

n.

mocktail

frozen • thick • sugary

n.

slushy

ice-cold • sparkling • boiling

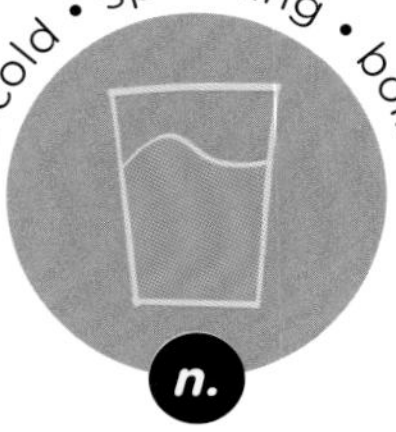

n.

water

spilled • lukewarm • chilled

n.

milk

FRUIT & VEGETABLES

whole • shredded • fermented

n.

cabbage

crunchy • rotten • tart

n.

apple

mashed • tropical • overripe

n.

banana

ripe • dried • chopped

n.

apricot

plump • frozen • hand-picked

n.

blueberries

diced • stuffed • fried

n.

eggplant

pickled • roasted • organic

n.

beet

raw • crunchy • roasted

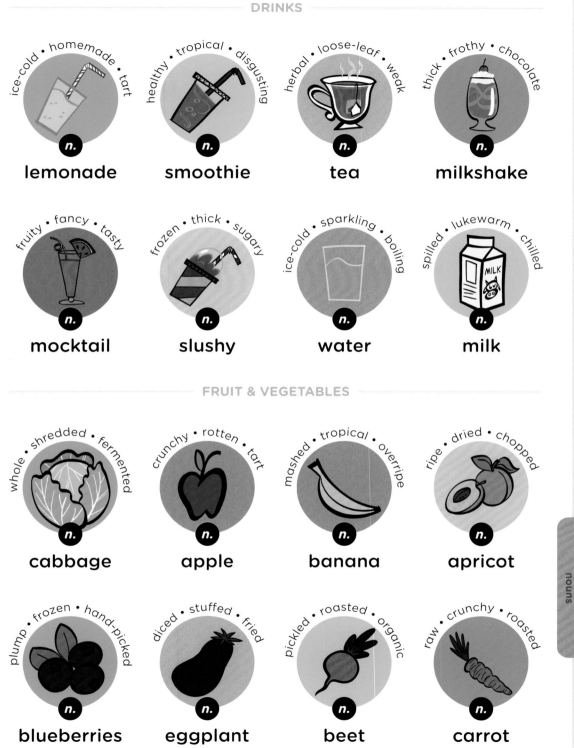

n.

carrot

FRUIT & VEGETABLES

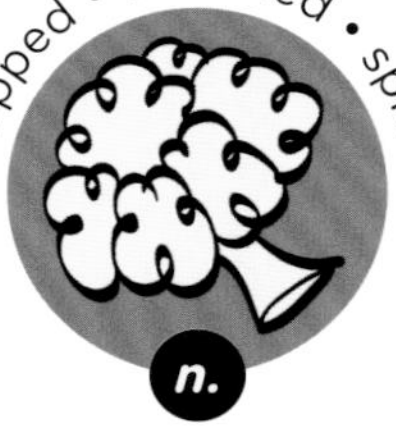
chopped • steamed • spiced
n.
cauliflower

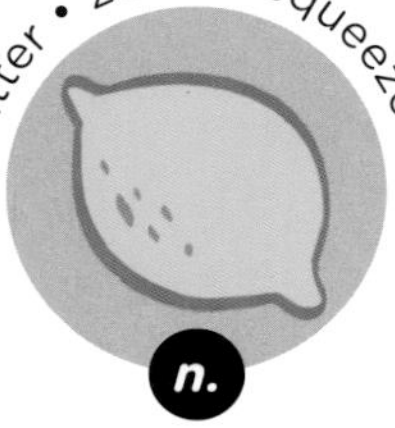
bitter • zesty • squeezed
n.
lemon

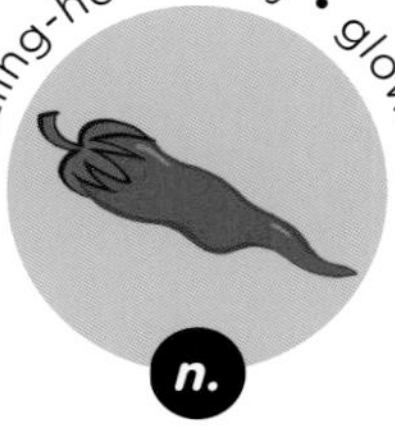
sizzling-hot • fiery • glowing
n.
chili

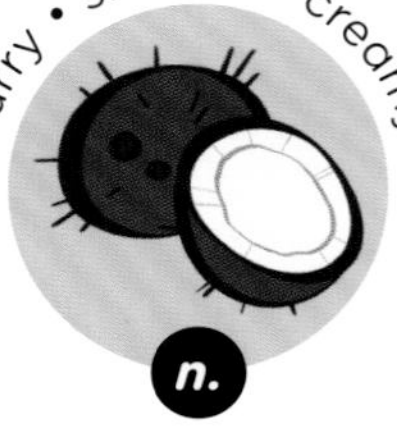
furry • shaved • creamy
n.
coconut

wild • grilled • poisonous
n.
mushrooms

sweet • roasted • scarlet
n.
pepper

canned • charred • roasted
n.
corn

halved • citric • zingy
n.
lime

frozen • mushy • creamed
n.
peas

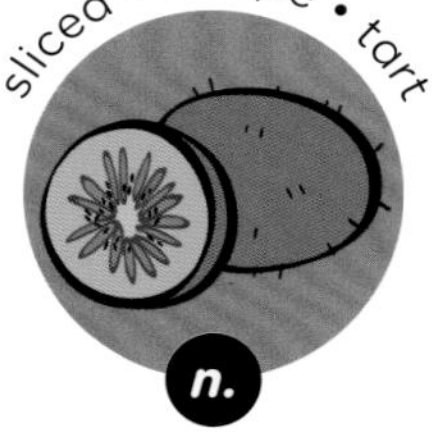
sliced • unripe • tart
n.
kiwi

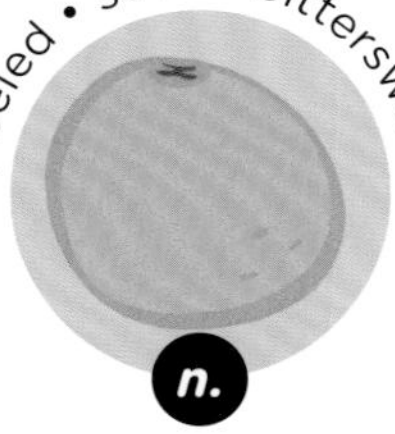
peeled • sour • bittersweet
n.
orange

bruised • luscious • succulent
n.
peach

curly • raw • steamed
n.
kale

juicy • seedless • shriveled
n.
grapes

dark • sour • pitted
n.
cherries

sweet • grilled • tropical
n.
pineapple

FRUIT & VEGETABLES

chopped • creamed • wilted

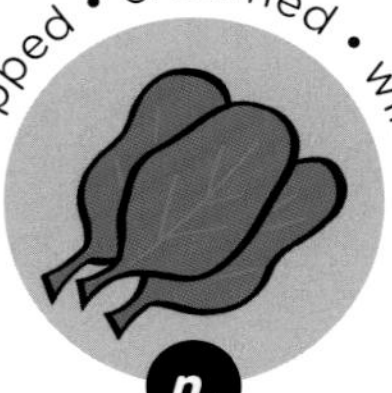

n.

spinach

sour • stewed • delicious

n.

plum

healthy • strict • ethical

n.

vegan

a person who doesn't eat anything from animals; like someone who never eats meat, cheese, or eggs

juicy • seedless • sliced

n.

watermelon

wild • local • preserved

n.

strawberries

INGREDIENTS

melted • burnt • salted

n.

butter

sliced • candied • pickled

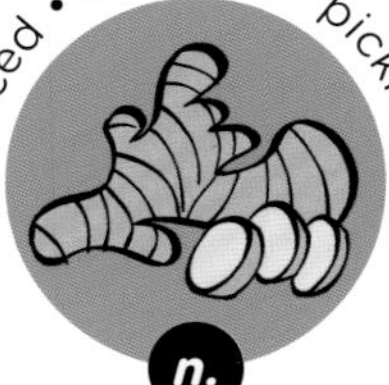

n.

ginger

fresh • dried • aromatic

n.

herbs

grated • pungent • crumbly

n.

cheese

crushed • raw • roasted

n.

garlic

sifted • self-rising • gluten-free

n.

flour

spicy • mild • homemade

n.

curry powder

fiery • drizzled • delectable

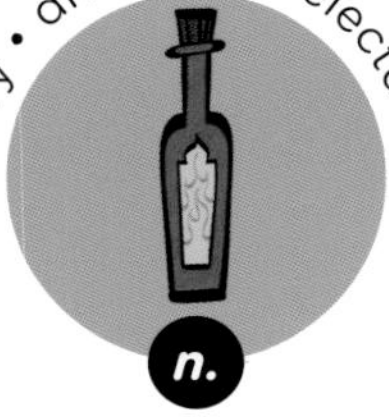

n.

hot sauce

INGREDIENTS

black • cracked • whole

n.
peppercorns

extra-virgin • healthy • organic

n.
olive oil

table • excess • sea

n.
salt

raw • caramelized • fried
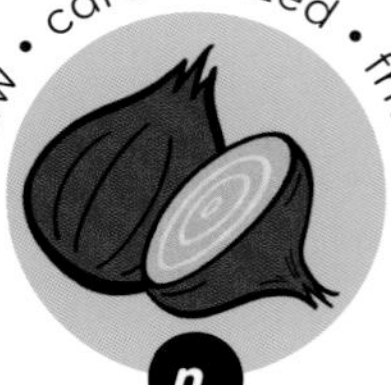
n.
onion

dark • aged • low-sodium

n.
soy sauce

vegetable • chicken • salty

n.
stock

strong • balsamic • rice
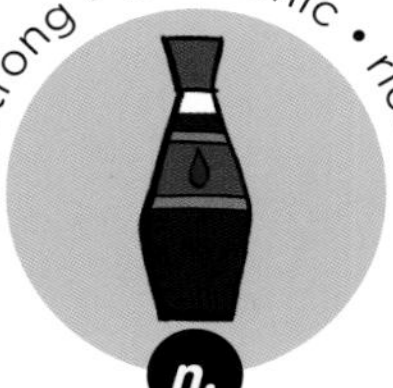
n.
vinegar

pure • delicate • expensive
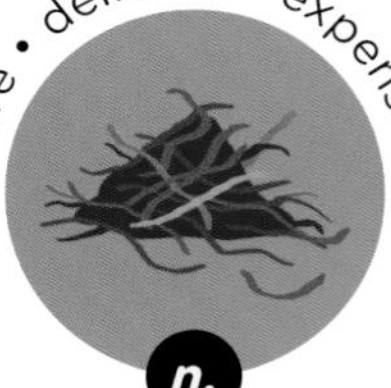
n.
saffron

MEAT & FISH

crispy • fatty • roasted

n.
duck

stewed • fatty • tough

n.
beef

frozen • crispy • baked

n.
chicken nuggets

expensive • boiled • grilled

n.
lobster

cold • sliced • cured
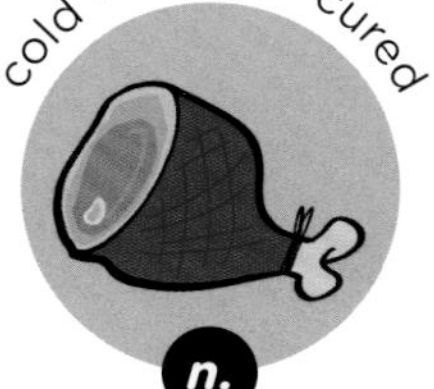
n.
ham

deep-fried • rubbery • seasoned

n.
calamari

spicy • enormous • hearty

n.
meatballs

fried • free-range • plucked

n.
chicken

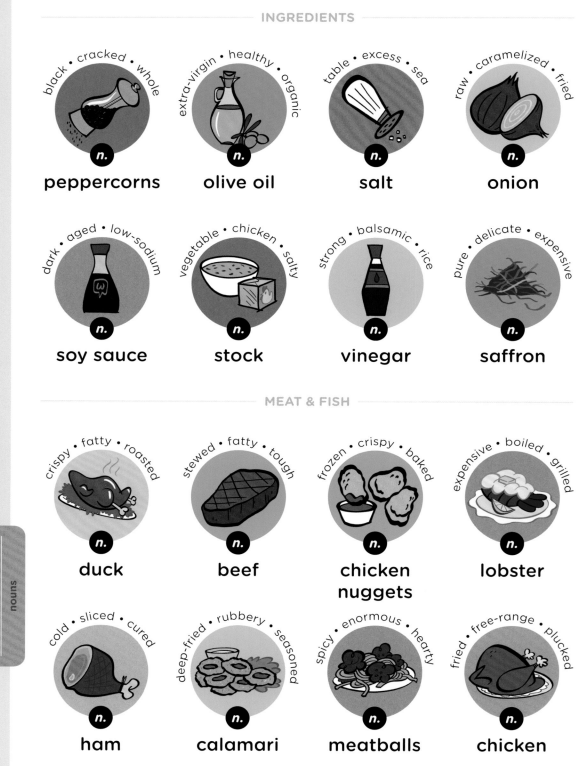

MEAT & FISH

wild • farmed • poached
n.
salmon

salty • local • exquisite
n.
oysters

plump • seared • marinated
n.
scallop

jumbo • frozen • imported
n.
shrimp

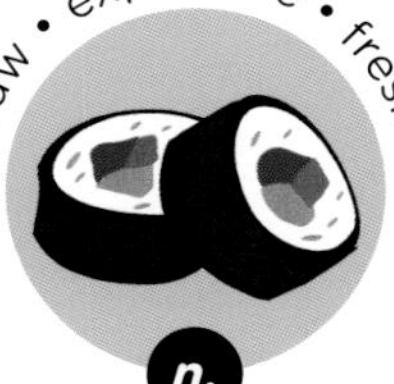
raw • expensive • fresh
n.
sushi

canned • seared • sustainable
n.
tuna

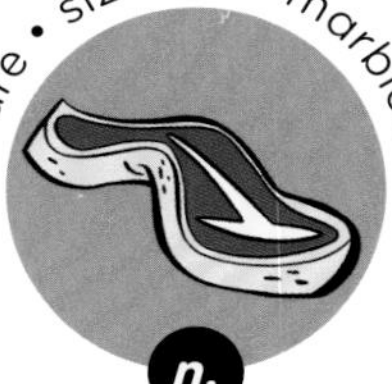
rare • sizzling • marbled
n.
steak

stuffed • oversized • leftover
n.
turkey

EATING OUT

empty • popular • upscale
n.
restaurant

shocking • unpaid • extortionate
n.
bill

head • renowned • temperamental
n.
chef

white • ruffled • embroidered
n.
tablecloth

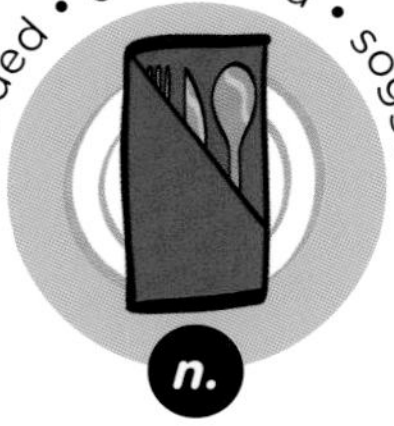
folded • crumpled • soggy
n.
napkin

daily • seasonal • vegetarian
n.
menu

busy • snooty • attentive
n.
waiter

free • all-you-can-eat • elaborate
n.
buffet

FAST FOOD

steamed • deep-fried • vegetable

n.

dumplings

frozen • wood-fired • leftover

n.

pizza

grilled • half-eaten • foot-long

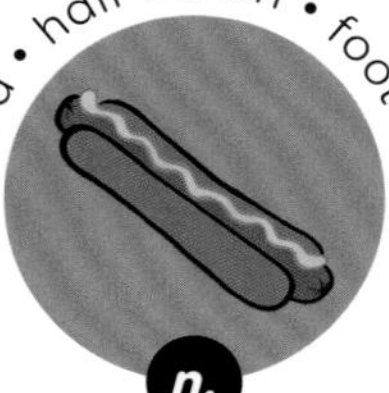

n.

hot dog

fried • instant • spicy

n.

noodles

spicy • authentic • magnificent

n.

kebab

soft • spicy • crunchy

n.

taco

salty • greasy • soggy

n.

fries

juicy • towering • succulent

n.

hamburger

CARBOHYDRATES

roasted • deep-fried • parboiled

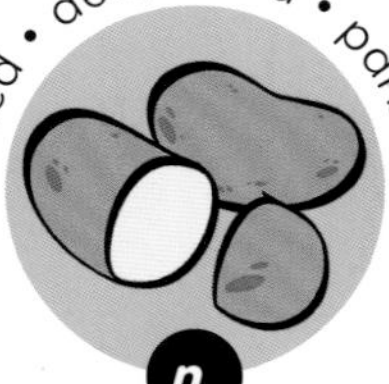

n.

potatoes

mashed • baked • leftover

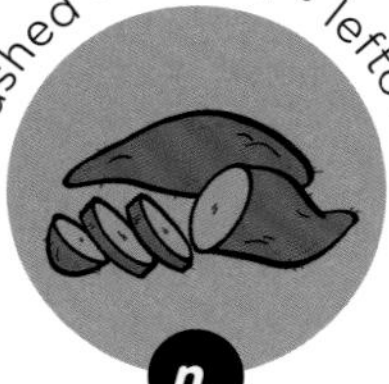

n.

sweet potato

rolled • organic • crunchy

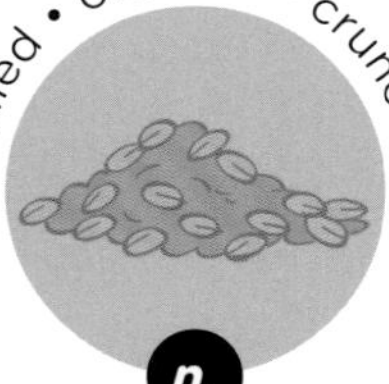

n.

oats

puffed • expensive • trendy

n.

quinoa

fresh • sourdough • moldy

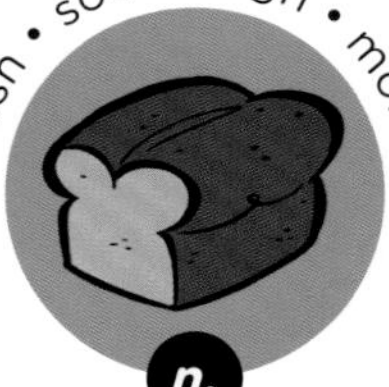

n.

bread

golden • wild • stone-ground

n.

wheat

sticky • fried • curried

n.

rice

handmade • cheesy • fresh

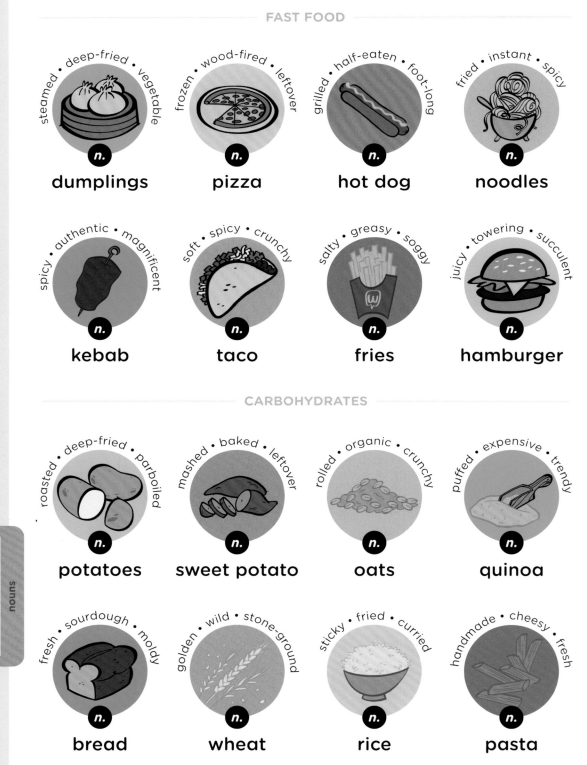

n.

pasta

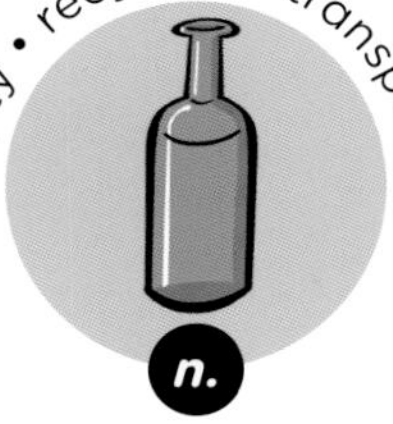
empty • recycled • transparent
n.
bottle

dirty • chipped • steaming
n.
mug

plastic • flattened • corrugated
n.
carton

walk-in • locked • unplugged
n.
freezer

steaming • piping-hot • reusable
n.
coffee cup

mixing • ceramic • overturned
n.
bowl

rusty • unopened • discarded
n.
can

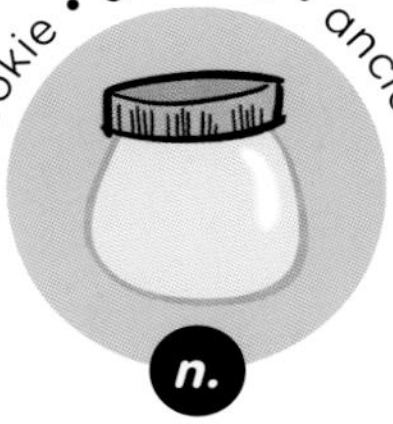
cookie • airtight • ancient
n.
jar

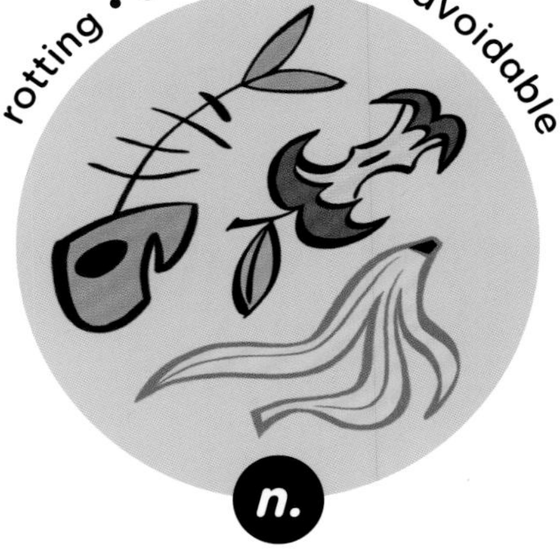
rotting • composting • avoidable
n.
food waste

scraps or uneaten leftovers;
like fish bones and apple cores that are thrown away after a meal

sealed • metal • ceramic
n.
flask

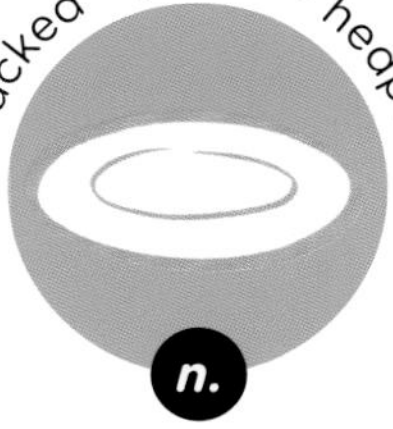
cracked • paper • heaped
n.
plate

oversized • fully stocked • faulty
n.
fridge

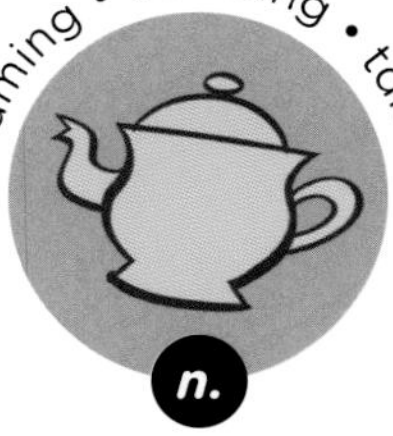
steaming • scalding • talking
n.
teapot

flurry

WEATHER

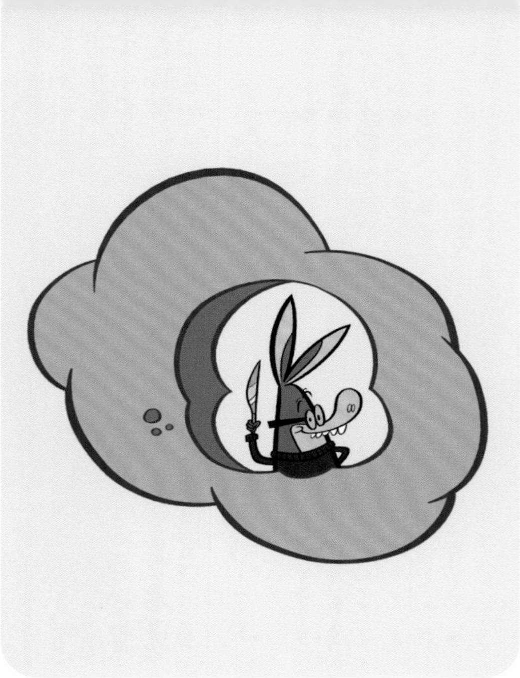

billowing *adj*. moving, flowing, or swelling; like rolling clouds that fill the sky

word pairs: clouds, sails, waves

dense *adj*. thick, solid, or heavy; like a cloud so thick you need a knife to cut through it

word pairs: fog, clouds, forest

---

overcast *adj*. cloudy or gray; how the sky looks when dark clouds block out all the sunshine

word pairs: morning, weather, conditions

swirling *adj*. spiraling or twirling; like clouds spinning around after a plane whizzes past

word pairs: mist, smoke, snowflakes

hazy *adj*. cloudy or misty; like a fog that makes it hard to see clearly

word pairs: sky, sunshine, memories

---

wispy *adj*. thin or fine; like clouds that are feathery and light

word pairs: clouds, beard, voice

cloudy words

word pair after:

billowing clouds
dense fog
hazy sky
overcast morning
swirling mist
wispy clouds

biting *adj*. bitter cold or harsh; so cold it feels like an icy monster is sinking its teeth into you

word pairs: wind, frost, comment

brisk *adj*. sharp or crisp; like the cold air on your face when you go for a winter walk

word pairs: air, walk, trade

---

frosty *adj*. freezing or icy; the kind of cold that feels like you have a layer of ice all over you

word pairs: breath, air, silence

numbing *adj*. taking away feeling; like ice that makes your tongue so cold you can't feel it

word pairs: pain, cold, boredom

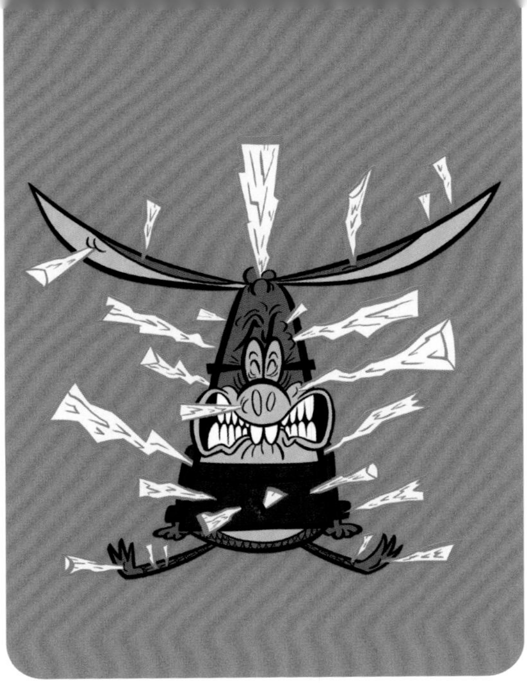

excruciating *adj.* extremely painful; how it would feel to be pricked all over by sharp icicles

word pairs: agony, cold, experience

---

penetrating *adj.* piercing or sharp; like freezing air that goes straight to your bones

word pairs: cold, gaze, odor

cold words

word pair after:

biting wind
brisk air
excruciating agony
frosty breath
numbing pain
penetrating cold

bleak *adj*. gloomy or depressing; like opening a box of doughnuts to find that it's empty

word pairs: reality, day, future

downpour *n*. a heavy rainstorm; like a big burst of rain that soaks you to the skin

word pairs: heavy, torrential, thundery

dreary *adj*. boring or miserable; like a dull job doing the same thing over and over again

word pairs: work, winter, afternoon

ominous *adj*. scary, threatening, or menacing; like a huge, dark tornado spinning toward you

word pairs: clouds, sign, shadow

drab *adj*. dull or gray; like a dark, gloomy day

word pairs: day, uniform, existence

---

splattered *adj*. splashed or sprinkled; like heavy raindrops that ruin your painting

word pairs: water, paint, mud

dark & rainy words

word pair before:

heavy **downpour**

word pair after:

bleak reality
drab day
dreary work
ominous clouds
splattered water

blistering *adj.* harsh or scorching; like sun so strong it makes your skin hurt

word pairs: sunburn, speed, critique

oppressive *adj.* heavy, harsh, or overpowering; like heat so strong you feel like it is crushing you

word pairs: heat, laws, silence

clammy *adj.* soggy or moist; like your skin when you are sweaty or feverish

word pairs: sweat, weather, handshake

perspire *v.* to drip with sweat; like what you do when you sit in a very hot sauna

word pairs: heavily, profusely, visibly

gleaming *adj*. shining or bright; like teeth that have been scrubbed clean by the dentist

word pairs: smile, light, sword

---

radiant *adj*. bright, brilliant, or glowing; like a very large and powerful light bulb

word pairs: glow, skin, beauty

hot words

word pair after:

blistering sunburn
clammy sweat
gleaming smile
oppressive heat
perspire heavily
radiant glow

relentless *adj*. constant or nonstop; like the sun when it beats down until you almost melt

word pairs: heat, rain, pressure

scorching *adj*. red-hot or blazing; like the kind of heat that will roast a marshmallow

word pairs: rays, summer, desert

---

stifling *adj*. smothering or suffocating; like a day so hot it makes your skin pour with sweat

word pairs: atmosphere, heat, smoke

suffocating *adj*. stuffy or smothering; like clothes so tight around your neck you can't breathe

word pairs: feeling, heat, fumes

searing *adj*. burning or scorching; like a day so hot that you can fry an egg on the pavement

word pairs: hot, pain, honesty

---

sweltering *adj*. very hot or baking; like weather that makes you desperate to find shade

word pairs: heatwave, heat, day

hot words

word pair after:

relentless heat
scorching rays
searing hot
stifling atmosphere
suffocating feeling
sweltering heatwave

balmy *adj*. mild or warm; like weather that makes you want to lie down and daydream

word pairs: night, weather, breeze

serene *adj*. peaceful or calm; like how you feel when you've done some relaxing yoga

word pairs: moment, beauty, weather

dewy *adj*. moist or damp; like grass that is covered in droplets of water in the morning

word pairs: grass, cobweb, complexion

temperate *adj*. mild or pleasant; like a place where the weather is never too hot or too cold

word pairs: weather, climate, person

rustling *adj.* crackling or swishing; like the sound of fall leaves being shaken from a tree

word pairs: leaves, papers, fabric

tranquil *adj.* peaceful or blissfully quiet; like how you feel when you take a nap in the shade

word pairs: surroundings, garden, atmosphere

pleasant words

word pair after:

balmy night
dewy grass
rustling leaves
serene moment
temperate weather
tranquil surroundings

deluge *n.* a flood or overflowing water; like gushing water from a blocked toilet

word pairs: sudden, torrential, catastrophic

electrifying *adj.* thrilling or stunning; like an exciting storm full of lightning and thunder

word pairs: storm, story, performance

lashing *adj.* thrashing or beating; like heavy rain smacking you in the face

word pairs: rain, wind, tail

tempestuous *adj.* stormy, wild, or violent; when the wind and the sea are out of control

word pairs: weather, sea, relationship

incessant *adj*. endless or nonstop; like rain that just never stops

word pairs: rainfall, chatter, repetition

---

torrential *adj*. falling heavily or forcefully; like the rain in a violent storm

word pairs: downpour, rain, thunderstorm

stormy words

word pair before:

sudden **deluge**

word pair after:

electrifying storm
incessant rainfall
lashing rain
tempestuous weather
torrential downpour

blustery *adj.* windy or gusty; like gusts of wind that turn your umbrella inside out

word pairs: conditions, wind, afternoon

flurry *n.* a short, swirling gust; like a burst of whirling snow that flies around your head

word pairs: brief, initial, constant

howl *v.* to cry or wail; like wind so strong that it makes a sound

word pairs: loudly, fiercely, miserably

whirlwind *n.* a hurricane or tornado; like wind that spins and sweeps everything up

word pairs: violent, sudden, destructive

gust *n.* a blast of air or strong breeze; like wind so strong that it blows your picnic away

word pairs: sudden, strong, violent

---

windswept *adj.* windblown and untidy; like how you look after being blown around by the wind

word pairs: beach, hair, island

windy words

word pair before:

brief **flurry**
sudden **gust**
violent **whirlwind**

word pair after:

blustery conditions
howl loudly
windswept beach

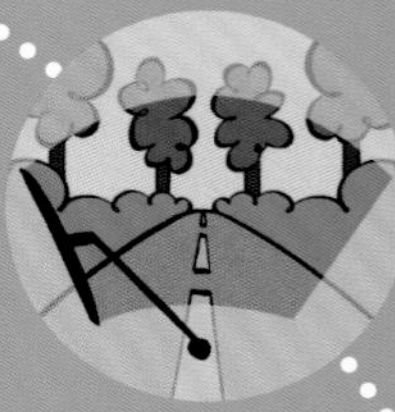

97

whistling weather nouns

Discover the nouns and word pairs that will transform your story from a **refreshing breeze** into a **powerful typhoon**. This section has something for everyone, whatever the weather.

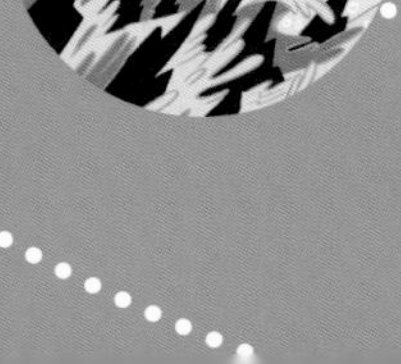

floating • lost • sensitive

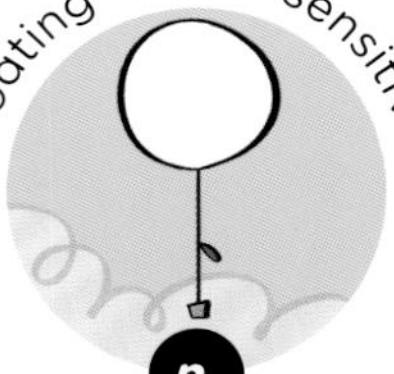

n.

weather balloon

useful • marine • reliable

n.

barometer

powerful • early-warning

n.

radar

extreme • man-made • accelerated

n.

global warming

old • global • interactive

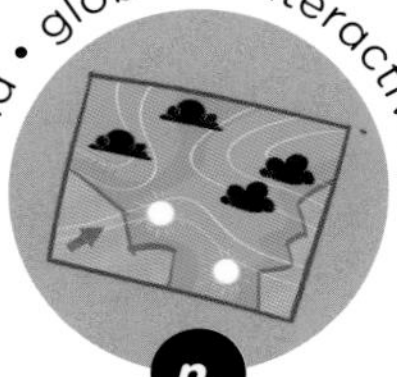

n.

map

colorful • geographical • global

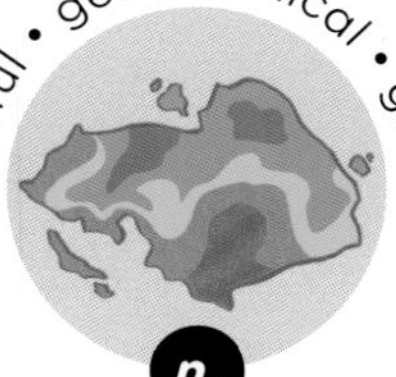

n.

heat map

respected • renowned • incompetent

n.

meteorologist

poor • limited • reduced

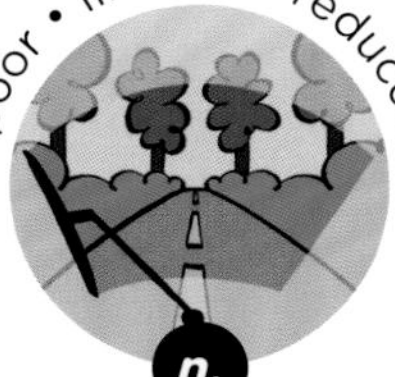

n.

visibility

daily • pessimistic • local

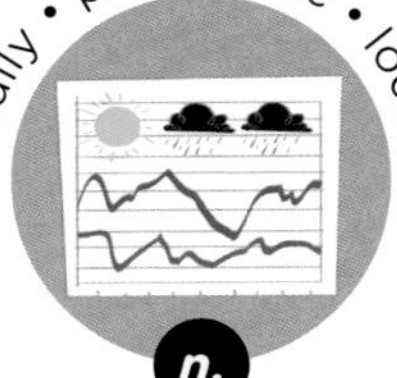

n.

forecast

low • above-average • atmospheric

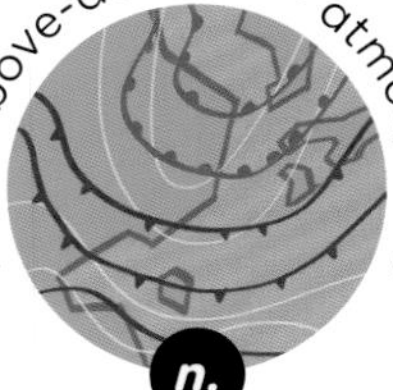

n.

pressure

rising • freezing • boiling

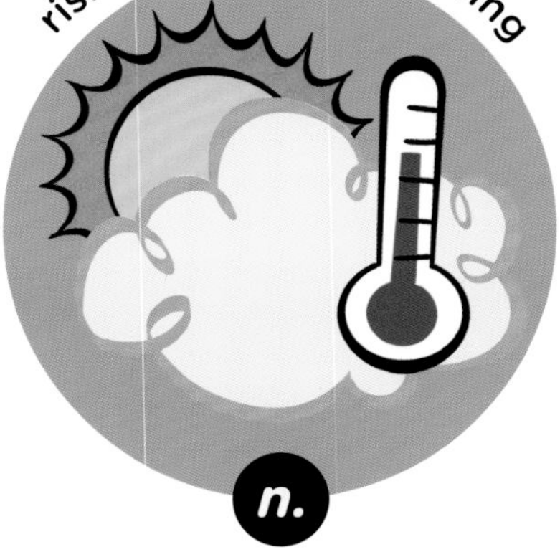

n.

temperature

how hot or cold something is;
like the difference in how the air feels between winter and summer

environmental • electronic • network

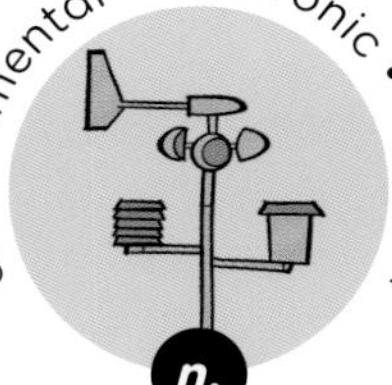

n.

sensor

bent • rusty • motionless

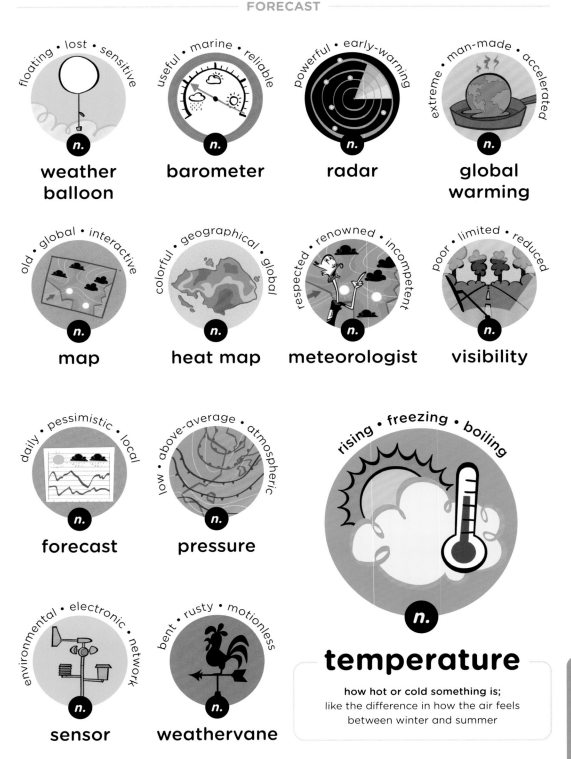

n.

weathervane

innocent • orphaned • helpless

n.

baby birds

April • brief • scattered

n.

showers

rapid • stunted • sluggish

n.

growth

the process of getting bigger or better;
like a plant bursting from the ground in spring

yellow • bright • blooming

n.

daffodil

golden • sticky • abundant

n.

pollen

tiny • newborn • vulnerable

n.

hatchlings

early • fragrant • delicate

n.

blossom

seasonal • chronic • debilitating

n.

hay fever

fallen • delicate • withered

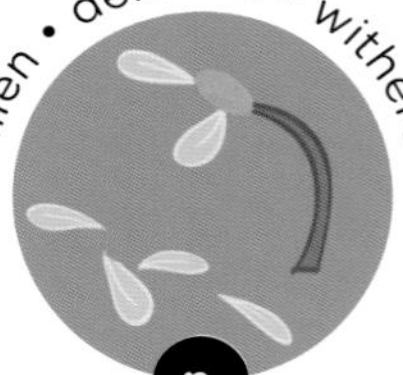

n.

petals

unopened • fresh • swelling

n.

buds

green • leafy • slender

n.

shoots

rapid • gradual • delayed

n.

thaw

heavy • light • plentiful

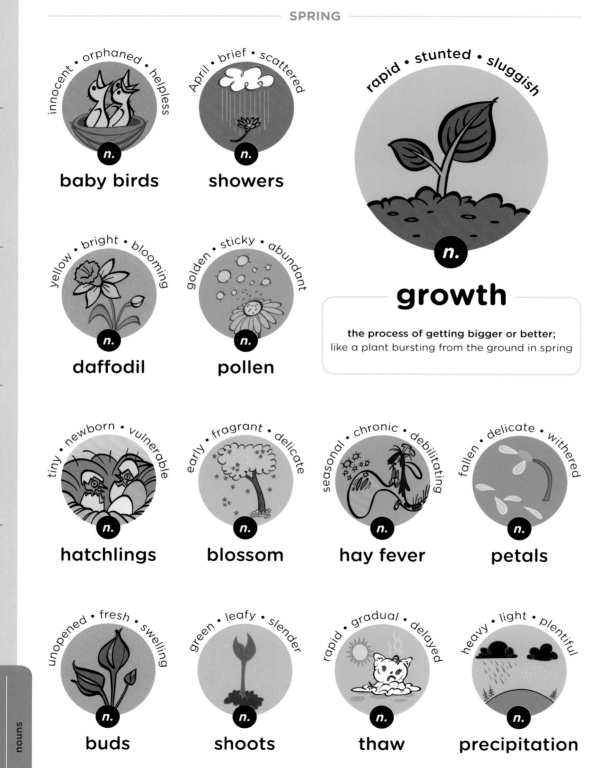

n.

precipitation

retro • musical • parked

n.

ice cream truck

sandy • sun-kissed • picturesque

n.

seaside

dry • tropical • stifling

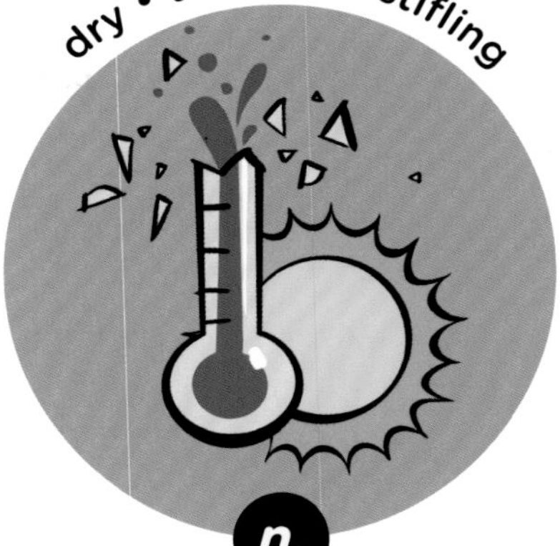

n.

heat

the energy that makes things hotter; like the warmth coming from the sun on a summer's day

delicious • melting • half-finished

n.

ice pop

magical • brilliant • glowing

n.

fireflies

giant • flamingo • inflatable

n.

float

broken • noisy • powerful

n.

air conditioner

plump • poisonous • organic

n.

berries

absolute • record-breaking

n.

scorcher

folding • empty • striped

n.

deck chair

heavy • clammy • profuse

n.

perspiration

afternoon • well-earned

n.

siesta

fake • glowing • fading

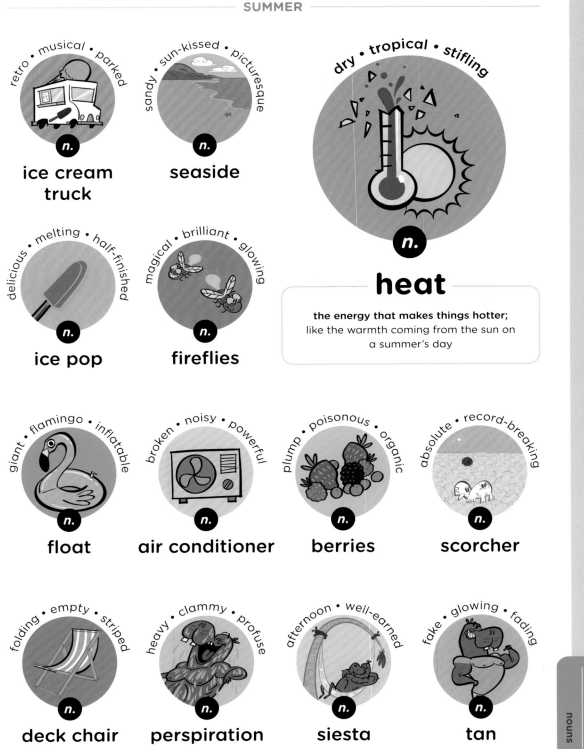

n.

tan

FALL

ugly • ragged • animated

n.
scarecrow

ripe • fallen • poisonous
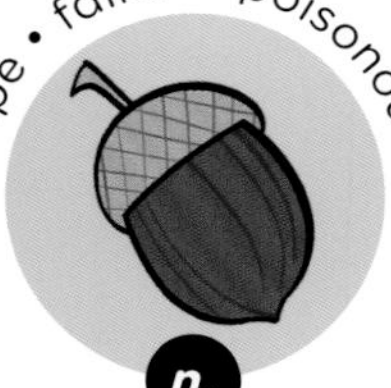
n.
acorn

glossy • graceful • overhanging

n.
foliage

steady • patchy • dreary
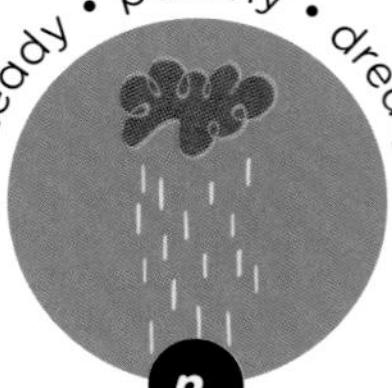
n.
drizzle

roaring • crackling • illegal

n.
bonfire

bad • annual • bountiful

n.
harvest

crunchy • scarlet • dead

n.
leaves

high • hanging • fallen

n.
branches

WINTER

slippery • cracked • thawing

n.
ice

heavy • intense • damaging
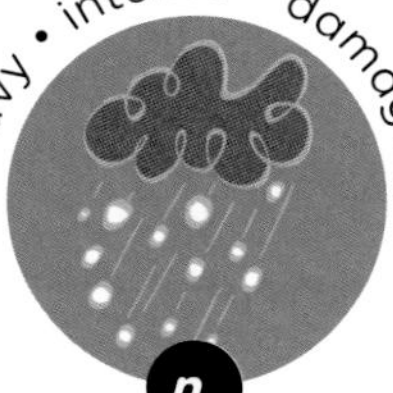
n.
hail

painful • mild • severe
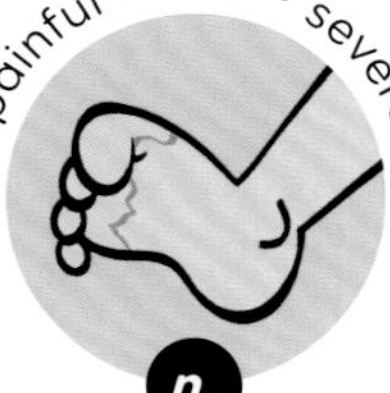
n.
frostbite

heavy • fresh • powdery

n.
snow

glittering • jagged • hazardous
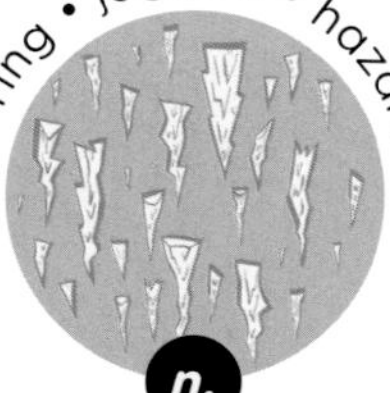
n.
icicles

bitter • widespread • sudden

n.
frost

fluffy • whirling • feathery

n.
snowflakes

muddy • ankle-deep • wintry
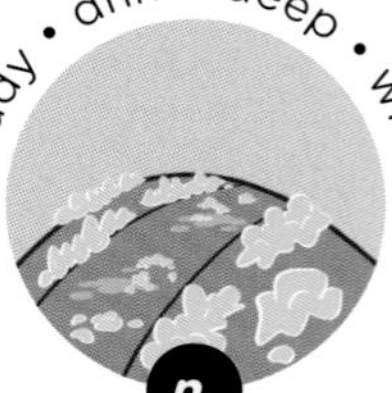
n.
slush

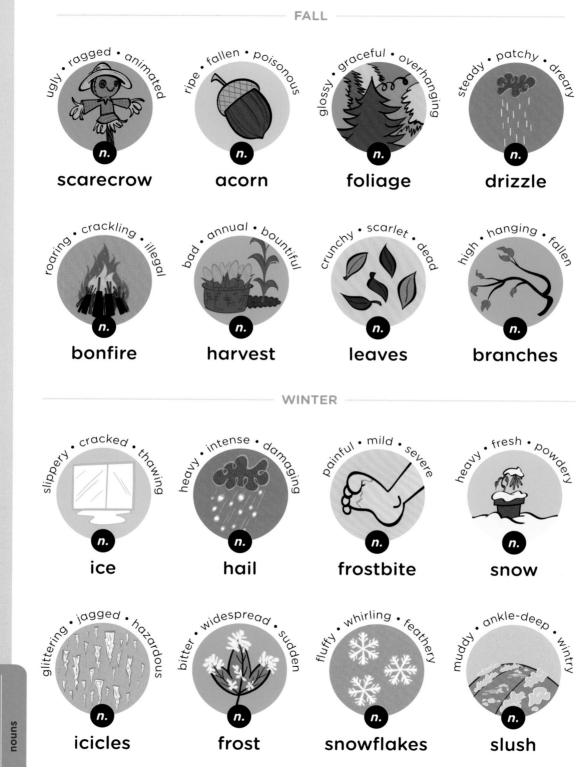

CLOUDY WEATHER

excessive • unbearable • seasonal

n.

humidity

dampness in the air;
like steamy air that's full of water droplets after a hot shower

gloomy • threatening • menacing

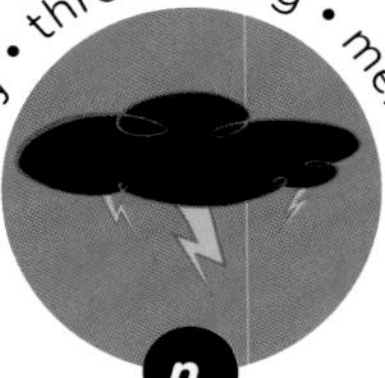

n.

thunder cloud

slender • floating • delicate

n.

wisp

drifting • dense • ominous

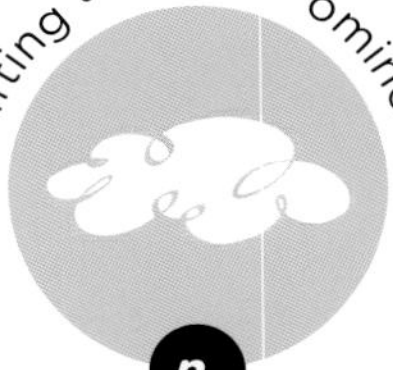

n.

cloud

soft • misty • faint

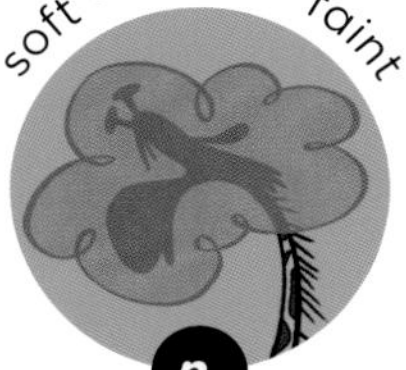

n.

haze

EXTREME WEATHER

rumbling • muffled • deafening

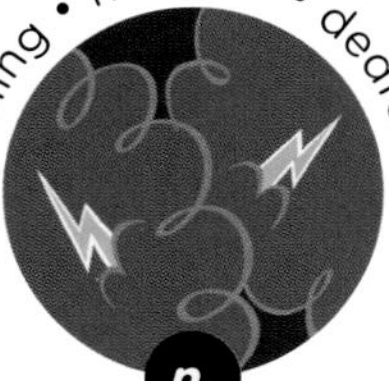

n.

thunder

tropical • fierce • approaching

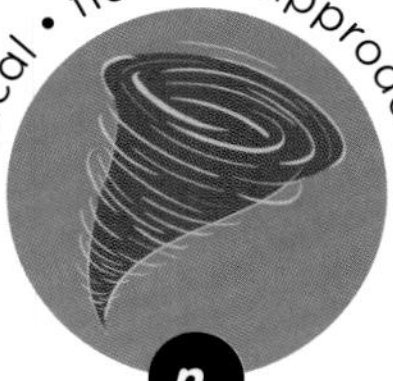

n.

tornado

deadly • horrific • catastrophic

n.

tsunami

jagged • deadly • blinding

n.

lightning bolt

powerful • deadly • destructive

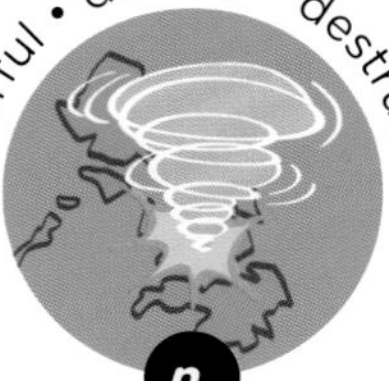

n.

typhoon

swirling • invisible • vast

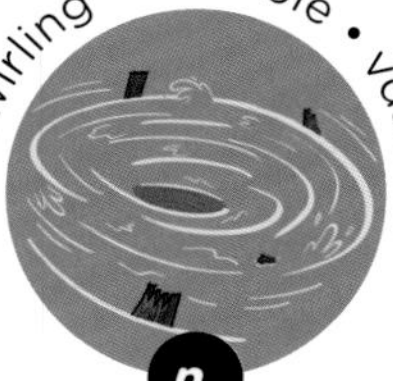

n.

maelstrom

rapid • raging • relentless

n.

torrent

raging • fast-moving

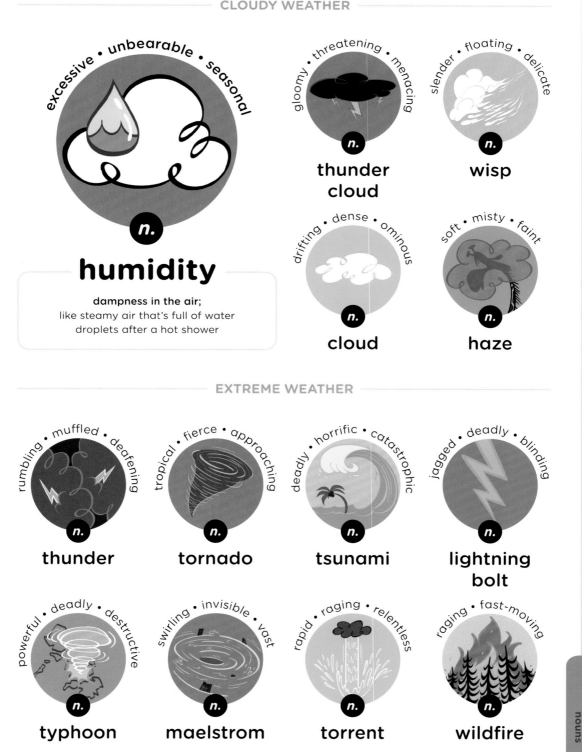

n.

wildfire

FOGGY WEATHER

harmful • plastic • industrial

n.

pollution

harmful fumes or dirty waste;
like the smoke from a factory that's bad for the environment

toxic • suffocating • choking

n.

smog

silvery • strange • impenetrable

n.

mist

fine • salty • iridescent

n.

spray

dense • mysterious • luminous

n.

fog

RAINY WEATHER

heavy • incessant • torrential

n.

rain

lucky • faint • vivid

n.

rainbow

sudden • rising • catastrophic

n.

flood

shallow • ankle-deep • rippling

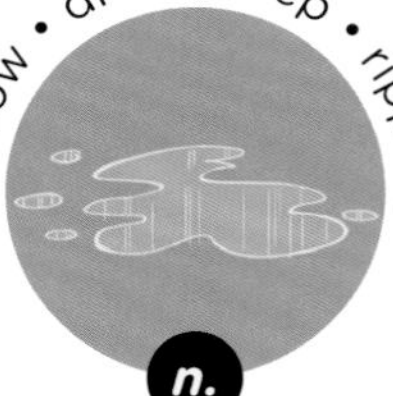

n.

puddle

serious • steady • possible

n.

leak

whistling • pelting • blinding

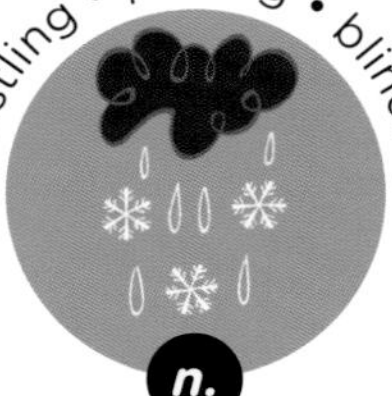

n.

sleet

fine • heavy • dispersed

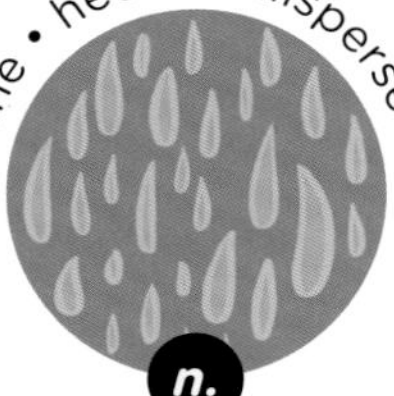

n.

droplets

gentle • mighty • sudden

n.

splash

SUNNY WEATHER

beautiful • perfect • endless
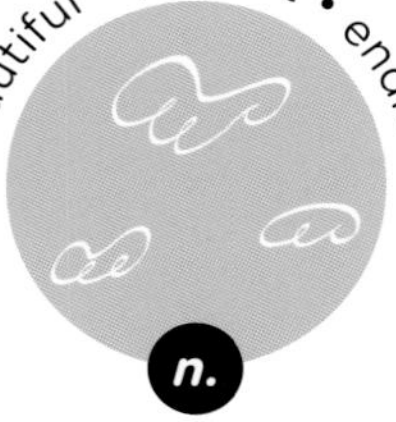
n.
blue sky

bright • perfect • distorted
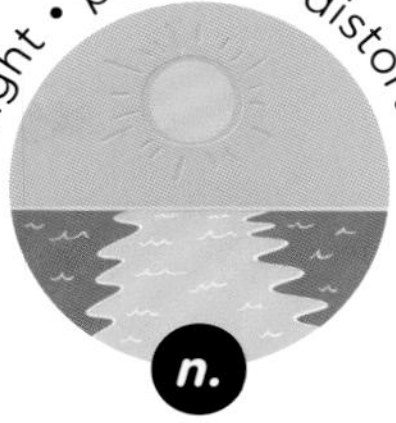
n.
reflection

rising • blazing • sinking
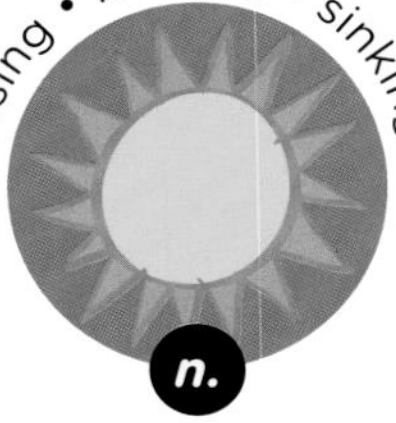
n.
sun

nasty • painful • blistering

n.
sunburn

enormous • wilting • perennial

n.
sunflower

scorching • dappled • slanting

n.
sunbeam

waterproof • tinted • effective
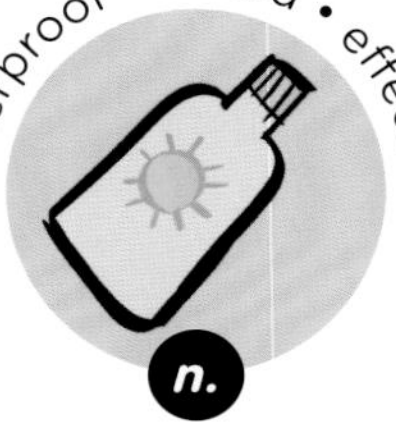
n.
sunscreen

natural • golden • blinding
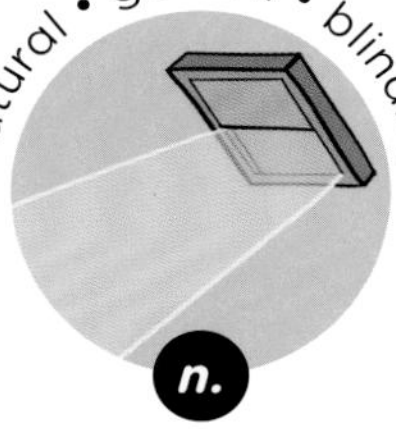
n.
light

WINDY WEATHER

sudden • furious • passing

n.
squall

strong • coastal • howling

n.
gale

warm • brisk • refreshing

n.
breeze

steady • harsh • vicious

n.
crosswind

runaway • soaring • free-flying
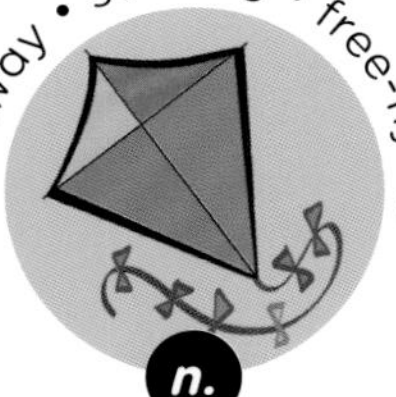
n.
kite

dangerous • considerable • restless

n.
turbulence

offshore • experimental • advanced

n.
wind turbine

white • billowing • threadbare

n.
sails

A

abandoned
adj. left or deserted

abnormal
adj. unusual or uncommon

above-average
adj. more than the normal amount

absolute
adj. total or complete

abstract
adj. showing ideas, not real things

abundant
adj. having a large amount or plenty

accelerated
adj. quicker or happening faster

accidental
adj. happening by chance

accomplished
adj. highly trained or skilled

accumulated
adj. piled up over time

accurate
adj. showing correct information

accusatory
adj. suggesting someone has done something wrong

aching
adj. in constant dull pain

activated
adj. made to start working

addictive
adj. something you want more of

adjustable
adj. able to be resized or adjusted

adorable
adj. cute, charming, or lovable

advanced
adj. using the latest technology

advancing
adj. moving forward

afternoon
n. time between noon and evening

aged
adj. allowed to mature

agile
adj. able to move quickly and easily

airborne
adj. in the air or flying

airtight
adj. sealed so that no air gets in

airy
adj. open and full of fresh air

alien
n. a creature from outer space

all-you-can-eat
adj. with unlimited portions

alleged
adj. reported or said without proof

alluring
adj. tempting or drawing you in

alpine
adj. relating to high mountains

amazing
adj. stunning or astonishing

ambushed
adj. victim of a surprise attack

amphibious
adj. suited for both land and water

ancient
adj. very old or from long ago

angelic
adj. like an angel

angry
adj. wild, raging, or out of control

animated
adj. lively or full of life

ankle-deep
adj. deep enough to cover your feet

annoying
adj. irritating or maddening

annual
adj. every year or in one year

anonymous
adj. unnamed or unknown

antigravity
adj. acting against gravity

antique
adj. old and precious

approaching
adj. coming closer

April
n. the fourth month of the year

arch
adj. main or chief

arched
adj. curved or bent

architectural
adj. to design buildings with

arid
adj. very dry or barren

aristocratic
adj. belonging to a grand family

armed
adj. carrying a weapon

armored
adj. protected or covered by metal

aromatic
adj. having a strong, pleasant smell

artisan
n. highly skilled worker or maker

artistic
adj. creative or imaginative

aspiring
adj. ambitious, hopeful, or budding

asthmatic
adj. suffering from asthma

athletic
adj. fit and strong

atmospheric
adj. in the air or atmosphere

A–B

atomic
adj. used for looking at atoms

attentive
adj. helpful and paying attention

austere
adj. harsh and bare

authentic
adj. real or made in the proper way

automated
adj. done using machines

automatic
adj. working by itself

available
adj. free to use

average
adj. ordinary or typical

avid
adj. very eager or enthusiastic

avocado
n. a pear-shaped, green fruit

avoidable
adj. unnecessary or needless

award-winning
adj. having won awards or prizes

babbling
adj. making a continuous noise

back-up
adj. used if the original doesn't work

bad
adj. not good or low-quality

baggy
adj. too big or hanging loosely

baked
[1] *adj.* cooked in an oven
[2] *adj.* dried in an oven

bald
adj. without hair

balmy
adj. pleasantly warm or mild

balsamic
adj. dark, sweet, and strong-tasting

bamboo
Go ask a panda!

bandaged
adj. wrapped in protective cloth

barbed-wire
adj. wire with lots of sharp spikes

bare
adj. naked or not covered

barren
adj. with nothing growing in it

basic
adj. only with the important parts

battered
adj. beaten and damaged

beached
adj. lying stranded on a beach

beachfront
adj. looking out over a beach

beachside
adj. next to a beach

beaded
adj. in small, round drops

beady-eyed
adj. with small, shiny, round eyes

beastly
adj. unkind, savage, or cruel

beaten
adj. whisked into a smooth liquid

beating
adj. pounding or drumming

beautiful
You!

bedraggled
adj. messed up and untidy

bejeweled
adj. decorated with jewels

belching
adj. sending out smoke or flames

beloved
adj. deeply loved or precious

bent
adj. twisted, curved, or crooked

big-city
adj. found in a large city

billionaire
n. a person with billions of pounds

billowing
adj. swelling or bulging in the wind

biodegradable
adj. rotting away naturally in soil

bitter
[1] *adj.* angry or grudging
[2] *adj.* cold or harsh
[3] *adj.* sharp or not sweet

bittersweet
[1] *adj.* tasting both bitter and sweet
[2] *adj.* making you feel sad and happy

black
adj. the darkest color

blackened
adj. turned black

blank
adj. empty or plain

blaring
adj. loud or booming

blazing
adj. very hot or burning

bleak
adj. gloomy or depressing

bleating
adj. making a crying sound

blind
adj. without thinking or judging

blinding
[1] *adj.* so bright that you can't see
[2] *adj.* so thick you can't see through

blinking
adj. quickly turning on and off again

B

blistered
adj. having sore, swollen bubbles

blistering
adj. so hot that your skin blisters

bloated
adj. full and swollen

blocked
adj. not letting things go through

bloodshot
adj. red, sore, and tired

bloodsucking
adj. blood-drinking

bloody
adj. stained or smeared with blood

blooming
adj. producing a flower

blotchy
adj. uneven or patchy

blueberry
n. a small and sweet berry

Bluetooth
n. wireless, short-range connection

blunt
adj. not having a sharp edge

boiled
adj. cooked in very hot water

boiling
adj. very hot or scorching

bold
adj. brave or daring

bony
[1] *adj.* skinny or scrawny
[2] *adj.* made of bone or bonelike

booming
adj. loud or thundering

borrowed
adj. taken to be used for a short time

botched
adj. done badly or messed up

bottomless
adj. very deep or endless

bouncing
adj. springing off the ground

bouncy
Like all the best castles.

boundless
adj. never-ending or limitless

bountiful
adj. generous or abundant

bowed
adj. lowered or looking down

branded
adj. stamped or marked with a logo

brave
adj. bold and daring

breathtaking
adj. beautiful or stunning

brief
adj. lasting for a short time

bright
adj. shining, radiant, or colorful

brilliant
adj. bright or shiny

brimming
adj. full to the point of overflowing

brisk
adj. cold and fresh

bristly
adj. short, stiff, and spiky

brittle
adj. fragile or breakable

broad
adj. wide or long from side to side

broken
[1] *adj.* not working or injured
[2] *adj.* hurt or despairing
[3] *adj.* smashed or shattered

bronzed
adj. tanned or bronze-colored

brooding
adj. looking intense and sad

broody
adj. ready to lay eggs and sit on them

brown
adj. the color of caramel or chocolate

bruised
adj. bashed and discolored

brutal
adj. violent, cruel, or savage

bubbling
adj. frothing, foaming, or gurgling

bug-eyed
adj. with bulging, sticking-out eyes

built-in
adj. fixed or fitted in

bulging
adj. swollen or sticking out

bulky
adj. big or taking up a lot of space

bulletproof
adj. able to block bullets

bumbling
adj. awkward or useless

buoyant
adj. light and able to float

burning
adj. on fire or very hot

burnt
[1] *adj.* spoiled by heat or overcooked
[2] *adj.* charred and destroyed by fire

burnt-out
adj. completely ruined by fire

burst
adj. broken, torn, or split open

bursting
adj. breaking or splitting open

bushy
adj. thick and full

bustling
adj. crowded or lively

busy
[1] *adj.* full of people
[2] *adj.* with lots of jobs to do

buttered
adj. covered in butter

buttery
adj. rich and creamy, like butter

buzzing
adj. making a continuous, low noise

caffeinated
adj. containing caffeine

caged
adj. kept in a cage

callused
adj. hardened or roughened

calm
adj. still and peaceful

camouflaged
adj. blending into the background

candied
adj. preserved in sugar syrup

canned
adj. kept in a sealed can

capsized
adj. upside down or flipped

captive
adj. kept prisoner or caged in

captured
adj. caught or taken by force

caramelized
adj. cooked slowly and sweet

carpeted
adj. covered with a carpet

cascading
adj. gushing or falling down quickly

cast-iron
adj. easily molded black metal

catastrophic
adj. disastrous or destructive

celebrated
adj. admired or praised

celebrity
No, you can't have my autograph.

ceramic
adj. made of baked clay

challenging
adj. difficult or dangerous

chaotic
adj. wild and confusing

charming
adj. attractive or delightful

charred
adj. burned or blackened by heat

cheap
adj. low-priced or not expensive

cheesy
adj. with cheese on top or inside

chemical
adj. made of chemicals or man-made

chewy
adj. tough or hard to chew

chic
adj. stylish or fashionable

chicken
n. a bird used in cooking

chilled
adj. cooled in a fridge

chipped
adj. with a small piece broken off

chiseled
adj. perfectly carved or sculpted

chocolate
Charlie's favorite type of factory.

choking
adj. making it hard to breathe

chopped
adj. cut or sliced into pieces

choppy
adj. with lots of little waves

chronic
adj. continuous or long-lasting

chubby
adj. plump or round

chunky
adj. thick or with big pieces

cinematic
adj. like something from a movie

circling
adj. moving around in circles

citric
adj. acidic, lemony, and sharp

clammy
adj. soggy, moist, and sticky

clandestine
adj. undercover or secret

clanking
adj. rattling, jangling, or clattering

classic
adj. popular since a long time ago

clattering
adj. noisy and rattling

clean
adj. washed or without any dirt

clear
[1] *adj.* easy to hear or understand
[2] *adj.* easy to see through
[3] *adj.* easy to spot or notice

clenched
adj. tense or gripping tightly

clever
[1] *adj.* skillful and cunning
[2] *adj.* smart or cunning
[3] *adj.* well-designed or high-tech

clipped
adj. cut short or trimmed

clogged
adj. blocked or stuffed

C

close
[1] *adj.* knowing each other very well
[2] *adj.* only won by a few points

clotted
[1] *adj.* dried or thickened into chunks
[2] *adj.* thickened or mixed until it's stiff

cloudless
adj. clear or without clouds

cluttered
adj. messy or littered

coarse
adj. rough or scratchy

coastal
adj. on the coast or beside the sea

cold
Brrrrrrrrr.

collapsed
adj. fallen down or crumpled

collected
adj. picked or brought together

colonized
adj. taken as a new place to live

colorful
adj. brightly colored or not dull

colossal
adj. massive or gigantic

comfortable
[1] *adj.* cozy or snug
[2] *adj.* easy to wear and the right size

comfy
adj. soft or nice to wear

comical
adj. funny or amusing

common
adj. ordinary or usual

communal
adj. used by everyone or shared

compact
adj. small and neat

competitive
[1] *adj.* related to winning and losing
[2] *adj.* wanting to be the best

complete
adj. has all the parts

composting
adj. rotting to be used as fertilizer

concealed
adj. hidden or secret

concealing
adj. hiding something

concrete
n. a very hard, stone building material

confusing
Huh?

congested
adj. blocked or too crowded

considerable
adj. big and noticeable

contaminated
[1] *adj.* spoiled or ruined
[2] *adj.* spoiled by dirt or pollution

contemporary
adj. in a modern style

cooing
adj. making a soft, murmuring sound

cookie
Heavenly circles of deliciousness.

cool
adj. popular or fashionable

corroded
adj. worn down or burnt away

corrosive
adj. harmful or burning

corrugated
adj. ridged or wavy

corrupt
[1] *adj.* ruined or full of mistakes
[2] *adj.* dishonest or misusing power

countless
adj. too many to be counted

covert
adj. secret or undercover

coveted
adj. wanted by lots of people

cowardly
adj. afraid or not confident

cowboy
Yee-haw!!!

cozy
adj. warm and comfortable

cracked
adj. split or with broken lines

crackling
adj. making small, sharp noises

crackly
adj. making short, harsh noises

cramped
adj. small, without enough room, or stuffy

crashed
[1] *adj.* fallen to the ground or smashed
[2] *adj.* smashed into something

crashing
adj. smashing loudly against things

creaky
adj. noisy when stepped on

creamed
adj. blended, smooth, and soft

creamy
adj. as smooth and soft as cream

credible
adj. easy to believe or reliable

creeping
adj. moving slowly over a surface

creepy
adj. scary or unnerving

crescent
adj. curved or in a semicircle shape

crisp
adj. cold and fresh

crispy
adj. thin, dry, and crunchy

crooked
adj. bent or wonky

crowded
adj. full of people or things

crude
adj. made very simply or badly

cruel
adj. mean or unkind

cruising
adj. sailing or traveling

crumbling
adj. falling down bit by bit

crumbly
adj. easily broken into little bits or crumbs

crumpled
adj. crushed out of shape

crunchy
[1] *adj.* making a noise when you bite it
[2] *adj.* making a crushing noise

crushed
adj. broken by squeezing or pressing

crushing
adj. squashing or smashing

cuddly
adj. soft and huggable

cunning
adj. clever or crafty

curdled
adj. separated into lumpy bits

cured
adj. dried or smoked to last longer

curious
adj. wanting to find out more

curly
adj. curved or spiraled

curried
adj. flavored with spices

curved
adj. rounded or bent

custom-made
adj. made especially for you

cute
adj. sweet or lovable

cutting-edge
adj. using advanced technology

cynical
adj. negative or full of doubt

daily
adj. for each new day

dairy-free
adj. free from animal milk products

damaging
adj. harmful or destructive

damp
adj. slightly wet or soggy

dangerous
adj. unsafe or likely to cause harm

dapper
adj. neat and stylish

dappled
adj. marked with spots or patches

daring
adj. brave or bold

dark
[1] *adj.* with little or no light
[2] *adj.* any color close to black

dated
adj. old-fashioned or from the past

daunting
adj. seems scary or intimidating

daytime
adj. while the sun is up

dazzling
adj. very bright or amazing

dead
[1] *adj.* out of energy
[2] *adj.* fallen and no longer alive

dead-end
adj. with no way out the other side

deadly
adj. dangerous or life-threatening

deafening
adj. very loud or noisy

debilitating
adj. weakening or holding you back

decadent
adj. very luxurious or indulgent

decorated
adj. made prettier by adding things

dedicated
adj. eager or devoted

deep
adj. goes far down below the top

deep-fried
adj. cooked by being dipped in hot oil

deep-set
adj. fixed or firmly in something

deep-water
adj. growing in very deep water

defective
adj. broken or not working properly

defined
adj. obvious, clear, or outlined

deflated
adj. flat or with the air let out

delayed
adj. later than expected

delectable
adj. very tasty or delicious

delicate
[1] *adj.* fine, elegant, and detailed
[2] *adj.* fragile and breakable
[3] *adj.* with a mild or subtle flavor

delicious
adj. tasty or enjoyable to eat or drink

dense
adj. thick, solid, or heavy

D–E

dented
adj. pushed in from being hit

dependable
adj. reliable or always works well

derailed
adj. driven off the tracks

derelict
adj. run down or left to fall apart

deserted
adj. empty or abandoned

desolate
adj. bleak, bare, and empty

desperate
adj. anxious, frantic, or without hope

destructive
adj. damaging or devastating

detached
adj. not joined onto another building

detailed
adj. packed with info and facts

devastating
adj. very damaging and destructive

devious
adj. cheating, sneaky, or sly

dewy
adj. covered in little water droplets

diced
adj. chopped into small cubes

die-hard
adj. unchanging or never giving up

digital
adj. using electronics or computers

dilapidated
adj. ruined, run down, or shabby

dim
adj. faint or not shining brightly

dim-witted
adj. silly or not clever

dimmed
adj. turned down

dingy
adj. dark or gloomy

direct
adj. straight or uninterrupted

dirty
adj. unclean or mucky

discarded
adj. thrown away or rejected

disgusting
adj. gross or revolting

dismal
adj. dark and depressing

disorganized
adj. messy or cluttered

dispersed
adj. spread out over a big area

disposable
adj. thrown away after it's used

distant
adj. far away or faint

distinctive
adj. easy to identify or recognize

distorted
adj. twisted or bent out of shape

disused
adj. not used anymore

doomed
adj. unlucky or heading for disaster

double-breasted
adj. with overlapping flaps at the front

double-decker
adj. with two floors or decks

downward
adj. toward the ground

drafty
adj. breezy and cold inside

drained
adj. run down or empty

drawn
adj. closed or pulled shut

dreadful
adj. very bad or very serious

dreary
adj. dull and miserable

dried
[1] *adj.* dehydrated or sun-baked
[2] *adj.* dehydrated to make it last

drifting
adj. floating gently away

dripping
adj. wet and with droplets falling off

driverless
adj. automatic and without a driver

drizzled
adj. sprinkled or poured carefully

droning
adj. constantly humming or buzzing

drooling
adj. dribbling or slobbering

drooping
adj. hanging down or sagging

dry
adj. not wet or damp

dull
adj. blunt or not sharp

durable
adj. strong and lasting a long time

dusty
adj. full of dust, dried mud, or soot

dwindling
adj. getting smaller and weaker

eager
adj. ambitious or enthusiastic

ear-splitting
adj. so loud that it hurts your ears

early
adj. sooner than expected

early-warning
adj. giving a warning ahead of time

eclipsed
adj. blocked out by another thing

eerie
adj. weird, ghostly, or creepy

effective
adj. working well

ejectable
adj. can be kicked out or sent flying

elaborate
adj. complex, detailed, or fancy

elbow-length
adj. reaching up to your elbows

electric
adj. powered by electricity

electrified
adj. charged with electricity

electronic
adj. powered by electricity

elegant
adj. graceful and grand

elongated
adj. made longer or stretched

elusive
adj. difficult to find or catch

embedded
adj. fixed, lodged, or planted firmly

embroidered
adj. with a stitched design

empty
adj. with nothing inside

enchanted
adj. under a magic spell

encrypted
adj. hidden or protected by a code

endangered
adj. likely to go extinct soon

endless
adj. unlimited or with no end

engraved
adj. with a design carved in

enormous
adj. really big or huge

enraged
adj. very angry or furious

entire
adj. complete or whole

enviable
adj. making other people jealous

environmental
adj. to do with the natural world

epic
adj. awesome or extraordinary

erratic
adj. unpredictable or unreliable

escaped
adj. running free

essential
adj. very important or necessary

eternal
adj. with no end or lasting forever

ethical
adj. moral, honest, and fair

evil
adj. bad or wicked

excess
adj. more than you need

excessive
adj. too much or over the top

excited
adj. lively or enthusiastic

exclusive
adj. only letting a few people in

exhausted
adj. worn-out or very tired

exotic
adj. unusual and from far away

expensive
adj. costing a lot of money

experimental
adj. testing or based on new ideas

exposed
adj. bare or not covered

expressive
adj. showing a lot of emotion

exquisite
adj. excellent or magnificent

external
adj. outside or separate

extortionate
adj. too much or overly expensive

extra
adj. more than the usual

extra-virgin
adj. when olive oil is very pure and high quality

extreme
adj. strong, intense, or severe

fabulous
adj. amazing or wonderful

faded
adj. faint or worn-out

fading
adj. slowly losing its color

failing
adj. not working properly

faint
adj. slight or barely noticeable

faithful
adj. loyal and devoted

fake
adj. not real or not natural

fallen
adj. having dropped to the ground

falling
adj. dropping to the ground

family-owned
adj. owned by one family

F

famous
adj. known by lots of people

fancy
adj. decorative or expensive

faraway
adj. distant or not nearby

farmed
adj. produced on a farm or fishery

fast
Blink and you might miss it!

fast-growing
adj. getting bigger quickly

fast-moving
adj. moving or spreading quickly

fatty
adj. with a lot of fat

faulty
adj. not working properly

favorite
adj. liked more than all the others

fearless
adj. brave or not afraid

fearsome
adj. frightening or menacing

feathered
adj. soft and cut at different lengths

feathery
adj. light and soft, like feathers

fenced-in
adj. surrounded by a fence

fermented
adj. gone sour

ferocious
adj. fierce or violent

fertile
adj. fruitful or able to grow things

fierce
adj. violent or savage

fiery
[1] *adj.* very spicy or hot-tasting
[2] *adj.* burning or producing fire

filthy
adj. disgustingly dirty or mucky

fine
[1] *adj.* light, thin, or wispy
[2] *adj.* excellent or top-quality

finest
adj. best or nicest

fireproof
adj. protected against fire

firm
adj. hard or solid

first
adj. at the beginning or before others

first-degree
adj. mild or not very harmful

fishy
adj. tasting or smelling like fish

fitted
adj. made to be the right shape

five-star
adj. of the highest standard

flaky
adj. breaking easily into flakes

flaming
adj. on fire or burning

flamingo
n. a bright pink bird with a long neck

flammable
adj. easy to set on fire

flapping
adj. moving quickly up and down

flared
adj. opened or made wider

flashing
adj. quickly switching on and off

flat
adj. smooth and even

flat-screen
adj. thin and not curved

flattened
adj. squashed or made flat

flattering
adj. making you look good

fleeing
adj. running away or escaping

flesh-eating
adj. eating the meat of humans

flexible
adj. able to bend without breaking

flickering
adj. burning or shining unsteadily

flightless
adj. not able to fly

flimsy
adj. weak, thin, or easy to break

floating
[1] *adj.* sitting on top of the water
[2] *adj.* staying up in the air

flooded
adj. covered with too much water

floppy
adj. limp or hanging loosely

floral
adj. with a flowery pattern

floured
adj. dusted with a layer of flour

flowering
adj. producing flowers

flowing
adj. hanging loosely and smoothly

fluffy
adj. woolly, fleecy, and soft
adj. light and full of air

fluorescent
[1] *adj.* producing a bright light
[2] *adj.* vividly colorful and bright

fluttering
adj. with wings flapping up and down

F–G

flying
adj. moving through the air

foaming
adj. frothing or making tiny bubbles

folded
adj. with one part turned over

folding
adj. able to be made smaller or neater

fond
adj. loving or affectionate

foolish
adj. silly or unwise

foot-long
adj. 12 inches or 30.48 cm long

forensic
adj. using science to find the truth

formal
adj. appropriate for important occasions

formidable
adj. impressive and intimidating

fortune
n. luck or chance in life

fossilized
adj. preserved in a rock

foul
adj. disgusting or revolting

fragile
adj. easy to break or ruin

fragrant
adj. sweet-smelling or perfumed

frayed
adj. with worn-out edges

free
adj. without any cost or payment

free-flying
adj. able to move easily in the air

free-range
adj. not raised in small cages

freezing
adj. below zero or very cold

frenzied
adj. wildly excited or frantic

fresh
adj. made or created recently

freshly baked
adj. just out of the oven

freshly squeezed
adj. recently pressed from fruit

fried
adj. cooked in a pan with oil

friendly
adj. kind, sociable, and welcoming

frightened
adj. scared or fearful

front
adj. on the side that faces forward

frosty
adj. freezing or icy

frothy
adj. foamy and bubbly

frozen
adj. iced over or kept in a freezer

fruit
n. a sweet, healthy food from plants

full
adj. complete or without empty space

full-length
adj. as long as your body

fully stocked
adj. with everything you might need

fur-lined
adj. with a layer of fur inside

furious
adj. wild, angry, and violent

furry
adj. soft, fluffy, and hairy

futuristic
[1] *adj.* using the latest technology
[2] *adj.* with a very modern design

fuzzy
adj. woolly, fluffy, or frizzy

galloping
adj. racing or sprinting

gaping
adj. open very wide

gargantuan
adj. huge or enormous

garish
adj. much too bright and flashy

gaudy
adj. bright, glaring, or flashy

gaunt
adj. far too thin and scrawny

general
adj. common or from all around

genetic
adj. involving DNA or genes

gentle
adj. calm, soft, or mild

geographical
adj. to do with a certain area

ghostly
[1] *adj.* creepy or scary
[2] *adj.* creepy or like a ghost

giant
Fee, fi, fo, fum!

gifted
adj. talented or skilled

gigantic
adj. huge or enormous

gladiator
n. an armed Roman warrior

glass
adj. made of a clear, hard material

glazed
adj. with a thin layer of icing

G–H

gleaming
adj. shining or bright

glimmering
adj. glowing faintly or twinkling

glistening
adj. shining or sparkling

glitching
adj. not working properly

glitchy
adj. often working incorrectly

glittering
adj. shiny or sparkling

global
adj. of the whole world

gloomy
adj. dark and depressing

gloopy
adj. thick and sticky

glorious
adj. beautiful and magnificent

glossy
adj. shiny and smooth

glowing
[1] *adj.* bright or shining
[2] *adj.* bright and healthy-looking

gluten-free
adj. without gluten

gnarled
adj. knobby, rough, and twisted

golden
adj. the color of gold

gooey
adj. with a soft and sticky texture

gossipy
adj. talking about other people

graceful
adj. elegant and beautiful

gracious
adj. polite, kind, and pleasant

gradual
adj. happening slowly

grand
adj. big and impressive

grassy
adj. like grass or covered in grass

grated
adj. cut into thin slices by a grater

grazed
adj. lightly scraped and bleeding

grazing
adj. slowly eating grass

greasy
adj. oily or waxy

greedy
adj. wanting too much food

green
adj. the color of grass

greenish
adj. slightly green

grilled
adj. cooked on a hot grill

grim
adj. serious, gloomy, or unpleasant

grimy
adj. dirty or covered with grime

gristly
adj. with hard-to-chew tough bits

grizzly
adj. with patches of gray

groaning
adj. creaking under heavy weight

groomed
adj. looked after or styled

growling
adj. making noise due to hunger

grubby
adj. a little dirty or grimy

gruesome
adj. horrible or disgusting to look at

grunting
adj. making a short, low sound

gushing
adj. coming out quickly

hacked
adj. accessed a computer illegally

hairy
adj. covered with hairs

half-eaten
adj. only partly eaten

half-finished
adj. only partly finished

halved
adj. cut into two equal pieces

hand-painted
adj. painted by a person

hand-picked
adj. picked by a person

handheld
adj. small enough to hold

handmade
adj. made by a person

handwritten
adj. written with a pen or pencil

handy
adj. helpful or convenient

hanging
adj. drooping or dangling

hard
adj. solid or firm

hard-fought
adj. played with lots of effort

hardened
adj. harder than before or not soft

harmful
adj. dangerous or unhealthy

harmless
adj. not causing harm or damage

harnessed
adj. wearing straps for guiding

H–I

harsh
adj. unpleasantly strong or intense

haunted
adj. lived in by ghosts

hazardous
adj. dangerous or unsafe

head
adj. chief or main

headless
adj. without a head

healthy
[1] *adj.* fit and well
[2] *adj.* good for you

heaped
adj. in a big pile or completely full

heart-shaped
adj. in the shape of a heart

hearty
adj. filling and wholesome

heated
adj. made hot or warm

heavy
[1] *adj.* sad or miserable
[2] *adj.* weighty, thick, or hard to lift
[3] *adj.* forceful or in big amounts

heavy-duty
adj. not easily worn out

heavyweight
adj. above the normal weight

helpful
adj. useful or giving help

helpless
adj. weak, powerless, or unprotected

herbal
adj. made using herbs

hidden
adj. secret or kept out of sight

high
adj. tall or near the top

high-definition
adj. with a very detailed or clear picture

high-end
adj. expensive or luxury

high-powered
adj. with a lot of power or energy

high-rise
adj. in a tall, multistory building

high-security
adj. strictly guarded or protected

high-speed
adj. very fast

high-tech
adj. using the latest science

hilarious
adj. very funny or hysterical

hilly
adj. with lots of hills

hissing
adj. making a "sssss" sound

historic
adj. famous or significant in history

holey
adj. full of holes

hollow
adj. empty or with nothing inside

homemade
adj. made at home

homing
adj. able to find and hit a target

honking
adj. beeping or hooting

hooked
adj. curved or bent

hopping
adj. jumping or leaping

horned
adj. with a horn on its head

horrific
adj. terrible and shocking

horse-drawn
adj. pulled by horses

hostile
adj. unfriendly and aggressive

hot
adj. having a high temperature

hovering
adj. floating or fluttering in the air

howling
adj. crying or wailing

huge
adj. very big or enormous

hulking
adj. big and heavy

human
Look in a mirror!

humble
adj. modest, plain, and simple

humid
adj. muggy or with damp air

humming
adj. making a continuous sound

hunched
adj. bent over or arched

hungry
Warning: This dictionary is not edible.

hurtling
adj. moving very fast or rushing

hydroelectric
adj. using water to make electricity

hypnotic
adj. mesmerizing or captivating

ice-cold
adj. as cold as ice

iced
[1] *adj.* covered with icing
[2] *adj.* served cold and with ice

I–J

iconic
adj. famous and recognizable

icy
adj. with ice or covered in ice

idyllic
adj. ideal or perfect

illegal
adj. against the law

immaculate
adj. perfect or spotless

immense
adj. very large or huge

immersive
adj. making you completely involved

immortal
adj. living forever or never dying

immune
adj. not affected by certain illnesses

impenetrable
adj. dense or inaccessible

important
adj. valuable or significant

imported
adj. brought from another country

imposing
adj. grand or impressive

impractical
adj. not useful or sensible

impregnable
adj. impossible to break into or take over

impressive
adj. admirably good or big

inadequate
adj. too few or not enough

incessant
adj. constant or never stopping

incoming
adj. approaching or arriving

incompetent
adj. lacking skill or useless

incorrect
adj. wrong or not accurate

incurable
adj. unable to be made better

indecipherable
adj. impossible to understand

indestructible
adj. impossible to break or destroy

indulgent
adj. luxurious or pampering

industrial
adj. relating to factories or industry

industrious
adj. hard-working

infected
adj. affected by a virus or disease

infinite
adj. going on forever

inflatable
adj. able to be filled with air

inflated
adj. filled with air

infrared
adj. using invisible light rays

ingenious
adj. clever and inventive

ingrown
adj. growing backward or sideways

injured
adj. hurt or wounded

innocent
adj. harmless or not guilty

innovative
adj. new, advanced, and original

inquisitive
adj. wanting to discover things

inspiring
adj. exciting and motivating

instant
adj. immediate or very quick to make

intelligent
adj. clever or able to work things out

intense
adj. strong, powerful, or extreme

interactive
adj. responding to what you do

international
adj. involving different countries

interplanetary
adj. going between planets

interstellar
adj. going between stars

intoxicating
adj. making you dizzy or light-headed

intrusive
adj. unwelcome or going where not wanted

intuitive
adj. easily understood without training

invasive
adj. growing aggressively

invigorating
adj. making you feel lively and alert

invisible
adj. impossible to see

inviting
adj. attractive or tempting

iridescent
adj. colored like a rainbow

isolated
adj. alone or far from others

ivy-covered
adj. covered with a climbing plant

jagged
adj. with sharp or pointy edges

jealous
adj. wanting what someone else has

jittery
adj. nervous, scared, and jumpy

jolly
adj. happy and joyful

jolting
adj. moving suddenly and roughly

juicy
adj. full of juice or moisture

jumbo
adj. especially big or large

key
adj. important or essential

khaki
adj. grayish-green or brownish-yellow

killer
adj. deadly or dangerous

kind
adj. friendly, generous, and caring

knee-high
adj. reaching up to your knees

knitted
adj. made by knitting wool

knobby
adj. with lumps and bumps

lakeside
adj. next to a lake

lanky
adj. tall and slim

lapping
adj. gently flowing or splashing

large
adj. big or great in size

late-night
adj. staying open late at night

latest
adj. newest or most recent

lazy
adj. not working hard

leafless
adj. bare and without leaves

leafy
adj. with lots of leaves

leaky
adj. letting water in through holes

leather
adj. made of animal skin

leather-clad
adj. covered in leather

leering
adj. gaping or gawking

leftover
adj. uneaten by the end of a meal

legendary
adj. famous or told of in stories

lethal
adj. deadly or very harmful

life-changing
adj. improving life significantly

life-saving
adj. able to cure people

life-size
adj. full-size or the actual size

lifelike
adj. very like a living thing

lifelong
adj. for your whole life

light
adj. not thick or heavy

lightweight
adj. thin or not weighing much

limited
adj. restrictive or not very good

lingering
adj. lasting or not ending

lit
adj. on fire or burning

littered
adj. covered in trash or messy

little
adj. small or tiny

livid
adj. raging or furious

loaded
adj. full or carrying a lot

loathsome
adj. making you feel hatred

local
adj. in or from a nearby area

locked
adj. sealed shut with a lock and key

lone
adj. on its own or solitary

lonely
adj. alone or isolated

long
[1] *adj.* lasting a while or not fast
[2] *adj.* far from beginning to end

long-lasting
adj. not ending quickly

longtime
adj. for many years

loose
adj. baggy or not tight

loose-leaf
adj. made using loose tea leaves

lopsided
adj. drooping or leaning to one side

lost
Where am I? HELP!

loud
adj. noisy or easy to hear

lovable
adj. adorable or sweet

low
adj. less than the normal amount

low-fat
adj. not containing much fat

low-flying
adj. flying low in the sky

L–M

low-sodium
adj. not containing much sodium

loyal
adj. faithful and reliable

lucky
adj. bringing good luck

lukewarm
adj. quite warm

luminous
adj. bright, shining, or glowing

lumpy
adj. uneven or with lots of bumps

lurking
adj. hiding and waiting to attack

luscious
adj. rich, sweet, and delicious

lush
adj. rich and growing healthily

luxurious
adj. very comfortable and expensive

luxury
n. richness or comfort

magic
n. mysterious or unexplained power

magical
[1] *adj.* with mysterious power
[2] *adj.* wonderful or special

magnificent
adj. very beautiful or impressive

majestic
adj. beautiful or powerful

makeshift
adj. temporary and not very good

malfunctioning
adj. not working properly

malicious
adj. spiteful or meaning harm

mammoth
adj. very large or giant

man-eating
adj. likes feeding on human flesh

man-made
adj. created by humans

manicured
adj. tidy and well looked after

marauding
adj. looking for things to kill or steal

marbled
adj. streaky like marble

marinated
adj. soaked in spices or flavors

marine
adj. used at sea

marshy
adj. wet and boggy

mashed
adj. crushed or blended into a pulp

masked
adj. disguised or covered

massive
adj. very large or giant

matted
adj. tangled or knotted

meandering
adj. wandering or taking a long path

mechanical
adj. controlled by a machine

meddling
adj. getting involved or interfering

medical
adj. relating to medicine or doctors

medieval
adj. from the Middle Ages

mellow
adj. soft and soothing

melted
adj. turned from solid to liquid

melting
adj. turning from solid to liquid

menacing
adj. threatening to do harm

mesmerizing
adj. very attractive or bewitching

messy
adj. untidy or dirty

metal
n. a hard, shiny material

metallic
adj. looking like metal

mighty
adj. big, strong, and powerful

migrating
adj. moving from one place to another

mild
adj. not very strong or not spicy

military
adj. to do with the army or soldiers

mindless
adj. foolish or senseless

mini
adj. smaller than usual

mint
n. a plant used in cooking

miraculous
adj. wonderful or magical

mirrored
[1] *adj.* shiny or mirrorlike
[2] *adj.* reflective or with a mirror

mischievous
adj. naughty and playful

mismatched
adj. not the same color or pattern

misplaced
adj. in the wrong place

mistreated
adj. treated badly or cruelly

misty
adj. like a thin fog

M–O

misunderstood
adj. not understood or appreciated

mixing
adj. combining things together

mobile
adj. able to be carried around

modern
adj. in the latest or current style

moist
adj. damp or not dry

moldy
adj. rotten or covered with mold

monstrous
adj. horrible or like a monster

moonlit
adj. lit up by the moon

moored
adj. tied up with a rope or anchor

moth-eaten
adj. full of holes made by moths

motionless
adj. still or not moving

motorized
adj. powered by a motor

mournful
adj. very sad or full of regret

much-needed
adj. very important and necessary

mud
n. a mixture of water and soil

muddled
adj. confused or mixed up

muddy
adj. covered in mud

muffled
adj. quiet and not heard properly

multistory
adj. made up of several floors

murky
adj. dark, muddy, or cloudy

muscular
adj. strong and powerful

mushy
adj. mashed or pulpy

musical
adj. melodic or related to music

musty
adj. stuffy, moldy, or stale

mutated
adj. changed into something else

mysterious
adj. strange, eerie, or unexplained

mythical
adj. existing only in stories

narrow
adj. small or not far from side to side

nasty
adj. very bad or unpleasant

natural
adj. made by nature

neglected
adj. not well looked after

neon
adj. very bright or fluorescent

nesting
adj. building a home or nest

network
n. a system of connected things

new
adj. just made or just bought

newborn
adj. born very recently

nimble
adj. moving quickly and skillfully

nocturnal
adj. active at night

noise-canceling
adj. blocking out other sounds

noisy
WHAT? I CAN'T HEAR YOU.

nondescript
adj. not unusual or not memorable

nonstick
adj. not letting food stick

nuclear
adj. relating to splitting atoms

number-one
adj. the best or highest rated

nutty
adj. tasting of nuts or with nuts in

oak
n. a large tree that bears acorns

oaty
adj. made with oats

obscure
adj. hidden or unclear

obsessive
adj. too interested or addicted

obvious
adj. easy to see or notice

odd-looking
adj. looking unusual or strange

offshore
adj. out at sea

old
adj. having existed for a long time

ominous
adj. scary, threatening, or menacing

oncoming
adj. moving toward you

oozing
adj. slowly trickling or leaking

open
[1] *adj.* not shut or not closed
[2] *adj.* wide and exposed

open-air
adj. outside or not walled in

open-plan
adj. with no dividing walls

O–P

oppressive
adj. cruel, harsh, and overpowering

optical
adj. relating to eyes and sight

opulent
adj. rich and luxurious

orbiting
adj. circling or moving around

organic
adj. made without using chemicals

ornamental
adj. fancy or decorative

ornate
adj. detailed and decorated

orphaned
adj. without a mother or father

outdoor
adj. not inside

outer
adj. on the outside

outspread
adj. spread open or wide apart

overcast
adj. cloudy or gray

overcrowded
adj. full of too many people

overflowing
adj. too full and spilling over

overgrown
adj. grown too big or thick

overhanging
adj. above or hanging over

overhead
adj. above your head or in the sky

overloaded
adj. carrying too much stuff

overnight
adj. during the night

overripe
adj. too ripe or past its best

oversized
adj. bigger than normal

overstocked
adj. filled with too many things

overstuffed
adj. stuffed with too many things

overturned
adj. tipped upside down

packed
adj. full or overcrowded

padded
adj. stuffed with a soft material

painful
adj. causing pain or distress

painted
adj. covered with paint

palatial
adj. vast or splendid

paper
n. thin sheets made from trees

parboiled
adj. boiled until partly cooked

parked
adj. left somewhere without moving

passing
[1] *adj.* moving or going past
[2] *adj.* not lasting long

patchy
adj. uneven or not everywhere

patterned
adj. with a repeated design

peaceful
adj. calm and tranquil

pebbly
adj. with a lot of pebbles

peeled
adj. with the outer peel removed

peeling
adj. coming off or shedding

peep
adj. showing or poking out

pelting
adj. bombarding or battering

perennial
adj. living for many years

perfect
adj. ideal or flawless

perilous
adj. dangerous and full of risk

personal
adj. belonging to you or for you

pesky
adj. causing trouble or annoying

pessimistic
adj. gloomy or negative

phenomenal
adj. fantastic or extraordinary

photographic
adj. using photos or in photos

pickled
adj. preserved in a vinegary liquid

picturesque
adj. attractive or scenic

pink
adj. the color of red and white mixed together

pinstripe
adj. with very thin stripes

pioneering
adj. new and innovative

piped
adj. applied in thin stripes

piping-hot
adj. extremely hot

pirate
Ahoy, matey!

pitted
adj. with the stones removed

P

pivotal
adj. very important or critical

plastic
n. an easily molded material

platform
n. a raised level or surface

playful
adj. fun-loving and lively

pleasant
adj. enjoyable or nice

plentiful
adj. in large amounts

plowed
adj. with the soil turned over

plucked
adj. with feathers or hairs pulled off

plump
adj. round and fat

plush
adj. rich, soft, and luxurious

poached
adj. cooked in a hot liquid

pointed
adj. ending in a sharp point

pointy
adj. with a pointed tip

poisoned
adj. with a harmful substance added

poisonous
adj. deadly or toxic

polar
adj. near the North or South Pole

polished
adj. made shiny by being rubbed

polluted
adj. dirty or full of waste

poor
adj. low-quality or not very good

pop-up
adj. spring-loaded

popular
adj. liked by many people

porcelain
n. a white ceramic material

portable
adj. easy to carry or move

possible
adj. likely or able to happen

potted
adj. grown in a pot

pounding
adj. beating hard and repeatedly

powdery
adj. fine and powderlike

powerful
adj. strong, mighty, or effective

precious
adj. loved, valued, or expensive

precipitous
adj. steep or dangerously high

precise
adj. exact or accurate

predatory
adj. hunting other creatures

preening
adj. grooming itself with its beak

pregnant
adj. going to have a baby soon

preheated
adj. already heated up

preserved
adj. protected from going off

pressed
adj. flattened to get rid of creases

prestigious
adj. important and respected

prickly
adj. covered in sharp spikes

primitive
adj. basic, rough, or crude

princely
adj. good enough for a prince

pristine
adj. brand-new or spotless

private
adj. for one person or not for everyone

prized
adj. valued very highly

professional
adj. trained or expert

profitable
adj. making money

profuse
adj. a lot of or abundant

projectile
adj. pushed forward forcefully

prolific
adj. producing a lot

prominent
adj. easy to see or noticeable

promising
adj. hopeful or having potential

prosthetic
adj. made to replace the real thing

protected
adj. kept safe from harm

protective
adj. keeping you safe from harm

proud
adj. feeling important and confident

prowling
adj. roaming and looking for prey

pruned
adj. with the branches cut back

public
adj. for everyone to use

P–R

puffed
adj. swollen or bigger than before

puffed-up
adj. sticking out proudly

punctured
adj. damaged by making a hole

pungent
adj. having a very strong smell or taste

pure
adj. not mixed with anything else

purple
adj. the color of red and blue mixed together

purring
adj. a soft, low, and happy hum

quaint
adj. charming and picturesque

quaking
adj. shaking or trembling

queasy
adj. feeling sick or nauseous

quiet
Shhhh!

quilted
adj. with a layer of soft padding

quirky
adj. in an unusual or eccentric style

rabid
adj. wild and violent

radiant
adj. bright, brilliant, or glowing

radioactive
adj. sending out toxic waves

ragged
adj. old and torn

raging
adj. furious or uncontrollable

rainbow-billed
adj. with a beak full of colors

ramshackle
adj. falling to pieces

random
[1] *adj.* odd or irregular
[2] *adj.* chosen without a reason

ransacked
adj. damaged and robbed

rapid
adj. very fast or quick

rapid-fire
adj. firing quickly one after another

rare
[1] *adj.* very few or not often seen
[2] *adj.* very lightly cooked

ravenous
adj. hungry or starving

raw
adj. uncooked or unprocessed

razor-sharp
adj. able to cut things very easily

reborn
adj. made new again

rechargeable
adj. able to be refilled with energy

reclining
adj. able to be tilted backward

record-breaking
adj. more than ever before

recycled
adj. reused again for something new

red-brick
adj. made with red-colored bricks

red-hot
adj. so hot that it glows red

reduced
adj. lowered or lessened

reedy
adj. with tall grass everywhere

refreshing
adj. making you feel energized

refurbished
adj. repaired, fixed, or revamped

regular
adj. always at the same time

reinforced
adj. made stronger or tougher

rejuvenating
adj. making you feel better or younger

relentless
adj. constant or nonstop

reliable
adj. trusted and dependable

remote
adj. far away or distant

renowned
adj. well-known and respected

rented
adj. paid to be used for a short time

reputable
adj. well-respected and reliable

rescued
adj. saved from danger

respected
adj. admired or thought highly of

responsible
adj. sensible and trusted

restless
adj. unsettled or desperate to move

restored
adj. repaired or fixed

retired
adj. no longer employed or working

retractable
adj. able to be drawn back in

retro
adj. old-style and cool

reusable
adj. working more than once

R–S

revolutionary
adj. bringing about a big change

revolving
adj. moving in a circle

rice
n. a cereal grain

rich
[1] *adj.* creamy, heavy, and delicious
[2] *adj.* lush, fertile, and full of life

rickety
adj. wobbly, shaky, or poorly made

ridiculous
adj. funny, silly, or absurd

ripe
adj. soft and ready to eat

ripped
adj. torn or pulled apart

rippling
adj. flowing in small waves

rising
adj. getting higher or moving up

roaring
[1] *adj.* making a loud and deep noise
[2] *adj.* full of loud and powerful flames

roasted
adj. cooked for a long time

roasting
adj. used to roast things

robotic
adj. mechanical or like a robot

robust
adj. strong and tough

rocky
adj. made of rock or stone

rogue
adj. rebellious and different

rolled
adj. turned over and flattened

rolling
[1] *adj.* rippling, wavy, or tumbling
[2] *adj.* turning around and around

romantic
adj. showing love and passion

roof-mounted
adj. attached to the top of a roof

rotating
adj. spinning or turning

rotten
adj. decayed, old, and stinking

rotting
adj. going bad or decaying

rough
adj. carelessly made or badly made

rounded
adj. smooth and curved

royal
adj. for the family of a king or queen

rubber
n. a soft, bendy material

rubbery
adj. flexible and tough

rude
You smell.

ruffled
adj. scrunched up in a design

rugged
adj. rough, uneven, or craggy

rumbling
adj. making a deep and continuous sound

rumpled
adj. wrinkled or creased

run-down
adj. old and needing repairs

runaway
adj. escaped or out of control

running
n. moving quickly on foot

runny
adj. liquid or flowing easily

ruptured
adj. broken open or burst

rustic
adj. typical of the countryside

rusty
adj. covered in rust or red flakes

sabotaged
adj. broken or ruined on purpose

sacred
adj. holy, religious, or spiritual

sad
:(

safari
n. a trip to look at or hunt animals

sagging
adj. drooping or hanging loosely

salted
adj. containing or covered in salt

saltwater
adj. containing salty water

salty
adj. tasting of salt

salvaged
adj. saved or rescued

sandy
adj. covered with sand

satin
n. a smooth, glossy fabric

savage
adj. cruel, violent, and uncontrolled

scalding
adj. extremely hot or burning

scaly
adj. covered in scales

scampering
adj. scurrying or dashing

scarlet
adj. vivid red in color

S

scattered
adj. spread randomly

scenic
adj. with beautiful views

scented
adj. with a nice smell

scheming
adj. plotting devious tricks

scientific
adj. to do with science

scorching
adj. red-hot or blazing

scraped
adj. grazed or scratched

scrappy
adj. determined and feisty

scrawny
adj. thin and bony

screeching
adj. squawking or squealing

scruffy
adj. shabby or untidy

scrumptious
adj. tasty or delicious

scuffed
adj. lightly damaged from scraping

sculpted
adj. beautifully shaped or carved

scuttling
adj. running with short steps

sea
How do we know the sea is friendly? It waves.

sealed
adj. shut tightly

seared
adj. quickly cooked on the surface

seaside
adj. by the sea

seasonal
adj. happening in certain seasons

seasoned
adj. with salt, pepper, or spices

secluded
adj. quiet or kept hidden

secret
My lips are sealed.

secure
adj. safe against danger or attacks

seedless
adj. without seeds

self-rising
adj. with a raising agent already added

self-service
adj. letting people serve themselves

sensible
adj. wise and responsible

sensitive
adj. able to notice small changes

sentient
adj. able to feel things

serene
adj. peaceful or calm

serious
adj. important or not to be ignored

serrated
adj. sharp, rough, and jagged

serving
adj. used for giving out portions

severe
adj. very serious or harsh

shabby
adj. scruffy and worn

shaded
adj. sheltered from the sun

shady
adj. giving shelter from the sun

shaggy
adj. long, thick, and messy

shallow
adj. not deep

sharp
[1] *adj.* able to cut or pierce things easily
[2] *adj.* quick, clear, and noticeable

sharp-eyed
adj. quick to spot things

sharpened
adj. made more pointy

shattered
adj. smashed into small pieces

shaved
adj. shredded into thin flakes

sheltering
adj. protecting or covering

shifting
adj. moving in different directions

shimmering
adj. glinting and flickering

shocking
adj. surprising and distressing

shooting
adj. moving very fast

shorn
adj. with its fleece cut off

short
adj. not very long

shredded
adj. cut or torn into thin pieces

shrill
adj. sharp or very high-pitched

shriveled
adj. wrinkled or shrunken

shuttered
adj. closed with shutters

sifted
adj. put through a sifter

S

silk
n. a strong, soft, and thin fabric

silver
adj. pale gray and shiny

silvery
adj. light gray and reflective

simple
adj. basic and plain

singing
adj. whistling sounds made by birds

single
adj. only one or with no others

sinking
adj. moving slowly downward

sizzling
adj. very hot or hissing with heat

sizzling-hot
adj. hot or extremely spicy

skilled
adj. trained or experienced

skillful
adj. talented or expert

skimpy
adj. small and revealing

skinny
[1] *adj.* thin or scrawny
[2] *adj.* slim and tight-fitting

sky-high
adj. very tall or very high

sky-piercing
adj. taller than the sky

slanting
adj. sloping at an angle

slathered
adj. spread on thickly or heavily

sleek
adj. smooth and shiny

sleeping
adj. asleep or not awake

sleepy
adj. quiet and peaceful

slender
adj. slim and graceful

sliced
adj. cut into thin pieces

slimy
adj. slippery, wet, and gooey

slippery
adj. smooth, wet, or difficult to grip

slithering
adj. slipping, sliding, or moving smoothly

slobbering
adj. drooling or dripping saliva

slouchy
adj. hunched or drooping

slow
adj. taking a long time or not fast

slow-moving
adj. moving slowly or barely moving

sluggish
adj. slow, lazy, or lifeless

sly
adj. clever and dishonest

small
adj. little in size or not big

smart
[1] *adj.* intelligent technology
[2] *adj.* clean, tidy, and well-dressed

smashed
adj. very broken or shattered

smelly
Whoever smelt it, dealt it.

smoked
adj. preserved using smoke

smoky
adj. sending out smoke

smudged
adj. blurred, rubbed, or smeared

snarling
adj. making a growling noise

sneaky
adj. good at lying and hiding

snooty
adj. rudely looking down on others

snow-capped
adj. covered with snow at the top

snowy
adj. covered with snow

snug
adj. cozy and comfortable

soaked
adj. extremely wet

soaring
adj. high, flying, or gliding

sodden
adj. soaking or completely wet

soft
[1] *adj.* faint or dim
[2] *adj.* mild and mellow
[3] *adj.* mushy or not hard

soggy
adj. wet and soft

solar
adj. powered by sunlight

solemn
adj. serious and formal

solid
[1] *adj.* hard and thick
[2] *adj.* firm and reliable

solitary
adj. living or spending time alone

somber
adj. sad, gloomy, or dark

soothing
adj. comforting and calming

sore
[1] *adj.* painful or aching
[2] *adj.* angry or annoyed

S

soundproofed
adj. not letting sound in or out

sour
adj. bitter, sharp, and acidic

sourdough
n. a sour or bitter type of dough

spacious
adj. big or with a lot of room inside

spare
adj. extra or back-up

sparkling
adj. shining or glimmering

sparkly
adj. shiny or glittery

spattered
adj. splashed, stained, or speckled

special
adj. important or unique

speckled
adj. marked with small dots

speeding
adj. moving too fast

speedy
adj. fast or quick

spiced
adj. with added flavor from spice

spicy
adj. tasting hot and fiery

spiked
adj. with sharp points or spikes

spilled
adj. falling out or overflowing

spiral
adj. coiled, twisted, or curved

spiraling
adj. winding around and around

spirited
adj. lively and determined

spiritual
adj. religious and emotional

splendid
adj. bright, glorious, or impressive

splintered
adj. broken into thin, sharp pieces

spooked
adj. scared, frightened, and jumpy

spotless
adj. completely clean

spouting
adj. sending out a jet of water

sprawling
adj. stretching over a large area

spray-painted
adj. painted using a spray

springy
adj. bouncy or moving like elastic

square
n. a shape with four equal sides and four right angles

squashed
adj. crushed or squeezed

squat
adj. short and stubby

squawking
adj. screeching or shrieking

squeaky
adj. making a high-pitched noise

squealing
adj. making a loud, high noise

squeezed
adj. with the juice pressed out

squirming
adj. wriggling uncomfortably

stacked
adj. piled up, one on top of the other

stagnant
adj. still and stale

stained
adj. marked or discolored

stale
adj. old, hard, and crusty

stampeding
adj. rushing wildly in a group

startled
adj. surprised or frightened

steady
adj. constant and unchanging

steak
n. a thick slice of meat

stealthy
adj. sneaky or secretive

steamed
adj. cooked with heat from steam

steaming
adj. giving off misty fumes

steamy
adj. clouded by misty fumes

steep
adj. going sharply up or down

sterile
adj. completely free from germs

stewed
adj. cooked slowly in liquid

sticky
adj. gluey or attaching to things

stiff
[1] *adj.* unbending or hard to move
[2] *adj.* straight and severe

stifling
adj. so hot you can barely breathe

stinging
adj. painful to touch

stinking
adj. smelling nasty

stolen
adj. taken illegally or without asking

stone-ground
adj. crushed up finely using stones

S–T

stony
[1] *adj.* unfriendly or unfeeling
[2] *adj.* covered in small rocks

stormy
adj. rainy, thundery, and windy

strained
adj. tense, tired, or painful

stranded
adj. left, stuck, or abandoned

strange
adj. odd or unusual

strapless
adj. without straps

strappy
adj. held together with straps

stray
adj. escaped or without an owner

streaky
adj. marked with stripes

streamlined
adj. made simple and easy to use

stretched
adj. pulled tight and not loose

strict
adj. sticking to the rules

striped
adj. patterned with lines

strong
[1] *adj.* firm and muscular
[2] *adj.* intense and full of flavor
[3] *adj.* powerful, tough, and mighty

strutting
adj. walking upright and confidently

stubborn
adj. difficult to get rid of or move

stubby
adj. short and thick

studded
adj. decorated with pieces of metal

stuffed
adj. filled or packed with something

stumpy
adj. short, thick, and squat

stunning
adj. beautiful and impressive

stunted
adj. stopped from growing fully

sturdy
adj. strong and solidly built

stylish
adj. fashionable or elegant

submerged
adj. completely underwater

subtle
adj. faint and delicate

succulent
adj. juicy, fresh, and tasty

sudden
adj. unexpected or without warning

suffocating
adj. making it hard to breathe

sugary
adj. very sticky and sweet

sulfurous
adj. smelling like rotten eggs

sun-kissed
adj. warmed or browned by the sun

sunken
[1] *adj.* lower or beneath a surface
[2] *adj.* underwater or submerged

sunny
adj. lit up by the sun

super-strong
adj. very powerful or lasting longer

superfast
adj. extremely speedy

surfacing
adj. coming up above the water

surgical
adj. used in surgery

suspected
adj. thought to be guilty

sustainable
adj. caught safely and responsibly

swarming
adj. moving together in a big group

swaying
adj. moving gently from side to side

sweet
adj. pleasant and sugary

sweetened
adj. made to taste sugary

swelling
adj. growing bigger or expanding

sweltering
adj. very hot or baking

swimming
adj. moving through water

swirling
adj. spiraling or twirling

swollen
adj. bulging, expanded, or inflamed

swooping
adj. flying downward quickly

sympathetic
adj. understanding and comforting

table
n. a surface for eating or working

tailored
adj. specially made to fit you

tainted
adj. spoiled or contaminated

talented
adj. skilled and gifted

talkative
adj. chatty or talks a lot

talking
adj. saying words out loud

tall
adj. high off the ground

T

tame
adj. well-trained and obedient

tangled
adj. twisted or knotted

tart
adj. sharp and sour

tasty
adj. delicious or yummy

tattered
adj. old, torn, and worn-out

teeming
adj. full or crowded

teen
n. a person aged 13 to 19

telepathic
adj. reading thoughts

televised
adj. shown on the television

temperamental
adj. emotional, moody, or fiery

tempestuous
adj. wild, stormy, and unpredictable

temporary
adj. lasting for a short time

tempting
adj. attractive or hard to say no to

terrible
adj. very bad or awful

tethered
adj. tied up or chained

thatched
adj. made with straw or hay

thawing
adj. melting into water

therapeutic
adj. healing or making you feel better

thick
[1] *adj.* not very runny
[2] *adj.* chunky, wide, and heavy
[3] *adj.* closely packed in or dense

thieving
adj. robbing or stealing

thirsty
adj. in need of water

thorny
adj. has lots of thorns

threadbare
adj. old and worn thin

threatening
adj. ominous or scary

three-legged
adj. with three legs

thriving
adj. growing and doing very well

throbbing
adj. pulsing in pain

thundering
adj. making a sound like thunder

thunderous
adj. very loud or like thunder

ticking
adj. a short and repetitive sound

ticklish
adj. making you wriggle and giggle

tie-dyed
adj. with round color patterns

tiered
adj. with one row on top of another

tight
[1] *adj.* dense or pressed firmly together
[2] *adj.* close-fitting or figure-hugging

tiled
adj. covered in flat stone slabs

timid
adj. shy or fearful

tinted
adj. with a faint color

tiny
adj. very small

tired
adj. worn out and sleepy

toasted
adj. heated until crispy and brown

toasty
adj. keeping you warm

top
adj. best or of the highest standard

toppling
adj. tumbling or about to fall over

torn
adj. cut or split

torrential
adj. falling heavily and forcefully

total
adj. complete or absolute

touch-screen
adj. controlled by pressing a screen

tough
[1] *adj.* difficult to cut or chew
[2] *adj.* strong and resilient

towering
adj. extremely tall

toxic
adj. poisonous or deadly

trained
adj. prepared and practiced

trampled
adj. walked over and crushed

trampling
adj. stomping and crushing

tranquil
adj. peaceful or blissfully quiet

tranquilized
adj. made sleepy or calm with a drug

transparent
adj. clear or see-through

transplanted
adj. moved from another body

trapped
adj. stuck or caught

treacherous
[1] *adj.* dangerous or unsafe
[2] *adj.* lying and not to be trusted

treasured
adj. loved and valued

trembling
adj. shaking with nerves or fear

trendy
adj. fashionable or in style

trophy
n. a prize cup given to winners

tropical
adj. in or from a hot country

trusted
adj. loyal, reliable, and honest

trusty
adj. reliable or tried and tested

turbocharged
adj. made extra fast or strong

turbulent
adj. violent and unpredictable

twinkling
adj. sparkling and flickering

twirling
adj. spinning or swirling

twisting
adj. bending or curling around

twitching
adj. fluttering or jerking

two-headed
adj. with two heads

two-person
adj. with space for two people

two-pronged
adj. with just two sharp points

two-time
adj. having happened twice before

ugly
adj. unattractive or hideous

unattended
adj. left alone or not watched

unbearable
adj. impossible to take or put up with

unbeatable
adj. impossible to be beaten or bettered

unbreakable
adj. very strong or not easily broken

unbuttoned
adj. with the buttons undone

uncharted
adj. unexplored or not mapped

uncomfortable
adj. unpleasant or not comfortable

unconvincing
adj. not very believable

undefeated
adj. never beaten before

undercover
adj. working secretly or in disguise

underground
adj. under the surface of the ground

undetectable
adj. impossible for others to see

undrinkable
adj. too disgusting to drink

uneven
adj. bumpy or not level

unexpected
adj. surprising or without warning

unfeeling
adj. without emotions

unflushed
adj. not flushed and left full of waste

unforgiving
adj. showing no mercy

unidentified
adj. unknown or unrecognized

uninflated
adj. not filled with air

uninhabitable
adj. not possible to live in

unique
adj. the only one of its kind

unkempt
adj. messy or untidy

unknowable
adj. impossible to know about

unlikely
adj. unexpected or not probable

unlit
adj. dark and without lights

unlocked
adj. not shut with a lock

unlucky
adj. unfortunate or out of luck

unmade
adj. not arranged neatly

unmanned
adj. without people on board

unopened
adj. closed or not opened

unpaid
adj. still needing to be paid

unpatrolled
adj. not checked by inspectors

unplugged
adj. not plugged in to electricity

unripe
adj. not ready to be eaten

unscooped
adj. left or not picked up

unsightly
adj. ugly or not pleasant to look at

unsinkable
adj. impossible to drop underwater

U–W

unstoppable
adj. impossible to stop

unsuccessful
adj. failed or giving bad results

unsung
adj. uncelebrated or not praised

unsuspecting
adj. not realizing what is going on

unswept
adj. unchecked or uncleared

untidy
adj. messy or cluttered

untuned
adj. sounding wrong

unwanted
adj. rejected or not wanted

unwavering
adj. steady or constant

unwieldy
adj. large and difficult to use

unwitting
adj. not aware of the facts

upcoming
adj. happening soon

upright
adj. standing up straight

upscale
adj. fashionable and expensive

upturned
adj. tipped over or upside down

useful
adj. handy or helpful

useless
adj. pointless or without use

user-friendly
adj. easy for anyone to use

vacant
adj. empty or not lived in

valiant
adj. brave or fearless

varicose
adj. painfully swollen or twisted

vast
adj. very large or enormous

vegetable
Yummy bundles of goodness.

vegetarian
adj. not including meat or fish

velvety
adj. soft, smooth, and silky

vengeful
adj. wanting revenge

venomous
adj. poisonous or toxic

versatile
adj. able to do lots of different things

vicious
adj. cruel, brutal, and violent

vintage
adj. old, high-quality, and stylish

visceral
adj. deeply felt and uncontrolled

viscous
adj. thick and sticky

vivid
adj. full of bright colors

volcanic
adj. made by volcanoes

voluminous
adj. large and full

vulnerable
adj. exposed to being attacked or harmed

waddling
adj. walking in short, wobbly steps

wagging
adj. shaking or waving up and down

walk-in
adj. big enough to walk into

warm
[1] *adj.* keeps in the heat
[2] *adj.* hot, but not too hot

wary
adj. careful or cautious

washed-up
adj. dumped on a beach by the tide

watchful
adj. alert or observant

waterproof
[1] *adj.* won't stop working in water
[2] *adj.* not letting water through

weak
adj. watery or not very strong

weekly
adj. happening every week

weightless
adj. not held down by gravity

welcome
adj. wanted or pleasing

welcoming
adj. making people want to go in

well-cut
adj. well-made and of high quality

well-done
adj. cooked for longer than normal

well-earned
adj. deserved after hard work

well-lit
adj. covered in light and easy to see

well-run
adj. efficient and organized

well-worn
adj. old and worn-out

wet
adj. covered in water or full of water

wheezy
adj. panting, gasping, and hissing

whipped
adj. thickened using a whisk

W–Z

whirling
adj. moving around in quick circles

whistling
adj. making a high-pitched sound

white
adj. of the color of snow

whitewashed
adj. painted with a thin white liquid

whole
adj. in one piece or not cut up

whole-grain
adj. made using complete grains

wicked
adj. evil or bad

wide
adj. broad or with the sides far apart

widespread
adj. covering a large area

wild
[1] *adj.* violent or uncontrolled
[2] *adj.* not grown on a farm

willing
adj. eager or happy to agree

wilted
adj. cooked until slightly soft

wilting
adj. dying from lack of water

winding
adj. bending or moving in a curve

windowless
adj. without any windows

windswept
adj. windblown or beaten by winds

winning
adj. first in a contest or competition

wintry
adj. looking or feeling like winter

wire-framed
adj. with thin metal frames

wireless
adj. without any wires

wise
adj. clever and sensible

wispy
adj. thin or fine

withered
adj. wilted, dried up, and drooping

wobbly
adj. shaky or unsteady

wood-burning
adj. using wood as fuel

wood-fired
adj. burning wood for heat

wooden
adj. made of wood

woolly
adj. made of wool

world-class
adj. one of the best in the world

worn-out
adj. damaged from being used a lot

worthy
adj. respectable and deserving

wounded
adj. hurt or injured

woven
adj. made by weaving materials together

wriggling
adj. twisting and turning

wrinkled
adj. with lots of little creases

writhing
adj. wriggling or squirming

yellow
adj. the color of a banana

young
adj. not having lived for long

zesty
adj. fruity and sharp-tasting

zingy
adj. lively or sharp-tasting

zooming
adj. moving very quickly

0-9

A

A B C D E F G H I J K L M N O P Q R S T U V W X Y Z

C

D

A B **C** **D** E F G H I J K L M N O P Q R S T U V W X Y Z

E

F

A B C D **E** **F** G H I J K L M N O P Q R S T U V W X Y Z

A B C D E F G H I J K L M N O P Q R S T U V W X Y Z

G

H

I

M

N

O

P

Q

R

S

A B C D E F G H I J K L M N O P Q R **S** T U V W X Y Z

T

A B C D E F G H I J K L M N O P Q R S **T** U V W X Y Z

U

V

W

A B C D E F G H I J K L M N O P Q R S T U V W X Y Z

X

Y

Z

COOKED UP BY MRS WORDSMITH'S CREATIVE TEAM

Creative Director
Craig Kellman

Academic Advisors
Emma Madden
Prof. Susan Neuman

Producer
Leon Welters

Techies
Josh Bhurruth
Rob Koeling
Benj Pettit
Stanislaw Pstrokonski

Pedagogy
Federico Espinosa
Rochelle McClymont
Eleni Savva

Writers
Tatiana Barnes
Justin Blanchard
Katie Davis
Becky Fuller
Mark Holland
Amelia Mehra
Jill Russo

Designers
Sarah Bennion
Fabrice Gourdel
Gemma Kindness
Jess Macadam
James Sales
Lady San Pedro
Evelyn Wandernoth
James Webb

Artists
Sara Anderson
Leah Artwick
Ellen Bae
Francis Boncales
Brett Coulson
Giovanni D'Alessandro
Dustin d'Arnault
Adam Fay
Suzy Gonzalez
Tracy Hui
Holly Jones
Megan Kelly
Wendell Luebbe
Phil Mamuyac
Aghnia Mardiyah
André Medina
Nicolò Mereu
Fernando Peque
Daniel J. Permutt
Rachel Smith
Joan Varitek
Serena Wu
Maggie Ziolkowska

No animals were harmed in
the making of these illustrations.

DK | Penguin Random House

Project Managers
Project Editor Lisa Stock
Senior Editor Helen Murray
Senior US Editor Kayla Dugger
Senior Designer Anna Formanek

Senior Production Editor Jennifer Murray
Senior Production Controller Lloyd Robertson
Publishing Director Mark Searle

First American Edition, 2022
Published in the United States by DK Publishing
1745 Broadway, 20th Floor, New York, NY 10019

Storyteller's Illustrated Dictionary
was previously published by Mrs Wordsmith in 2018

24 25 26 10 9 8 7 6 5 4 3 2
002-328659-Nov/2022

A catalog record for this book
is available from the Library of Congress.
ISBN 978-0-7440-5806-2

Printed and bound in China

www.dk.com

mrswordsmith.com

For the curious